Annie's Favorite Special Occasions Crochet Projects™

Annie's Attic®

Contents

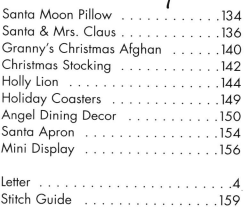

Product Development Director . . . .
Andy Ashley

Publishing Services Director . . . . .
Ange Van Arman

Crochet Design Manager . . . . . .
Deborah Levy-Hamburg

Product Development Staff . . . . . .
Mickie Akins, Darla Hassell, Sandra Miller Maxfield, Alice Vaughan, Elizabeth Ann White

Senior Editor . . . .
Donna Scott

Crochet Editorial Staff . . . .
Shirley Brown, Liz Field, Skeeter Gilson, Sharon Lothrop, Nina Marsh, Lyne Pickens

Book Design/Supervisor . . . .
Minette Smith

Graphic Artist . . . .
Debby Keel

Photography Manager . . . .
Scott Campbell

Photographers . . . .
Tammy Coquat-Payne, Keith Godfrey, Andy J. Burnfield

Color Specialist . . . .
Betty Holmes

Production Coordinator . . . .
Glenda Chamberlain

Library of Congress Cataloging-in-Publication Data ISBN: 0-9655269-7-6 First Printing: 2000 Library of Congress Catalog Card Number: 00-133562 Published and Distributed by Annie's Attic, Big Sandy, Texas 75755 **www.anniesattic.com** Printed in the United States of America

Dear Friends,

When asked to think about the special occasions that have taken place in my life, certain key events spring to mind. Most of these are tied together in some way with what I would consider milestones. The patterns chosen for this book have been carefully chosen while I was re-living some of those precious memories. Most of these will mean different things to each of us, but the common denominator will still be one of presenting family and friends with the here-and-now, wrapped up in the mists of nostalgia.

Memories such as keeping pressed flowers from that first Valentine bouquet. Even after so many years, the imagination still detects the scent of roses. Laughingly recalling the balloon toss from so many July 4th picnics. Always ending up soaking wet, but was it ever fun!

How about bringing home baby for the first time? How small he seemed. How frightening the feeling of responsibility! The contentment felt holding him cuddled into his special baby afghan, wearing the booties grandma crocheted for him on his tiny little feet. Fast forward to watching those same feet walk across the stage to receive the parchment that is a stepping stone to adulthood—high school graduation.

Can you remember what outfit your special little person wore for that first Trick or Treat jaunt? Being in Texas, mine naturally dressed as a cowboy. Another favorite memory is taking the children to the local mall to give Santa their Christmas wishes. Your only wish was for them to remember not to tug on Santa's beard.

We all like to sit and contemplate flashes of special times spent together, whether it's seeing who gets a pinch for not wearing green on St. Patrick's Day to the youngest member of the family helping Daddy cut the Thanksgiving turkey for the first time. All of these create a mental slide show we will never be tired of seeing over and over throughout the years. Keep these memories close to your heart while you crochet reminders of the past and anticipation for the future.

chapter 1

Romance

*Add dreamy morsels
to the memories
that will be savored
during some of life's
most romantic
moments.*

Cream Cheese Mints

3 oz. pkg. cream cheese,
  softened
½ tsp. peppermint extract
3 cups sifted powdered sugar
Few drops food coloring
Granulated sugar

Combine softened cream cheese and
peppermint extract. Gradually blend and
knead in powdered sugar until mixture is
smooth. Knead in food coloring until evenly
distributed. Form mixture into ½" balls; dip
each into granulated sugar; place on
waxed paper. Flatten each to form patties.
Lightly cover with plastic wrap and allow
to rest overnight before serving. Makes 4
dozen. Mints can be stored up to one
month in freezer.

Wedding Bells Pillow

Designed by Elizabeth White

Finished Size: Pillow Top is 13½" square.

Materials:
- 200 yds. ecru size 20 crochet cotton thread
- 13½" square pillow
- Sewing thread and needle
- No. 8 steel hook or hook needed to obtain gauge

Gauge: 11 dc = 1"; 9 dc rows = 2".

Basic Stitches: Ch, sc, dc.

Special Stitches: For **beginning block,** ch 3, dc in next 3 sts.
For **mesh,** ch 2, skip next 2 sts or chs, dc in next st or ch.
For **block,** 2 dc in next ch sp, dc in next st, **or,** dc in next 3 sts, **or,** 5 dc in next bar.
For **bar,** ch 5, skip next lacet, dc in next st.
For **lacet,** ch 3, skip next 2 sts, sc in next st, ch 3, skip next 2 sts, dc in next st, **or,** ch 3, sc in ch sp of next bar, ch 3, dc in next st.

Pillow Top
Row 1: Ch 159, dc in fourth ch from hook and in each ch across, turn. *(157 dc made)*
Rows 2–60: Ch 3, work according to graph across, turn. At end of last row, fasten off.
Sew Pillow Top to pillow. ●

■ = BLOCK
□ = MESH
□ = BAR
▽ = LACET

Bridal Tablecloth

Designed by Gloria Coombes

Finished Size: 60" square.

Materials:
- 4,050 yds. white size 20 crochet cotton thread
- No. 10 steel hook or hook needed to obtain gauge

Gauge: Motif is 3¾" square.

Basic Stitches: Ch, sl st, sc, dc.

Special Stitches: For **beginning dc cluster (beg dc cluster),** ch 3, (yo, insert hook in same ch sp as ch-3, yo, pull through ch sp, yo, pull through 2 lps on hook) 2 times, yo, pull through all 3 lps on hook.

For **dc cluster,** yo, insert hook in next ch-3 sp, yo, pull through ch sp, yo, pull through 2 lps on hook, (yo, insert hook in same ch-3 sp, yo, pull through ch sp, yo, pull through 2 lps on hook) 2 times, yo, pull through all 4 lps on hook.

For **treble cluster (tr cluster),** yo 2 times, insert hook in next ch-3 sp yo, pull through ch sp, (yo, pull through 2 lps on hook) 2 times, *yo 2 times, insert hook in same ch-3 sp, yo, pull through ch sp, (yo, pull through 2 lps on hook) 2 times; repeat from *, yo, pull through all 4 lps on hook.

For **picot,** ch 5, sl st in **front lp and left bar** of last st made *(see Stitch Guide).*

Tablecloth

Work First Motif; work Second Motif 12 times for a total of 13 Motifs in first row. *For next row, work one Second Motif onto bottom of first Motif made on last row; (work Third Motif onto bottom of next Motif on last row and side of last Motif made on this row) 12 times; repeat from * for a total of 13 rows.

First Motif

Rnd 1: Ch 8, sl st in first ch to form ring, ch 6 *(counts as dc and ch 3),* (dc in ring, ch 3) 7 times, join with sl st in third ch of ch-6. *(8 dc, 8 ch sps made)*

Rnd 2: Ch 1, sc in first st, 3 sc in next ch sp, (sc in next st, 3 sc in next ch sp) around, join with sl st in first sc. *(32 sc)*

Rnd 3: Ch 1, sc in first 5 sts, ch 15, skip next 3 sts, (sc in next 5 sts, ch 15, skip next 3 sts) around, join. *(20 sc, 4 ch sps)*

Continued on page 15

Flower Basket

Designed by Lucille LaFlamme

Finished Size: 8" high.

Materials:
- 285 yds. white size 10 crochet cotton thread
- Fabric stiffener
- Glass or plastic container with 3¼"-diameter bottom *(for shaping only)*
- Plastic wrap
- Rust-proof straight pins
- White sewing thread
- Embroidery needle
- No. 7 steel hook or hook needed to obtain gauge

Gauge: Rnds 1–4 = 3¼" across.

Basic Stitches: Ch, sl st, sc, hdc, dc, tr.

Special Stitches: For **beginning treble cluster (beg tr cluster)**, ch 4, *yo 2 times, insert hook in same st as ch-4, yo, pull through st, (yo, pull through 2 lps on hook) 2 times; repeat from *, yo, pull through all 3 lps on hook.
For **3-treble cluster (3-tr cluster)**, yo 2 times, insert hook in next st or sp, yo, pull through st or sp, (yo, pull through 2 lps on hook) 2 times, *yo 2 times, insert hook in same st or sp, yo, pull through st or sp, (yo, pull through 2 lps on hook) 2 times; repeat from *, yo, pull through all 4 lps on hook.
For **2-treble cluster (2-tr cluster)**, yo 2 times, insert hook in st, yo, pull through st, (yo, pull through 2 lps on hook) 2 times, yo 2 times, insert hook in same st, yo, pull through st, (yo, pull through 2 lps on hook) 2 times, yo, pull through all 3 lps on hook.

Basket
Rnd 1: Ch 7, sl st in first ch to form ring, ch 4 *(counts as dc and ch-1)*, (dc, ch 1) 11 times in ring, join with sl st in third ch of ch-4. *(12 dc, 12 ch sps made)*
Rnd 2: Ch 6 *(counts as dc and ch-3)*, (dc in next st, ch 3) around, join with sl st in third ch of ch-6.
Rnd 3: Ch 14 *(counts as dc and ch-11)*, (dc in next st, ch 11) around, join with sl st in third ch of ch-11.
Rnd 4: Sl st in first 6 chs, ch 4 *(counts as tr)*, *(tr, ch 3, tr, ch 3, tr, ch 3, tr) in center ch of next ch-11; repeat from * 10 more times, (tr, ch 3, tr, ch 3, tr, ch 3) in same ch as ch-4, join with sl st in top of ch-4. *(36 ch sps)*
Rnd 5: Sl st in next st, (sl st, ch 1, sc) in next ch sp, ch 3, (sc in next ch sp, ch 3) around, join with sl st in first sc.
Rnds 6–12: (Sl st, ch 1, sc) in first ch sp, ch 3, (sc in next ch sp, ch 3) around, join.
Rnd 13: Sl st in first 2 chs, **beg tr cluster**—*see Special Stitches*—in same ch as last sl st made, **3-tr cluster** in center ch of next ch-3 sp, *(ch 7, tr in second ch of each of next 2 ch-3 sps) 2 times, ch 7, 3-tr cluster in second ch of each of

next 2 ch-3 sps; repeat from * 4 more times; repeat between ( ) 2 times, ch 3, join with tr in top of beg tr cluster *(joining ch sp made). (12 cluster, 18 ch sps)*
Rnd 14: Ch 1, sc in joining ch sp, (tr, ch 4, sc) in same st as joining tr, ch 3, (sc, ch 4, tr) in next tr cluster, *sc in next ch sp, (ch 7, sc, ch 7, sc) in next ch sp, ch 7, sc in next ch sp, (tr, ch 4, sc) in next 3-tr cluster, ch 3, (sc, ch 4, tr) in next 3-tr cluster; repeat from * 4 more times, sc in next ch sp, (ch 7, sc, ch 7, sc) in last ch sp, ch 3, join with tr in first sc.
Rnd 15: Ch 1, sc in joining ch sp, *ch 5, (3-tr cluster, ch 5, 3-tr cluster) in next ch-3 sp, (ch 5, sc in next ch-4 sp) 3 times; repeat from * 4 more times, ch 5, (3-tr cluster, ch 5, 3-tr cluster) in next ch-3 sp, (ch 5, sc in next ch-4 sp) 2 times, ch 2, join with dc in first sc.
Rnds 16–17: Ch 1, sc in joining ch sp, (ch 6, sc in next ch sp) around, ch 3, join with dc in first sc.
Rnd 18: Ch 1, sc in joining ch sp, ch 6, (sc in next ch sp, ch 6) around, join with sl st in first sc.
Rnd 19: Ch 7 *(counts as tr and ch-3)*, (tr, ch 3, tr, ch 3, tr) in same st as ch 7, ch 4, sc in next sc, ch 4, *(tr, ch 3, tr, ch 3, tr, ch 3, tr) in next sc, ch 4, sc in next sc, ch 4; repeat from * around, join with sl st in fourth ch of ch-7.
Rnd 20: Ch 2 *(counts as hdc)*, *[3 dc in next ch sp, dc in next tr, 5 dc in next ch sp, dc in next tr, 3 dc in next ch sp, hdc in next tr, 4 sc in each of next 2 ch sps], hdc in next tr; repeat from * 13 more times; repeat between [ ], join with sl st in top of ch-2. Fasten off.

Handle
Row 1: *Ch 5, **2-tr cluster** *(see Special Stitches)* in fifth ch from hook; repeat from * 26 more times, **do not turn.** *(27 clusters made)*
Rnd 2: Working across first side, ch 5, 3-tr cluster in fifth ch from hook, skip last 2 clusters made, *(3-tr cluster, ch 5, sl st, ch 5, 3-tr cluster) in next space between clusters*; repeat between first and second * 25 more times, (3-tr cluster, ch 5, sl st, ch 5, 3-tr cluster) in first ch of first ch-5 made on row 1; working in remaining lps on opposite side of starting ch on row 1, repeat between first and second * 26 times, ch 5, 3-tr cluster in fifth ch from hook, join with sl st in first ch of first ch-5 made on this row. Fasten off.

Finishing
Dampen crochet pieces with fabric stiffener according to manufacturer's instructions. Place glass or plastic container covered with plastic wrap inside Basket and shape. Let dry completely, shaping rnds 19 and 20 as it dries.
Shape and pin Handle on a flat surface covered with plastic wrap. Let dry completely.
Remove pieces from plastic wrap. Bend Handle to fit inside Basket, sew in place. ●

Pew Marker

Designed by Wilma Bonner

Finished Sizes: Dove is 2¾" long. Small Bell is 4¾" tall, not including decorations.

Materials:
- Size 10 crochet cotton thread:
    100 yds. white
    15 yds. cream
- 1 yd. ivory bridal tulle
- 4 yds. white ⅛" ribbon
- ⅔ yd. white ⅜" ribbon
- 4 ivory 6mm pearl beads
- 32 ivory 4mm pearl beads
- Desired wedding floral spray
- Polyester fiberfill
- Fabric stiffener
- Rust-proof stainless steel pins
- 4" Styrofoam® bell
- 4" x 2"-thick Styrofoam® disc
- Plastic wrap
- Pew clip
- Two 5" pieces of ⅛" wooden dowel painted white
- 4" piece of white covered 20-gauge floral wire
- 22-gauge floral wire
- Fabric glue
- Hot glue
- No. 7 and No. 9 steel hooks or hooks needed to obtain gauges

Gauges: With **No. 7 hook,** 9 dc = 1"; 4 dc rows = 1"; 2 tr rows = 1".
With **No. 9 hook,** Small Flower is 1" across, Large Flower is 1⅝" across and Leaf is ⅞" long.

Basic Stitches: Ch, sl st, sc, hdc, dc, tr.

Special Stitch: For **picot,** (sc, ch 3, sc) in specified st or ch sp.

Dove Pick (make 2)
Head & Body
Rnd 1: With No. 7 hook and white thread, ch 4, 11 dc in fourth ch from hook, join with sl st in top of ch-4. *(12 dc made)*

Rnd 2: Ch 2, hdc in each st around, join with sl st in top of ch-2.

Rnd 3: Ch 3, dc in next 4 sts; for shaping at top of Head, 2 hdc in each of next 2 sts, dc in last 5 sts, join with sl st in top of ch-3. *(14 sts)*

Rnd 4: Ch 3, dc in next 5 sts, 2 hdc in each of next 2 sts, dc in last 6 sts, join. *(16 sts)*

Rnd 5: Ch 1, sc in each st around, join with sl st in first sc.

Rnd 6: Ch 3, dc in next 4 sts; for shaping at top of Body, 2 dc in next st, (3 dc in next st, 2 dc in next st) 3 times, dc in last 4 sts, join. *(26 dc)*

Rnds 7–8: Ch 3, dc in next 4 sts, hdc in next 17 sts, dc in last 4 sts, join.

Rnd 9: Ch 3, dc in next 3 sts, (hdc next 2 sts tog) 9 times, dc in last 4 sts, join. *(17 sts)*

Rnd 10: Ch 1, sc in each st around, join.

Rnd 11: Ch 3, dc in next 3 sts, hdc in next 9 sts, dc in last 4 sts, join.

Rnd 12: Ch 1, sc in each st around, join. Stuff.

Rnd 13: Ch 1, sc in first st, (skip next st, sc in next st) around, join. **Do not fasten off.** *(9 sc)*

Tail
Row 1: Ch 3, skip next 4 sts of last rnd on Body, sl st in next st, turn. *(1 ch sp made)*

Row 2: Ch 1, 7 sc in ch-3 sp, turn. *(7 sc)*

Row 3: Ch 3, dc in each st across, turn.

Row 4: Ch 5 *(counts as first dc and ch-2),* dc in next st, (ch 2, dc in next st) across, turn. *(7 dc, 6 ch sps)*

Row 5: Ch 5, **picot** *(see Special Stitch)* in first ch-2 sp, (ch 3, skip next st, picot in next ch-2 sp) 5 times, ch 2, dc in last st, turn.

Row 6: Ch 5, dc in first ch sp, (ch 3, skip next picot, dc in next ch-3 sp) 5 times, ch 3, skip next picot, dc in last ch sp, ch 2, dc in last st, turn. *(9 dc, 8 ch sps)*

Row 7: Ch 1, sc in first st, (3 hdc in next ch sp, sl st in next st) 7 times, 3 hdc in last ch sp, sc in last st, turn. *(2 sc, 7 sl sts, 24 hdc)*

Row 8: Ch 1, sc in first 2 sts, picot in next st, sc in next st, (sl st in next sl st, sc in next st, picot in next st, sc in next st) 7 times, sc in last st. Fasten off.

Wing (make 2)
Row 1: With No. 7 hook and white thread, ch 13, sc in second ch from hook, sc in next ch, hdc in next 2 chs, dc in next 2 chs, tr in next 2 chs, dc in next ch, hdc in next ch, sc in last 2 chs, turn. *(12 sts made)*

Row 2: Ch 1, sc in first 2 sts, hdc in next st, dc in next st, tr in next 2 sts, dc in next st, hdc in next st, sc in next st, sl st in last 3 sts. Fasten off.

Lightly paint fabric stiffener over Head and Body, then saturate crochet Tail and Wings with fabric stiffener. Shape Wings and Tail on padded surface covered with plastic wrap, pin in place, propping Head and Body up at a right angle to Tail with pins. Allow pieces to dry.

Glue Wings to each side of Body over rnds 6–8 with tips pointing up toward Tail.

For **eyes,** glue two 4mm beads to top of Head on rnd 2 about ⅜" apart.

For **beak,** cut one 2" piece from white covered wire, fold in half. Apply small amount of fabric glue to folded end of wire and insert about ½" of folded end in Head at center of rnd 1. Trim ends of wire to desired length and separate ends slightly.

Apply hot glue to end of one wooden dowel and insert into center bottom of Body.

Small Bell (make 2)
Rnd 1: With No. 7 hook and white thread, ch 6, sl st in first ch to form ring, ch 1, sc in ring, (ch 5, sc in ring) 3 times, ch 2, join with dc in first sc *(ch-2 and dc counts as last ch sp).* *(4 sc, 4 ch sps made)*

Rnd 2: Ch 1, sc in last ch sp, (ch 7, sc in next ch sp) around, ch 7, join with sl st in first sc.

Continued on page 14

Pew Marker
Continued from page 13

Rnd 3: Sl st in first ch sp, ch 4, 12 tr in same ch sp, ch 1, (13 tr in next ch sp, ch 1) around, join with sl st in top of ch-4. *(52 tr, 4 ch sps)*

Rnd 4: Sl st in next st, ch 4, tr in next 10 sts, ch 2, skip next st, next ch sp and next st, (tr in next 11 sts, ch 2, skip next st, next ch sp and next st) around, join.

Rnd 5: Sl st in next st, ch 4, tr in next 8 sts, ch 3, skip next st, picot in next ch-2 sp, ch 3, (skip next st, tr in next 9 sts, ch 3, skip next st, picot in next ch-2 sp, ch 3) around, join.

Rnd 6: Sl st in next st, ch 4, tr in next 6 sts, ch 3, skip next st, (picot in second ch of next ch-3, ch 3) 2 times, *skip next st, tr in next 7 sts, ch 3, skip next st, (picot in second ch of next ch-3, ch 3) 2 times; repeat from * around, join.

Rnd 7: Sl st in next st, ch 4, tr in next 4 sts, ch 3, skip next st, (picot in second ch of next ch-3, ch 3) 3 times, *skip next st, tr in next 5 sts, ch 3, skip next st, (picot in second ch of next ch-3, ch 3) 3 times; repeat from * around, join.

Rnd 8: Sl st in next st, ch 4, tr in next 2 sts, ch 3, skip next st, (picot in second ch of next ch-3, ch 3) 4 times, *skip next st, tr in next 3 sts, ch 3, skip next st, (picot in second ch of next ch-3, ch 3) 4 times; repeat from * around, join.

Rnd 9: Sl st in next st, ch 7 *(counts as first tr and ch-3),* (picot in second ch of next ch-3, ch 3) 5 times, *skip next st, tr in next st, ch 3, skip next st, picot in second ch of next ch-3, ch 3) 5 times; repeat from * around, join with sl st in fourth ch of ch-7.

Rnd 10: Ch 1, sc in first st, *[ch 5, skip next ch sp and picot, (picot in second ch of next ch-3, ch 3, skip next picot) 3 times, picot in second ch of next ch-3, ch 5, skip next picot and ch sp], sc in next st; repeat from * 2 more times; repeat between [ ], join with sl st in first sc.

Rnd 11: Ch 1, sc in first st, *[ch 8, skip next ch sp and picot, (picot in second ch of next ch-3, ch 3, skip next picot) 2 times, picot in second ch of next ch-3, ch 8, skip next picot and ch sp], sc in next st; repeat from * 2 more times; repeat between [ ], join.

Rnd 12: Ch 1, sc in first st, *[ch 10, skip next ch sp and picot, picot in second ch of next ch-3, ch 3, skip next picot, picot in second ch of next ch-3, ch 10, skip next picot and ch sp], sc in next st; repeat from * 2 more times; repeat between [ ], join.

Rnd 13: Ch 1, sc in first st, *[ch 12, skip next ch sp and next picot, picot in second ch of next ch-3, ch 12, skip next picot and next ch sp], sc in next st; repeat from * 2 more times; repeat between [ ], join. Fasten off.

Hanging Loop
Row 1: Working between any 2 sts of rnd 1 on Bell, with No. 7 hook and white thread, join with sl st in ring, ch 17, sl st in ring between 2 sts opposite first sl st, turn.

Row 2: Ch 1, skip first sl st, (10 sc, 5 dc, 10 sc) in ch-17, sl st in last sl st. Fasten off.

Cover Styrofoam® bell form with plastic wrap. Saturate crochet Bell with fabric stiffener, lightly press out any excess stiffener. Place Bell over form, shape and pin in place. Allow to dry.

Flower (make 4)
Layer of Petals
Rnd 1: With No. 9 hook and cream thread, ch 7, sl st in first ch to form ring, ch 1, (2 sc in ring, ch 5) 6 times, join with sl st in first sc. *(12 sc, 6 ch sps made)*

Rnd 2: Sl st in next st, (3 sc, hdc, 3 sc) in next ch-5 sp, *sl st in next 2 sts, (3 sc, hdc, 3 sc) in next ch-5 sp; repeat from * 4 more times, join with sl st in first sl st. Fasten off.

For each **Flower,** using fabric glue, attach one 6mm pearl bead to center of one Layer of Petals. Attach seven 4mm pearl beads to Layer of Petals around center bead. Let glue dry. *(To make handling beads easier, use a straight pin to pick up and place beads.)*

Leaf (make 8)
With No. 9 hook and cream thread, ch 9, sc in second ch from hook, sc in next ch, hdc in next 2 chs, dc in next 2 chs, tr in next ch, ch 4, sl st in last ch; working in remaining lps on opposite side of starting ch, ch 4, tr in next ch, dc in next 2 chs, hdc in next 2 chs, sc in next 2 chs, sl st in ch at tip. Fasten off.

Finishing
Note: Use fabric glue for all assembly unless otherwise stated.

1: Cut ⅜" ribbon in half. Tie one end of each piece to Hanging Loop on each Bell.

2: Using ⅛" ribbon, make four multi-loop bows to fit on top of Bells *(see photo).*

3: Glue one Flower and two Leaves to center of each bow.

4: Placing bows back to back, using hot glue, attach two bows to top of each Bell, covering Hanging Loops *(see photo).*

5: Using hot glue, attach pew clip to center of one side on Styrofoam® disc. Cut two pieces of floral wire and bend each in a U shape. Place each piece of wire over base of pew clip and push ends through Styrofoam® to other side. Twist ends of wires together to secure.

6: Attach flower spray to Styrofoam® disc.

7: Tie bridal tulle in a large bow. Using hot glue, attach bow to Styrofoam® disc below flower spray.

8: Using hot glue, attach ends of ribbons on Bells to Styrofoam® disc so they hang as desired from bottom of flower spray.

9: Insert each Dove Pick in flower spray as desired or as shown in photo. •

Bridal Tablecloth

Continued from page 9

Rnd 4: Ch 1, sc in first st, *[ch 5, skip next 3 sts, sc in next st, sl st in first ch of next ch-15, ch 3 *(counts as dc),* dc in next 4 chs, ch 3, tr in next 5 chs, ch 3, dc in next 4 chs, ch 3, sl st in next ch], sc in next st; repeat from * 2 more times; repeat between [ ], join.

Rnd 5: Sl st in first 2 chs of first ch-5 sp, ch 1, sc in next ch, *[ch 3, skip next sc, dc in top of ch-3, dc in each of next 3 dc, ch 7, skip next dc, tr in next 5 tr, ch 7, skip next dc, dc in each of next 3 dc, dc in top of next ch-3, ch 3], skip next sc, sc in center ch of next ch-5 sp; repeat from * 2 more times; repeat between [ ], join with sl st in first sc.

Rnd 6: Sl st in each ch of first ch-3 sp, sl st in next dc, ch 3, dc in each of next 2 dc, *[ch 7, skip next dc, sc in fourth ch of next ch-7 sp, ch 7, tr in next 5 tr, ch 7, sc in fourth ch of next ch-7 sp, ch 7, skip next dc, dc in each of next 3 dc, ch 3], skip next sc, dc in each of next 3 dc; repeat from * 2 more times; repeat between [ ], join with sl st in top of ch-3.

Rnd 7: Ch 3, dc next 2 sts tog, *(ch 7, sc in fourth ch of next ch-7 sp) 2 times, [ch 7, skip next tr, tr in each of next 3 tr, (ch 7, sc in fourth ch of next ch-7 sp) 2 times, ch 7, dc next 3 dc tog], ch 3, dc next 3 dc tog; repeat from * 2 more times, (ch 7, sc in fourth ch of next ch-7 sp) 2 times; repeat between [ ], skip beginning ch-3, join with dc in top of next dc.

Rnd 8: Sl st in joining ch sp, **beg dc cluster** *(see Special Stitches),* **picot** *(see Special Stitches),* *[ch 3, sc in fourth ch of next ch-7 sp, (ch 7, sc in fourth ch of next ch-7 sp) 2 times, ch 7, tr next 3 tr tog, picot, (ch 7, sc in fourth ch of next ch-7 sp) 3 times, ch 3], **dc cluster,** picot; repeat from * 2 more times; repeat between [ ], join with sl st in top of beg dc cluster. Fasten off.

Second Motif
(joined on one side)

Rnds 1–7: Repeat rnds 1–7 of First Motif.
Rnd 8: Sl st in joining ch sp, beg dc cluster, picot, ch 3, sc in fourth ch of next ch-7 sp, (ch 7, sc in fourth ch of next ch-7 sp) 2 times, ch 7, tr next 3 tr tog; for **corner joining, ch 2, sl st in corresponding picot at corner of previous Motif, ch 2, sl st in top of last st made on this Motif** *(corner joining completed);* ch 7, sc in fourth ch of next ch-7 sp; for **side joining, skip next ch sp on previous Motif, (ch 3, sl st in fourth ch of next ch-7 sp on previous Motif, ch 3, sc in fourth ch of next**

ch-7 sp on this Motif) 2 times; ch 3, dc cluster, picot, ch 3, sc in fourth ch of next ch-7 sp, work side joining, ch 7, tr next 3 tr tog, work corner joining, *(ch 7, sc in fourth ch of next ch-7 sp) 3 times, ch 3, dc cluster, picot, ch 3, (sc in fourth ch of next ch-7 sp, ch 7) 3 times, tr next 3 tr tog, picot; repeat from *, (ch 7, sc in fourth ch of next ch-7 sp) 3 times, ch 3, join with sl st in top of beg dc cluster. Fasten off.

Third Motif
(joined on two sides)

Rnds 1–7: Repeat rnds 1–7 of First Motif.
Rnd 8: Sl st in joining ch sp, beg dc cluster, picot, ch 3, sc in fourth ch of next ch-7 sp, (ch 7, sc in fourth ch of next ch-7 sp) 2 times, *ch 7, tr next 3 tr tog, work corner joining, ch 7, sc in fourth ch of next ch-7 sp, work side joining, ch 3, dc cluster, picot, ch 3, sc in fourth ch of next ch-7 sp, work side joining; repeat from *, ch 7, tr next 3 tr tog, work corner joining, (ch 7, sc in fourth ch of next ch-7 sp) 3 times, ch 3, dc cluster, picot, ch 3, (sc in fourth ch of next ch-7 sp, ch 7) 3 times, tr next 3 tr tog, picot, (ch 7, sc in fourth ch of next ch-7 sp) 3 times, ch 3, join with sl st in top of beg dc cluster. Fasten off.

Border

Rnd 1: Join with sl st in any corner picot, (ch 3, 2 dc, ch 3, 3 dc) in same picot, *◊(ch 7, sc in fourth ch of next ch-7 sp) 3 times, ch 7; for **shell, (3 dc, ch 3, 3 dc) in next picot;** (ch 7, sc in fourth ch of next ch-7 sp) 3 times, [ch 7, 3 dc in sl st of next corner joining, (ch 7, sc in fourth ch of next ch-7 sp) 3 times, ch 7, shell in next picot, (ch 7, sc in fourth ch of next ch-7 sp) 3 times]; repeat between [ ] across to next corner, ch 7◊, shell in next picot at corner*; repeat between first and second * 2 more times; repeat between first and second ◊, join with sl st in top of ch-3.

Rnd 2: Ch 4 *(counts as tr),* tr next 2 dc tog, ch 3, **tr cluster** *(see Special Stitches),* picot, ch 3, tr next 3 dc tog, *◊(ch 7, sc in fourth ch of next ch-7 sp) 4 times, ch 7, tr next 3 dc tog, ch 3, tr cluster, picot, ch 3, tr next 3 dc tog, (ch 7, sc in fourth ch of next ch-7 sp) 4 times, [ch 3, tr next 3 dc tog, picot, ch 3, (sc in fourth ch of next ch-7 sp, ch 7) 4 times, tr next 3 dc tog, ch 3, tr cluster, picot, ch 3, tr next 3 dc tog, (ch 7, sc in fourth ch of next ch-7 sp) 4 times]; repeat between [ ] across to next corner, ch 7◊, tr next 3 dc tog, ch 3, tr cluster, picot, ch 3, tr next 3 dc tog*; repeat between first and second * 2 more times; repeat between first and second ◊, skip ch-4, join with sl st in top of next tr. Fasten off. ●

Love Spoken Here

Designed by Lucille LaFlamme

Finished Size: 11" x 13½".

Materials:
- Size 10 crochet cotton thread:
  - 300 yds. white
  - 150 yds. lt. pink
  - Small amount each yellow and dk. pink
- Tapestry needle
- No. 7 steel hook or hook needed to obtain gauge

Gauge: 10 dc = 1"; 7 dc rows = 2".

Basic Stitches: Ch, sl st, sc, dc.

Special Stitches: For **beginning mesh (beg mesh)**, ch 5, skip next 2 chs or sts, dc in next st.
For **mesh**, ch 2, skip next 2 chs or sts, dc in next st or ch.
For **end mesh**, ch 2, dc in third ch of ch-5.
For **block**, 2 dc in next ch sp, dc in next st, **or,** dc in next 3 sts, **or,** 2 dc in next bar, dc in next st or ch.
For **picot lacet**, ch 3, skip next 2 chs or sts, sc in next ch or st, ch 3, sl st in third ch from hook, ch 3, skip next 2 chs or sts, dc in next st.
For **bar**, ch 5, skip next picot lacet, dc in next st.
For **shell**, (2 dc, ch 2, 2 dc).
For **picot**, ch 3, sl st in third ch from hook.
For **beginning cluster (beg cl)**, ch 3, yo, insert hook in ch sp, yo, pull through sp, yo, pull through 2 lps on hook, yo, insert hook in same ch sp, yo, pull through sp, yo, pull through 2 lps on hook, yo, pull through all 3 lps on hook.
For **cluster (cl)**, yo, insert hook in ch sp, yo, pull through sp, yo, pull through 2 lps on hook, (yo, insert hook in same ch sp, yo, pull through sp, yo, pull through 2 lps on hook) 2 times, yo, pull through all 4 lps on hook.
For **cluster shell (cl shell)**, (cl, picot, ch 2, dc, picot, ch 2, cl, picot) in ch sp of next shell.

Picture
Row 1: With white, ch 140, dc in eight ch from hook, (ch 2, skip next 2 chs, dc in next ch) across, turn. *(45 mesh made) First 7 chs count as first mesh.*
Row 2: Beg mesh *(see Special Stitches),* mesh 43 times, end mesh, turn.
Rows 3–35: Work according to graph on page 22. At end of last row, fasten off.

Continued on page 22

Turn-of-the-Century Bride

Designed by Beverly Mewhorter

Finished Size: Fits 11½" fashion doll.

Materials:
- 750 yds. white size 10 crochet cotton thread
- White bridal tulle:
    - 6" x 52" *(for Petticoat)*
    - 12" x 28" *(for Veil)*
- 20" white iridescent 3mm strung pearl beads
- 10 white flat flowers
- 18 white small roses
- White ribbon:
    - 24" of ⅛"
    - 24" of ¼"
- 10" wooden skewer
- White acrylic paint
- Small paint brush
- Hot glue gun and glue
- 5 small snaps
- 3 straight pins
- White sewing thread
- Embroidery and sewing needles
- No. 7 steel hook or hook needed to obtain gauge

Gauge: 7 sc = 1"; 7 sc rows = 1".

Basic Stitches: Ch, sl st, sc, hdc, dc, tr.

Gown
Bodice
Row 1: Starting at waist, ch 23, sc in second ch from hook, sc in each ch across, turn. *(22 sc made)*

Rows 2–3: Ch 1, sc in each st across, turn. *Front of row 2 is right side of work.*

Row 4: Ch 1, sc in first 4 sts, 2 sc in next st, sc in next 12 sts, 2 sc in next st, sc in last 4 sts, turn. *(24)*

Row 5: Ch 1, sc in first 5 sts, 2 sc in next st, sc in next 12 sts, 2 sc in next st, sc in last 5 sts, turn. *(26)*

Rows 6–7: Ch 1, sc in each st across, turn.

Row 8: Ch 1, sc in first 5 sts, 2 sc in next st, sc in next 14 sts, 2 sc in next st, sc in last 5 sts, turn. *(28)*

Row 9: Ch 1, sc in each st across, turn.

Row 10: Ch 1, sc in first 8 sts, 2 sc in each of next 2 sts, sc in next 8 sts, 2 sc in each of next 2 sts, sc in last 8 sts, turn. *(32)*

Row 11: Ch 1, sc in first 12 sts, 3 sc in each of next 2 sts, sc in next 4 sts, 3 sc in each of next 2 sts, sc in last 12 sts, turn. *(40)*

Rows 12–15: Ch 1, sc in each st across, turn.

Row 16: Ch 1, sc in first 7 sts, ch 10, skip next 4 sts *(armhole made),* sc in next 18 sts, ch 10,
skip next 4 sts *(armhole made),* sc in last 7 sts, turn. *(32 sc, 20 chs)*

Row 17: Ch 1, sc in each st and in each ch across, turn. *(52 sc)*

Row 18: Working this row in **back lps** *(see Stitch Guide),* ch 1, sc in each st across, turn.

Row 19: Ch 1, sc in first 3 sts, sc next 2 sts tog, (sc in next 3 sts, sc next 2 sts tog) 9 times, sc in last 2 sts, turn. *(42)*

Row 20: Ch 1, sc in first st, sc next 2 sts tog, (sc in next st, sc next 2 sts tog) across, turn. *(28)*

Row 21: Ch 1, sc first 2 sts tog, (sc next 2 sts tog) across, turn. *(14)*

Rows 22–25: Ch 1, sc in each st across, turn.

Row 26: Ch 1, (sc, ch 1, sc) in each st across. Fasten off.

Bodice Ruffle
Row 1: With top of Bodice facing you, working in **remaining lps** of row 17, join with sl st in first st, (ch 3, 2 dc) in same st as joining sl st, 3 dc in each st across, turn. *(First 3 chs counts as first dc—156 dc made.)*

Rows 2–3: Ch 3, dc in each st across, turn. At end of last row, **do not turn.** Fasten off.

Row 4: Join with sc in first st, ch 1, sc in same st as joining sc, (sc, ch 1, sc) in each st across. Fasten off.

Skirt
Row 1: With top of Bodice toward you, working in remaining lps on opposite side of starting ch on row 1, join with sc in first ch, sc in each ch across, turn. *(22 sc made)*

Row 2: Ch 1, sc in first 5 sts, hdc in next 3 sts, dc in next 2 sts, 2 tr in each of next 2 sts, dc in next 2 sts, hdc in next 3 sts, sc in last 5 sts, turn. *(24 sts)*

Row 3: Working this row in **back lps,** ch 1, 3 sc in each st across, turn. *(72 sc)*

Rows 4–8: Ch 3, dc in each st across, turn.

Row 9: Working this row in **back lps,** (ch 3, 2 dc) in first st, 3 dc in each st across, turn.

Rows 10–15: Ch 3, dc in each st across, turn.

Row 16: Working this row in **back lps,** (ch 3, 2 dc) in first st, 3 dc in each st across, turn.

Rows 17–24: Ch 3, dc in each st across, turn.

Row 25: Ch 1, (sc, ch 1, sc) in each st across. Fasten off.

First Ruffle
With top of Bodice toward you, working in **remaining lps** of row 2 on Skirt, join with sc in first st, ch 1, sc in same st as joining sc, (sc, ch 1, sc) in each st across. Fasten off.

Continued on page 20

Second Ruffle
Row 1: With top of Bodice toward you, working in **remaining lps** of row 8 on Skirt, join with sl st in first st, ch 3, dc in each st across, turn.
Row 2: Ch 3, dc in each st across, turn.
Row 3: Ch 1, (sc, ch 1, sc) in each st across. Fasten off.

Third Ruffle
Working in **remaining lps** of row 15 on Skirt, repeat same as Second Ruffle.

Sleeve (make 2)
Rnd 1: Ch 14, sl st in first ch to form ring, ch 1, sc in each ch around, join with sl st in first sc. *(14 sc made)*
Rnd 2: (Ch 3, dc) in first st, 2 dc in each st around, join with sl st in top of ch-3. *(28 dc)*
Rnds 3–8: Ch 3, dc in each st around, join.
Rnd 9: Ch 2 *(not counted or used as a st)*, dc in next st, (dc next 2 sts tog) around, join with sl st in first dc. *(14 dc)*
Rnd 10: (Ch 3, 2 dc) in first st, 3 dc in each st around, join with sl st in top of ch-3. *(42 dc)*
Rnd 11: Ch 3, dc in each st around, join.
Rnd 12: Ch 1, (sc, ch 1, sc) in each st around, join with sl st in first sc. Fasten off.
Easing to fit, sew first rnd of Sleeves to armholes.

Petticoat
With sewing needle and thread, gather across one long edge of 6" x 52" piece of tulle to fit around doll's waist. Place around waist, secure ends.

Finishing
With embroidery needle and crochet cotton thread, sew matching ends of rows 3–25 on Skirt together.
Sew ends of rows on Second and Third Ruffles together.
With sewing needle and thread, sew five snaps evenly spaced down back opening on Gown.
Place Gown on doll.
Cut two pieces each 12" long from ⅛" ribbon. Tie one 12" ribbon in bow around rnd 9 of each Sleeve.
Tie 24" of ¼" ribbon around waist with bow in back.
Cut 3" of strung beads, glue over row 21 of Bodice.
Cut two strands each ⅞" from strung beads. Center and glue one strand to center front of Bodice and one to center back of Bodice.
Arrange and glue one rose and three flowers to front of Skirt between First and Second Ruffle *(see photo)*.
Arrange and glue one rose and three flowers to front of Skirt between Second and Third Ruffle.

Bouquet Holder
Rnd 1: Ch 6, sl st in first ch to form ring, ch 1, 12 sc in ring, join with sl st in first sc. *(12 sc made)*
Rnd 2: (Ch 3, dc) in first st, 2 dc in each st around, join with sl st in top of ch-3. *(24 dc)*
Rnd 3: (Ch 3, dc) in first st, dc in next st, (2 dc in next st, dc in next st) around, join. *(36 dc)*
Rnd 4: Ch 1, (sc, ch 1, sc) in each st around, join with sl st in first sc. Fasten off.
Arrange and glue ten roses and five flowers to top of Holder.
Cut 6" piece of ⅛" ribbon. Weave ribbon through two sts at center back of Holder, tie ends of ribbon tightly around doll's wrist leaving long ends.

Hat
Rnd 1: Ch 4, 13 dc in fourth ch from hook, join with sl st in top of ch-4. *(14 dc made)*
Rnd 2: (Ch 3, dc) in first st, 2 dc in each st around, join with sl st in top of ch-3. *(28 dc)*
Rnd 3: Working this rnd in **back lps**, ch 1, sc in each st around, join with sl st in first sc.
Rnd 4: Ch 1, sc in each st around, join.
Rnd 5: Working this rnd in **front lps**, (ch 3, dc) in first st, 2 dc in each st around, join with sl st in top of ch-3. *(56 dc)*
Rnd 6: Ch 1, sc in each st around, join with sl st in first sc. Fasten off.
Cut 6½" strand and 2" strand of strung beads.
Glue 6½" strand over rnd 6 of Hat.
Glue 2" strand over rnd 5 *(for front of Hat—see photo)*.
Arrange and glue six roses to top back of Hat *(see photo)*.
For **veil**, fold one 28" edge of 12" x 28" piece of tulle down 1½", with sewing needle and thread, gather tulle 1" from fold to measure 1½" across, secure.
Glue veil to wrong side of Hat with folded edge at back.
Place veil and Hat on head, secure with straight pins.

Parasol

Paint skewer with white paint. Let dry completely.

Rnd 1: Starting at bottom, ch 4, sl st in first ch to form ring, ch 3, 9 dc in ring, join with sl st in top of ch-3. *(10 dc made)*

Rnds 2–4: Ch 3, dc in each st around, join.

Rnd 5: (Ch 3, dc) in first st, 2 dc in each st around, join. *(20)*

Rnds 6–14: Ch 3, dc in each st around, join.

Rnd 15: (Ch 3, 2 dc) in first st, 3 dc in each st around, join. *(60)*

Rnd 16: Ch 1, (sc, ch 1, sc) in each st around, join with sl st in first sc. Fasten off.

Insert pointed end of skewer from wrong side through opening at center of rnd 1, glue in place with ½" end extended past center.

Wrap 12" piece of crochet cotton thread over rnd 14 and skewer, secure e ds.

Wrap 6" piece of crochet cotton thread over rnd 2 and skewer, secure ends.

Slightly twist crochet piece on skewer, glue in place.

Wrap and glue 5" strand of strung beads twice around threaded wrap of rnd 14.

Wrap and glue 2" strand of strung beads around threaded wrap of rnd 2. ●

Hot Tips for Great Doll Hair

Does fussing with fashion doll hair that goes flat or frizzy or refuses to hold a curl make you do a slow boil? If so, then hold that thought because we're about to reveal a secret we've discovered that will practically eliminate bad hair days for dolls. What's more, this styling technique is so easy, inexpensive, and almost foolproof, that it turns hairdo woes into coiffure wonders!

The simple secret to setting doll hair so that it holds a smooth and long-lasting curl is boiling water. That's right, good old H20 straight from the tap and then heated!

First, start with rolling the hair. In the photo at left, this doll's long hair was rolled on medium-size perm rods. Then, prepare to set the curl by boiling water, either on the stovetop or in the microwave, and immediately pouring it into a heatproof bowl or other container large enough to immerse the doll's curlers.

Gently and carefully, lower the doll's curls into the water, making sure all the curls are submerged. Be careful not to wet areas such as bangs that you want to leave as they are (see photo below).

Prop the doll if necessary so that it remains stationary, and leave the curlers in the water until the water has completely cooled.

When the water is cool, carefully lift the doll out of the water and lay on several layers of absorbent toweling to blot excess moisture. Allow curls to dry completely, changing toweling if necessary. Depending upon the size of the curl and the ambient humidity, drying may take up to three days.

When curls are completely dry, unwind and arrange them as desired. It's as simple as that. Finished curls will be smooth, shiny and soft, with no gel or hairspray required to keep them in place!

A warning: curls made by boiling water are quite permanent, so it is best to experiment first to get the look you want. Also, since doll hair varies greatly from brand to brand, it is best to test!

This finished style (above left) is just an example of the beautiful results that using boiling water to set curls can create with ease!

Love Spoken Here
Continued from page 17

Edging
Rnd 1: Join lt. pink with sl st in bottom right-hand corner mesh, (ch 3, dc, ch 2, 2 dc) in same mesh; working in mesh around outer edge, *ch 3, skip next mesh, sc in next mesh, ch 3, skip next mesh, **shell** *(see Special Stitches)* in next mesh*; repeat between first and second * 7 more times, skip next mesh, (shell, ch 2, shell) in next corner mesh, skip next mesh, shell in next mesh; repeat between first and second * 10 times, skip next mesh, (shell, ch 2, shell) in next corner mesh, skip next mesh, shell in next mesh; repeat between first and second * 7 times, ch 3, skip next mesh, sc in next mesh, ch 3, skip next mesh, (shell, ch 2, shell) in next corner mesh; repeat between first and second * 10 times, ch 3, skip next mesh, sc in next mesh, ch 3, skip next mesh, shell in starting corner mesh, ch 2, join with sl st in top of ch-3.

Rnd 2: Sl st in next st, sl st in next ch sp, **beg cl** *(see Special Stitches)*, **picot**, ch 2, (dc, picot, ch 2, **cl**, picot) in same ch sp as beg cl, *ch 3, (sc, picot) in next sc, ch 3, **cl shell***; repeat between first and second * 7 more times, [ch 3, (sc, picot) in ch sp of next shell, ch 3, cl shell in next ch-2 sp between shells, ch 3, (sc, picot) in ch sp of next shell, ch 3, cl shell in ch sp of next shell]; repeat between first and second * 10 times; repeat between [ ]; repeat between first and second * 8 times, ch 3, (sc, picot) in next ch-2 sp between shells, ch 3, cl shell in ch sp of next shell; repeat between first and second * 11 times, ch 3, (sc, picot) in ch-2 sp between shells, ch 3, join with sl st in top of first cl. Fasten off.

Flower (make 2 lt. pink, 1 dk. pink, 1 yellow)
Rnd 1: Ch 6, sl st in first ch to form ring, ch 1, (sc in ring, ch 3) 6 times, join with sl st in first sc. *(6 ch sps made)*

Rnd 2: Ch 1, (sc, hdc, 2 dc, hdc, sc) in each ch sp around, join. Fasten off.

Sew Flowers to Picture according to dots on graph. ●

■ = BLOCK

□ = BEG MESH, MESH
    or END MESH

= BAR

= PICOT LACET

● = FLOWER PLACEMENT

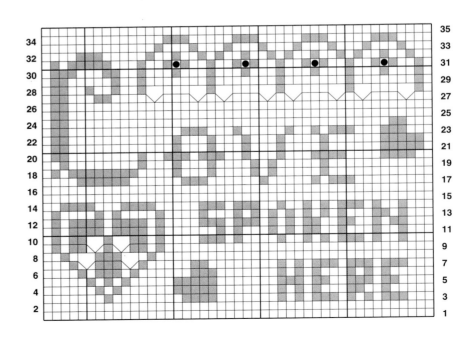

chapter 2

Irish Ayes

When Irish eyes are smiling, you can be sure they are usually cooking up something delicious!

Irish Creme
1¾ cup rum
14 oz. can sweetened condensed milk
1 cup whipping cream
4 eggs
2 tbs. chocolate syrup
2 tsp. instant coffee
1 tsp. vanilla
½ tsp. vanilla extract

Blend in blender. Refrigerate.

Leprechaun Doorstop

Designed by Cynthia Harris

Finished Size: Approximately 20½" tall, including Hat.

Materials:
- Worsted yarn:
  - 20 oz. green
  - 4 oz. lt. peach
  - 2 oz. black
  - 2 oz. white
  - 1 oz. bright orange
- 9" x 12" black felt
- 6" x 6" gold felt
- Scrap pieces of black and white felt
- 6" wooden ¼" dowel
- 1" x 1¼" cork
- About 15–20 oz. polyester fiberfill
- Minimum of 5 lbs. of any dried beans or sand
- Brown permanent marker
- Sharp knife
- One clean and dry plastic gallon milk jug with lid
- Craft glue
- Tapestry needle
- G and K hooks or hooks needed to obtain gauges

Gauges: With **G hook and two strands of yarn**, 4 loop sts = 1". With **K hook and two strands of yarn**, 3 sts = 1¼"; 3 sc rnds = 1¼".

Basic Stitches: Ch, sl st, sc, hdc, dc.

Notes: Work with K hook and two strands of yarn held together throughout unless otherwise stated.

Work in continuous rnds; do not join or turn unless otherwise stated. Mark first st of each rnd.

Body
Rnd 1: Beginning at bottom, with green, ch 3, sl st in first ch to form ring, ch 1, 2 sc in each ch around, **do not join**. *(6 sc made)*
Rnds 2–3: 2 sc in each st around. *(12, 24)*
Rnd 4: (Sc in next 2 sts, 2 sc in next st) around. *(32)*
Rnd 5: (Sc in next 3 sts, 2 sc in next st) around. *(40)*
Rnd 6: (Sc in next 4 sts, 2 sc in next st) around. *(48)*
Rnds 7–30: Sc in each st around.
Place plastic jug inside of Body. Stuff around sides and in front of jug. Handle will be at the center back of Body. *(Do not stuff too full; sts should not be stretched in front. Body should fit smoothly over back of jug.)*
Rnd 31: (Sc in next 4 sts, sc next 2 sts tog) around. *(40)*
Rnd 32: Sc in each st around.
Rnd 33: (Sc in next 3 sts, sc next 2 sts tog) around. *(32)*
Rnd 34: Sc in each st around.
Rnd 35: (Sc in next 2 sts, sc next 2 sts tog) around. *(24)*
Rnds 36–37: (Sc next 2 sts tog) around. At end of last rnd, join with sl st in first sc. Fasten off. *(12, 6)*
Note: *Top of Body does not have to be sewn together; the Head will cover this area.*
Fill jug with dried beans or sand. Place lid on jug, secure or glue in place.

Handle
Thread tapestry needle with two strands of green; press Body together through opening of jug handle and sew sides that have been pressed together, stitching back and forth through opening *(see illustration)*.

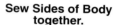
Sew Sides of Body together.

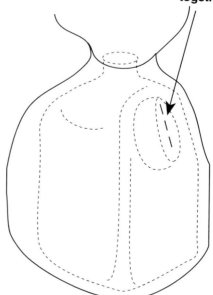

Head
Rnd 1: Beginning at top, with lt. peach, ch 3, sl st in first ch to form ring, ch 1, 2 sc in each ch around. *(6 sc made)*
Rnd 2: 2 sc in each st around. *(12)*
Rnd 3: (Sc in next st, 2 sc in next st) around. *(18)*

Continued on page 26

Leprechaun Doorstop
Continued from page 25

Rnd 4: (Sc in next 2 sts, 2 sc in next st) around. *(24)*

Rnd 5: (Sc in next 3 sts, 2 sc in next st) around. *(30)*

Rnd 6: (Sc in next 4 sts, 2 sc in next st) around. *(36)*

Rnd 7: (Sc in next 5 sts, 2 sc in next st) around. *(42)*

Rnds 8–14: Sc in each st around.

Rnd 15: (Sc in next 6 sts, 2 sc in next st) around. *(48)*

Rnds 16–18: Sc in each st around.

Rnd 19: (Sc in next 6 sts, sc next 2 sts tog) around. *(42)*

Rnd 20: (Sc in next 5 sts, sc next 2 sts tog) around. *(36)*

Rnd 21: (Sc in next 4 sts, sc next 2 sts tog) around. *(30)*

Rnd 22: (Sc in next 3 sts, sc next 2 sts tog) around. *(24)*

Rnds 23–24: Sc in each st around. At end of last rnd, join with sl st in first sc. Leaving 28" end for sewing, fasten off.

Stuff Head firmly leaving a small opening in the center bottom of Head to allow room for top of jug. Sew Head to rnd 35 of Body.

Leg (make 2)

Rnd 1: With black, ch 7, 2 sc in second ch from hook, sc in next 4 chs, 4 sc in last ch; working on opposite side of ch, sc in next 4 chs, 2 sc in next ch. *(16 sc made)*

Rnd 2: 2 sc in each of next 2 sts, sc in next 4 sts, 2 sc in each of next 4 sts, sc in next 4 sts, 2 sc in each of next 2 sts. *(24)*

Rnd 3: (Sc in next st, 2 sc in next st) 2 times, sc in next 4 sts, (2 sc in next st, sc in next st) 2 times, (sc in next st, 2 sc in next st) 2 times, sc in next 4 sts, (2 sc in next st, sc in next st) 2 times. *(32)*

Rnd 4: (Sc in next 3 sts, 2 sc in next st) around. *(40)*

Rnd 5: Working in **back lps** *(see Stitch Guide)*, sc in each st around.

Rnds 6–8: Sc in each st around.

Rnd 9: Sc in next 12 sts, (sc next 2 sts tog) 8 times, sc in next 12 sts. *(32)*

Rnd 10: Sc in next 10 sts; working in **back lps,** (sc next 2 sts tog) 6 times; working in **both lps,** sc in last 10 sts, join with sl st in first sc. Fasten off.

Rnd 11: Working in **back lps,** join white with sc in first st, sc in each st around.

Rnds 12–14: Working in **both lps,** sc in each st around.

Rnd 15: Sc in next 6 sts, 2 sc in next st, sc in next 12 sts, 2 sc in next st, sc in next 6 sts, join with sl st in next sc. Fasten off. *(28)*

Rnd 16: Join green with sc in any st, sc in next 6 sts, 2 sc in next st, sc in next 12 sts, 2 sc in next st, sc in next 7 sts. *(30)*

Rnd 17: Sc in next 7 sts, 2 sc in next st, sc in next 14 sts, 2 sc in next st, sc in next 7 sts. *(32)*

Rnd 18: Sc in next 8 sts, 2 sc in next st, sc in next 14 sts, 2 sc in next st, sc in next 8 sts. *(34)*

Rnd 19: Sc in next 8 sts, 2 sc in next st, sc in next 16 sts, 2 sc in next st, sc in next 8 sts, join with sl st in next sc. Leaving 18" end for sewing, fasten off.

Shoe Flap

Row 1: Working in **remaining lps** of row 10, join black with sl st in first st, sc first st and next st tog, sc in next 8 sts, sc next 2 sts tog, leaving remaining sts unworked, turn.

Rows 2–3: Ch 1, sc in each st across, turn. At end of last row, fasten off. Stuff Leg firmly.

Sew Legs to sides of Body 1¾" apart so Doorstop will be in a sitting position.

Arm (make 2)

Rnd 1: With lt. peach, ch 3, sl st in first ch to form ring, ch 1, 2 sc in each ch around. *(6 sc made)*

Rnd 2: 2 sc in each st around. *(12)*

Rnd 3: (Sc in next 2 sts, 2 sc in next st) around. *(16)*

Rnd 4: (Sc in next st, 2 sc in next st) around. *(24)*

Rnds 5–10: Sc in each st around. At end of last rnd, join with sl st in first sc. Fasten off.

Rnd 11: Join green with sc in any st, sc in each st around.

Rnds 12–23: Sc in each st around. At end of last rnd, join with sl st in first sc. Leaving an 18" end for sewing, fasten off.

Flatten top of Arm and sew closed. Sew one Arm to each side of Body two rnds below where Head and Body are joined *(see photo)*.

Shirt Ruffle

Row 1: With white, ch 13, sc in second ch from hook, sc in each ch across, turn. *(12 sc made)*

Row 2: Working in **back lps,** ch 1, sc in first st, (ch 2, sc in next st) across, turn.

Row 3: Keep ch-2 sps pulled toward you and skip them as you work; working in **back lps,** ch 1, sc first 2 sts tog, sc in each st across to last 2 sts, sc last 2 sts tog, turn. *(10)*

Rows 4–12: Repeat rows 2 and 3 alternately, ending with row 2. At end of last row, leaving end for sewing, fasten off. *(2)*

Sew Ruffle to front of Body, sewing row 1 to center front of neck below Head.

Jacket
Bottom

Row 1: With green, ch 62, sc in second ch from hook, sc in each ch across, turn. *(61 sc made)*

Row 2: Ch 1, 2 sc in first st, (sc in next 9 sts, 2 sc in next st) across, turn. *(68)*

Row 3: Ch 1, sc in each st across, turn.

Row 4: Ch 1, 2 sc in first st, (sc in next 10 sts, 2 sc in next st) 5 times, sc in next 11 sts, 2 sc in last st. Fasten off. *(75)*

Right Lapel

Row 1: Working in remaining lps on opposite side of starting ch on row 1 of Bottom, join green with sc in first ch, sc in next 3 chs leaving remaining chs unworked, turn. *(4 sc made)*

Rows 2–28: Ch 1, sc in each st across, turn. At end of last row, leaving long end for sewing, fasten off.

Left Lapel

Row 1: Working in remaining lps on opposite side of starting ch on row 1 of Bottom, skip next 53 chs, join green with sc in next ch, sc in last 3 chs, turn. *(4 sc made)*

Rows 2–28: Repeat rows 2–28 of Right Lapel.

Place Bottom of Jacket around waist. Keeping Lapels straight, sew row 28 of Lapels together behind neck.

Sew inner edge of Lapels across back of neck, over shoulder and down front of Body outlining Ruffle.

Sew top edge of Bottom around waist.

Nose

Rnd 1: With lt. peach, ch 3, sl st in first ch to form ring, ch 1, 2 sc in each ch around. *(6 sc made)*

Rnd 2: (Sc in next st, 2 sc in next st) around, join with sl st in first sc. Leaving end for sewing, fasten off.

Stuff lightly and sew to center front of Head.

Ear (make 2)

Rnd 1: With lt. peach, ch 2, 6 sc in second ch from hook. *(6 sc made)*

Rnd 2: 2 sc in each st around. *(12)*

Row 3: Fold piece in half with right side facing you; working through both thicknesses, matching sts, ch 1, sc in next 6 sts. Leaving end for sewing, fasten off.

Sew straight edge of one Ear to side of Head. Repeat on other side of Head.

Mouth

With tapestry needle and one strand of black yarn, embroider smile with backstitch *(see Stitch Guide)* centered below Nose over three rnds and across eight sts according to photo.

Beard

With orange, ch 41, **loop st** *(see Stitch Guide)* in second ch from hook, loop st in each ch across. Leaving long end for sewing, fasten off.

Working through top of sts, sew front of sts on Beard to Head beginning ½" above one Ear, going down below Mouth and up the other side, ending ½" above other Ear.

Eye (make 2)

Cut pieces from felt according to full-size pattern pieces on page 32. Glue Pupil to one side of Eye White, glue other side of Eye White to Eye Back.

Glue to Head with Eyes set downward *(see illustration)*.

Eyebrows

With tapestry needle and one strand of orange, embroider Eyebrows with outline stitch *(see Stitch Guide)* above Eyes as shown in photo.

Hat

Rnd 1: With green, ch 3, sl st in first ch to form ring, ch 1, 2 sc in each ch around. *(6 sc made)*

Rnds 2–3: 2 sc in each st around. *(12, 24)*

Rnd 4: (Sc in next 3 sts, 2 sc in next st) around. *(30)*

Rnd 5: (Sc in next 4 sts, 2 sc in next st) around. *(36)*

Rnd 6: (Sc in next 5 sts, 2 sc in next st) around. *(42)*

Rnds 7–15: Sc in each st around.

Rnd 16: Working in **front lps**, ch 1, (sc in next 5 sts, 2 sc in next st) 7 times. *(49)*

Rnd 17: (Sc in next 6 sts, 2 sc in next st) 7 times. *(56)*

Rnd 18: Working in **back lps**, ch 1, sc in each st around.

Rnd 19: Working in **back lps**, ch 1, (sc in next 6 sts, sc next 2 sts tog) around. *(49)*

Rnd 20: Working in **both lps**, (sc in next 5 sts, sc next 2 sts tog) around, join with sl st in first sc. Leaving long end for sewing, fasten off. *(42)*

Fold rnds 18–20 under; sew sts of rnd 20 to **remaining lps** of rnd 15. Stuff.

Sew rnd 20 of Hat to top of Head.

Buckle, Belt & Hat Band

For Belt and Hat Band, cut 1"-wide piece of black felt to fit around waist and around Hat piecing as needed. Glue Belt to waist. Glue Hat Band around Hat.

Using full-size pattern pieces, cut four Buckles from gold felt. Glue one to front of Hat Band, one to front of Belt and one to each Shoe Flap.

Cut one Prong according to full-size pattern piece, glue Prong to Belt Buckle as shown in photo.

Four-Leaf Clover (make 2)

With green, ch 23, sl st in third ch from hook, ch 2, sl st in same ch as first sl st, skip next 2 chs, sl st in next ch, (ch 5, sl st in third ch from hook, ch 2, sl st in same ch as last sl st made, skip next 2 chs on ch-5, sl st in same ch as last leaf in ch-23) 3 times; working in **back bar of ch** *(see Stitch Guide)*, for **stem**, sl st in each ch across ch-23. Fasten off.

Wrap end of right Arm around stems forming a hand and with lt. peach, tack hand in place.

Pipe

With brown marker, color entire cork and small wooden dowel. Let dry. With tip of knife blade, bore a small hole centered in side of cork. Insert dowel about ½". Remove dowel and apply glue. Insert dowel into cork again and let dry completely. Glue 1" of other end of dowel and place in one side of Mouth. ●

Continued on page 32

St. Patrick's Day Dress & Tam

Designed by Lucille LaFlamme

Finished Size: Fits 11½" fashion doll.

Materials:
- Size 10 crochet cotton thread:
  - 80 yds. dk. green
  - 70 yds. white
- 1 white 15mm pom-pom
- 3 small snaps
- Dk. green sewing thread
- Tapestry and sewing needles
- No. 7 steel hook or hook needed to obtain gauge

Gauge: 8 sts = 1"; 3½ dc shell rows = 1".

Basic Stitches: Ch, sl st, sc, dc.

Dress

Row 1: Starting at neckline, with dk. green thread, ch 30, sc in fourth ch from hook *(3 chs before the sc form a ch sp)*, (ch 3, skip next ch, sc in next ch) across to last 2 chs, ch 1, skip next ch, dc in last ch *(counts as a ch sp)*, turn. *(14 ch sps made)*

Rows 2–4: Ch 1, sc in first ch sp, (ch 3, sc in next ch sp) across to last ch sp, ch 1, dc in last ch sp, turn.

Row 5: Ch 3, 2 dc in same st as ch 3; *ch 1, 5 dc in next ch sp *(shell made)*; repeat from * across, ch 1, dc in last sc, turn.

Row 6: Ch 3; *5 dc in center st of next shell *(shell made)*; dc in next ch; repeat from * across to last 3 sts, skip next 2 sts, 3 dc in last st *(half shell made)*; turn.

Row 7: (Ch 3, 2 dc) in first st, (3 dc in next dc between shells, 5 dc in center st of next shell) across to last st, dc in last st, turn.

Row 8: (Ch 3, 2 dc) in first st, 5 dc in center st of each shell and in center st of each 3-dc group across to last 3 sts, skip next 2 sts, 3 dc in last st, turn.

Row 9: (Ch 3, 2 dc) in first st, 5 dc in center st of next 3 shells, ch 1, skip next 6 shells, 5 dc in center st of next shell *(armhole made)*; 5 dc in center st of next 6 shells, ch 1, skip next 6 shells, 5 dc in center st of next 2 shells, skip next 2 sts, 5 dc in last st, turn.

Row 10: Ch 3, 3 dc in center st of each shell across to last 3 sts, skip next 2 sts, dc in last st, turn.

Row 11: (Ch 3, dc) in first st, 2 dc in center st of each 3-dc group across with dc in last st, turn.

Row 12: Ch 3, dc in each st across, turn. **Fasten off.**

Row 13: With white thread, join with sc in first st on last row, sc in each st across, turn.

Row 14: Ch 1, sc in first st, (ch 4, sc) in each st across, turn.

Rows 15–21: Ch 1, sc in first ch sp; *ch 5, sc in next ch sp; for **picot, ch 3, sl st in front lp and left bar** *(see illustration)* of last sc made; repeat from * across, ch 1, dc in last sc *(counts as ch sp)*, turn.

Rnd 22: Working in rnds, ch 1, sc in first ch sp; (ch 6, sc in next ch sp, picot) around, **do not turn;** join with dc in first sc.

Rnds 23–29: Ch 1, sc around post *(see Stitch Guide)* of last dc made, picot, (ch 5, sc in next ch sp, picot) around, ch 2, join with dc in first sc. At end of last rnd, fasten off.

Rnd 30: With dk. green thread, join with sc in center back ch-5 sp of last rnd, 4 more sc in same ch-5 sp, ch 5, (5 sc in next ch-5 sp, ch 5) around, join with sl st in first sc.

Rnd 31: Sl st in next sc, ch-1, sc in next sc, *picot, ch 3, (dc, picot, dc) in next ch-5 sp, ch 3, sc in center st of next 5-sc group; repeat from * around, ending last repeat with ch 3, join with sl st in first sc. Fasten off.

Sew three snaps evenly spaced up back of bodice on Dress.

Sleeve Trim

Working in edge of one armhole on Dress, with white thread, join with sc in ch-1 at center bottom of armhole, picot, 3 sc in side of shell, picot, (sc in next 3 dc, picot) around to side of other shell at bottom of armhole, 3 sc in side of shell, join with sl st in first sc. Fasten off.

Repeat on other armhole.

Shamrock (make 11)

With dk. green thread, ch 3, sl st in first ch to form ring, sl st in ring, *ch 3, 2 dc in ring, ch 3, sl st in ring *(petal made)*; repeat from * 2 more times. Fasten off.

Sew Shamrocks evenly spaced around skirt of Dress staggering them as shown in photo.

Tam

Rnd 1: With No. 7 hook and dk. green thread, ch 5, sl st in first ch to form ring, ch 1, 14 sc in ring, join with sl st in first sc. *(14 sc made)*

Rnd 2: (Ch 3, dc) in first st, 2 dc in each st around, join with sl st in top of ch-3.

Rnd 3: (Ch 3, dc) in first st, 3 dc in next st, (2 dc in next st, 3 dc in next st) around, join.

Rnd 4: Working this rnd in **back lps** *(see Stitch Guide)*, ch 3, skip next st, (dc in next st, skip next st) around, join.

Rnd 5: Working this rnd in **back lps**, ch 3, dc in each st around, join. Fasten off.

Tack pom-pom to top of Tam, covering the opening at center of rnd 1. ●

Shamrock
Coasters & Irish
Crochet Bag

Designed by Dot Drake

Finished Sizes: Coaster is about 3½" x 3¾". Bag is about 3½" tall.

Materials:
- Size 10 crochet cotton thread:
    200 yds. white *(for Bag)*
    120 yds. green *(for Coasters)*
- No. 8 steel hook or hook needed to obtain gauge

Gauge: 9 sts = 1".

Basic Stitches: Ch, sl st, sc, hdc, dc, tr.

Special Stitches: For **picot**, ch 3, sl st in top of last st made.

For **inverted picot**, ch 6, drop lp from hook; keeping lp pointed down toward last rnd, insert hook through third ch from end of ch-6, pull dropped lp through, ch 3.

Coaster (make 4)
Rnd 1: With green, ch 12, sl st in first ch to form ring, ch 1, 3 sc in ring, *[**picot** *(see Special Stitches)*, 3 sc in ring; for **leaf**, ch 10, drop lp from hook, insert hook in third st before last picot, pull dropped lp through, work 17 sc in lp just made—*leaf made*], 8 sc in ring; repeat from * once; repeat between [ ], 5 sc in ring, join with sl st in first sc on first leaf.

Rnd 2: *[Sc in next st, hdc in next st, ch 1, (dc, ch 1) in next 11 sts, hdc in next st, sc in next st, sl st in next st, skip next st, sc in next 3 sts, skip next st], sl st in first sc of next leaf; repeat from * once; repeat between [ ], **do not join.**

Rnd 3: Skip first st, *[sl st in next 2 sts, sl st in each ch sp and dc around to next hdc on leaf, sl st in next 2 sts], skip next 2 sts, sl st in next st, skip next 2 sts; repeat from * once; repeat between [ ], skip next st; for **stem**, sl st in next st, ch 12, hdc in fourth ch from hook, hdc in each ch across, skip next st on last rnd, sl st in last st, **do not join.**

Rnd 4: Skip first st, *[sl st in next 2 sts, sc in next 21 sts, sl st in next 2 sts, skip next st], sl st in next st, skip next st; repeat from * once; repeat between [ ]; working in edge of stem, skip first sl st, sl st in each ch and in each st around to last sl st, skip last sl st, **do not join.**

Rnd 5: Skip first st, sl st in next st, *[sc in next 3 sts, (picot, sc in next 3 sts) 6 times], sl st in next 5 sl sts; repeat from * once; repeat between [ ], sl st in next 2 sl sts leaving remaining sts around stem unworked. Fasten off.

Bag
First Motif
Rnd 1: With white, ch 5, sl st in first ch to form ring, ch 1, 12 sc in ring, join with sl st in first sc. *(12 sc made)*

Rnd 2: Ch 6, skip next 2 sts, (sc in next st, ch 6, skip next 2 sts) around, join with sl st in first ch of first ch-6.

Rnd 3: For **petals**, work (sc, hdc, 5 dc, sc, 5 dc, hdc, sc) in each ch sp around, join with sl st in joining sl st of last rnd.

Rnd 4: *Skip first sc on next petal, ch 5, sl st in **back strands** *(see illustration)* of next sc on same petal, ch 5, sl st in back strands of last sc on same petal; repeat from * 3 more times, **do not join.**

Rnd 5: For **petals**, work (sc, hdc, 5 dc, hdc, sc) in each ch sp around, join with sl st in first sc.

Rnd 6: Sl st in next 4 sts, *[ch 5, (dc, ch 5, dc) in next sp between petals, ch 5, sc in fifth st of next petal], ch 5, sc in fifth st of next petal; repeat from * 2 more times; repeat between [ ], ch 2, join with dc in fifth sl st at beginning.

Rnd 7: Ch 5, sc in next ch sp, ch 5, (3 dc, ch 5 for corner, 3 dc) in next ch sp, *ch 5, (sc in next ch sp, ch 5) 3 times, (3 dc, ch 5 for corner, 3 dc) in next ch sp; repeat from * 2 more times, ch 5, sc in next ch sp, ch 5, join with sl st in top of dc on last rnd. Fasten off.

Second Motif
Rnd 1: With white, ch 10, sl st in first ch to form ring, 3 sc in ring; *[for **leaf**, ch 8, drop lp from hook, insert hook in eighth ch from hook, pull dropped lp through, work 15 sc in sp just made], 5 sc in ring; repeat from * 2 more times; repeat between [ ], 2 sc in ring, join with sl st in first sc.

Rnd 2: Ch 1, sc in first st, *[ch 9, sc in eighth st of next leaf, ch 9], sc in center st of next 5-sc group; repeat from * 2 more times; repeat between [ ], join.

Rnd 3: Ch 1, 11 sc in each ch-9 sp around, join.

Rnd 4: Sl st in next 5 sts, *[ch 5, (dc, ch 5, dc) in next sp between 11-sc groups, ch 5, sc in sixth st of next 11-sc group], ch 7, sc in sixth st of next 11-sc group; repeat from * 2 more times; repeat between [ ], ch 3, join with tr in sixth sl st at beginning.

Rnd 5: Ch 5, sc in next ch sp, ch 5, *(3 dc, ch 5 for corner, 3 dc) in next ch sp, ch 5, (sc in next ch sp, ch 5) 3 times; repeat from * once, 3 dc in next ch sp, ch 2, sc in corresponding corner ch sp on last Motif, ch 2, 3 dc in same ch sp on this Motif, (ch 2, sc in next ch sp on last Motif, ch 2, sc in next ch sp on this Motif) 3 times, ch 2, sc in next ch sp on last Motif, ch 2, 3 dc in next ch sp on this Motif, ch 2, sc in next corner ch sp on last Motif, ch 2, 3 dc in same ch sp on this Motif, ch 5, sc in next ch sp, ch 5, join with sl st in top of tr on last rnd. Fasten off.

Third Motif
Rnds 1–6: Repeat rnds 1–6 of First Motif.

Rnd 7: Ch 5, sc in next ch sp, ch 5, *(3 dc, ch 5 for corner, 3 dc) in next ch sp, ch 5, (sc in next ch sp, ch 5) 3 times; repeat from * once, 3 dc in next ch sp, ch 2, sc in corresponding corner ch sp on last Motif, ch 2, 3 dc in same ch sp on this Motif, (ch 2, sc in next ch sp on last Motif, ch 2, sc in next ch sp on this Motif) 3 times, ch 2, sc in next ch sp on last

Continued on page 32

Shamrock Coasters & Bag

Continued from page 31

Motif, ch 2, 3 dc in next ch sp on this Motif, ch 2, sc in next corner ch sp on last Motif, ch 2, 3 dc in same ch sp on this Motif, ch 5, sc in next ch sp, ch 5, join with sl st in top of dc on last rnd. Fasten off.

Last Motif

Rnds 1–4: Repeat rnds 1–4 of Second Motif.

Rnd 5: Ch 5, sc in next ch sp, ch 5, *3 dc in next ch sp, ch 2, sc in corresponding corner ch sp on First Motif, ch 2, 3 dc in same ch sp on this Motif, (ch 2, sc in next ch sp on First Motif, ch 2, sc in next ch sp on this Motif) 3 times, ch 2, sc in next ch sp on First Motif, ch 2, 3 dc in next ch sp on this Motif, ch 2, sc in next corner ch sp on First Motif, ch 2, 3 dc in same ch sp on this Motif*, ch 5, (sc in next ch sp, ch 5) 3 times; working in ch sps on Third Motif, repeat between first and second* once, ch 5, sc in next ch sp, ch 2, join with dc in top of tr on last rnd. **Do not fasten off.**

Top Section

Rnd 1: Working around top edge of joined Motifs, (ch 5, sc) in each ch sp and in each corner ch sp around, ch 2, join with dc in dc at end of last rnd on Last Motif.

Rnds 2–6: (Ch 5, sc) in each ch sp around, ch 2, join with dc in dc of last rnd.

Rnd 7: Inverted picot *(see Special Stitches),* (sc in next ch sp, inverted picot) around, join with sl st in first ch of first ch-6. Fasten off.

Drawstring

For **sc cord,** with green, ch 2, sc in second ch from hook; **turn** last st made to left so the back of the sc is facing you; sc in strand on left side of st *(see illustration 1);* *turn last st made to left; sc in parallel strands on left side of st *(see illustration 2);* repeat from * until piece measures 22" or desired length. Fasten off.

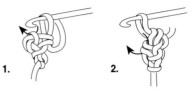

Beginning and ending at desired point, weave Drawstring through ch sps of rnd 4 of Top Section.

Bottom

Rnds 1–4: Repeat rnds 1–4 of Second Motif.

Rnd 5: Working in bottom edge of joined Motifs, ch 2, sc in corresponding ch sp on any Motif, ch 2, sc in next ch sp on this Motif, ch 2, sc in next ch sp on bottom edge, ch 2, *3 dc in next ch sp on this Motif, ch 2, sc in each of next 2 corner ch sps on bottom edge, ch 2, 3 dc in same ch sp on this Motif, (ch 2, sc in next ch sp on on bottom edge, ch 2, sc in next ch sp on this Motif) 3 times, ch 2, sc in next ch sp on bottom edge, ch 2; repeat from * 2 more times, 3 dc in next ch sp on this Motif, ch 2, sc in each of next 2 corner ch sps on bottom edge, ch 2, 3 dc in same ch sp on this Motif, ch 2, sc in next ch sp on bottom edge, ch 2, sc in next ch sp on this Motif, ch 2, sc in last ch sp on bottom edge, ch 2, join with sl st in top of tr on last rnd of this Motif. Fasten off. ●

Leprechaun Doorstop

Continued from page 27

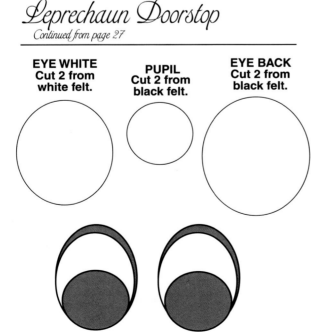

EYE WHITE
Cut 2 from white felt.

PUPIL
Cut 2 from black felt.

EYE BACK
Cut 2 from black felt.

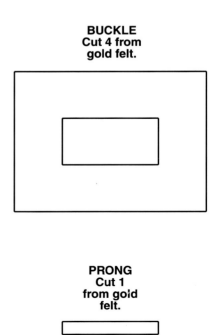

BUCKLE
Cut 4 from gold felt.

PRONG
Cut 1 from gold felt.

chapter 3

Spring Fling

*Cross your palette
with a flavorful
confection that
will pop you right into
chocolate heaven.*

Chocolate Cross Pops
1 pkg. white chocolate
 almond bark
Make 'n Mold cross mold
 #4062
Sucker sticks

Melt almond bark according to
package instructions. Lightly grease
mold with vegetable oil spray.
Carefully spoon melted chocolate into
mold. Insert sucker sticks into mold
slots. Spoon more melted chocolate
into mold as needed. Allow to harden
and then unmold.

BunnyAfghan

Designed by Ruby Gates

Finished Size: 42" x 54".

Materials:
- Worsted yarn:
  - 23 oz. pink *(bunny color)*
  - 12½ oz. blue *(bunny color)*
  - 12½ oz. variegated pastel *(background color)*
  - 10 oz. white *(background color)*
- G hook or hook needed to obtain gauge

Gauge: 4 sc = 1"; 4 sc rows = 1".

Basic Stitches: Ch, sl st, sc.

Notes: When **changing colors** *(see Stitch Guide)*, drop first color to wrong side of work, pick up next color, do not carry dropped color along back of work. Always change colors in last st made.

Use a separate ball of yarn for each section of color and fasten off each color when no longer needed.

Each square on graph equals one sc.

First Row
First Motif

Row 1: With white background color, ch 51, sc in second ch from hook, sc in each ch across, turn. *(50 sc made)*

Rows 2–4: Ch 1, sc in each st across, turn. *Front of row 2 is right side of work.*

Row 5: Ch 1, sc in first 18 sts changing to blue Bunny color *(see Notes),* sc in next 14 sts changing to white background color, sc in last 18 sts, turn.

Rows 6–66: Changing colors *(see Notes)* according to corresponding row of graph on page 50, ch 1, sc in each st across, turn. At end of last row, **do not turn.**

Rnd 67: Working around outer edge, ch 1, sc in each st and in end of each row around with ch 2 at each corner, join with sl st in first sc. Fasten off.

Notes: *The ch-10 lps and ch-4 lps alternate as you work; if two of the same size lps are next to each other the lacing instructions will not work; so periodically check to make sure they alternate.*

Rnd 68: With right side of work facing you, leaving 10" end, join pink with sc in any ch-2 sp at corner, ch 4, sc in same ch sp as last sc, *(ch 10, sc in next st, ch 4, sc in next st) across to next ch-2 sp at corner, ch 10, (sc, ch 4, sc) in ch-2 sp at corner; repeat from * 2 more times, (ch 10, sc in next st, ch 4, sc in next st) across to next corner, skip loose ch-10 end and join. Fasten off.

To **lace ch-10 lps** around outer edge, skipping over ch-4 lps as you work, reach through first ch-10 lp, pick up next ch-10 lp and pull through first lp; reaching through last lp, pick up next ch-10 lp and pull it through; repeat around Motif.

To **connect last lp to first lp,** using 10" strand at beginning of lps, ch 10, drop lp from hook,

weave loose end of ch-10 through first and last lp *(see illustration)* pulling remaining end of yarn completely through both lps; working behind laced ch-10 lps only *(do not get behind the ch-4 lps),* pick up lp at loose end of ch-10 and join with sl st in last sc. Fasten off.

Starting at blue arrow, weave ch through loops in direction of arrows.

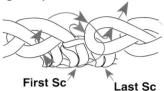

First Sc　　　**Last Sc**

Second Motif

Rows 1–67: Repeat rows 1–67 of First Motif, using variegated background color and pink bunny color.

Rnd 68: With right side of work facing you, leaving 10" end, join pink with sc in ch-2 sp at top right-hand corner; for **corner joining, ch 2, drop lp from hook, insert hook from front to back through adjacent ch-4 sp at corner of corresponding Motif, draw dropped lp through, ch 2;** sc in same ch sp as last sc on this Motif, (ch 10, sc in next st; for **side joining, ch 2, drop lp from hook, insert hook from front to back through adjacent ch-4 of corresponding Motif, draw dropped lp through, ch 2;** sc in next st on this Motif) across to next ch-2 sp at corner, ch 10, (sc, work corner joining, sc) in ch-2 sp at corner, *(ch 10, sc in next st, ch 4, sc in next st) across to next ch-2 sp at corner, ch 10, (sc, ch 4, sc) in ch-2 sp at corner; repeat from *, (ch 10, sc in next st, ch 4, sc in next st) across to next corner, skip loose ch-10 end and join. Fasten off.

Lace ch-10 lps and connect last lp to first lp same as First Motif.

Third Motif

Work same as Second Motif using white background color and blue bunny color.

Second Row
First Motif

Rows 1–67: Repeat rows 1–67 of First Motif, using variegated background color and pink bunny color.

Rnd 68: With right side of work facing you, leaving 10" end, join pink with sc in ch-2 sp at top right-hand corner, ch 4, sc in same ch sp as last sc, (ch 10, sc in next st, ch 4, sc in next st) across to next ch-2 sp at corner, ch 10, (sc, work corner joining on last Row, sc) in ch-2 sp at corner, (ch 10, sc in next st, work side joining on last Row, sc in next st on this Motif) across to next ch-2 sp at corner, ch 10, (sc, work corner joining on last Row, sc) in ch-2 sp at corner, (ch 10, sc in next st, ch 4, sc in next st) across to next ch-2 sp at corner, ch

Continued on page 47

Animal
Egg-stravaganza

Designed by June McWhirt

Basic Animal

Finished Size: 3" tall.

Basic Materials For Each:
- Small amount of each color worsted yarn listed in individual pattern
- Two 8mm glue-on moveable eyes *(for small children use sew-on eyes)*
- 2½" plastic egg
- Craft glue *(for glue-on eyes)*
- Sewing thread and needle *(for sew-on eyes)*
- Tapestry needle
- D and G hooks or hook needed to obtain gauge

Gauge: G hook, 4 sc = 1"; 4 sc rows = 1".

Basic Stitches: Ch, sl st, sc, hdc, dc, tr.

Basic Body
Note: Do not join rnds unless otherwise stated. Mark first st of each rnd.

Rnd 1: With G hook, ch 2, 6 sc in second ch from hook. *(6 sc made)*
Rnd 2: (Sc in next st, 2 sc in next st) around. *(9)*
Rnd 3: (Sc in next 2 sts, 2 sc in next st) around. *(12)*
Rnd 4: (Sc in next 3 sts, 2 sc in next st) around. *(15)*
Rnd 5: (Sc in next 4 sts, 2 sc in next st) around. *(18)*
Rnd 6: (2 sc in next st, sc in next 5 sts) around. *(21)*
Rnd 7: (2 sc in next st, sc in next 6 sts) around. *(24)*
Rnds 8–11: Sc in each st around.
Rnd 12: (Sc next 2 sts tog, sc in next 6 sts) around. *(21)*
Rnd 13: (Sc in next 5 sts, sc next 2 sts tog) around. *(18)*
Rnd 14: (Sc in next 4 sts, sc next 2 sts tog) around. *(15)*
Rnd 15: Sc in next 5 sts, (for **foot,** ch 6, dc in fourth ch from hook, hdc in next ch, sc in last ch), sl st in next 3 sts; repeat between ( ), sc in last 7 sts. Fasten off.

Basic Arm (make 2)
With G hook, ch 8, sc in second ch from hook, hdc in next ch, dc in next 2 chs, hdc in last 3 chs. Fasten off.
Sew one to each side of Body across rows 6–8.

Basic Wing (make 2)
With G hook, ch 8, sc in second ch from hook, hdc in next ch, dc in next 2 chs, tr in last 3 chs. Fasten off.
Sew one to each side of Body across rows 6–9. ●

Pink E. Pig

Materials:
- Small amount each lt. pink, yellow, lt. gold and black worsted yarn

Body
Rnds 1–14: With lt. pink, repeat rnds 1–14 of Basic Body. At end of rnd 14, fasten off.

Arms
With lt. pink, make Basic Arms.
For **hoofs,** with black, overcast *(see illustration)* in end st covering tip of each Arm.

Leg & Hoof (make 2)
With G hook and lt. pink, ch 4, sl st in second ch from hook, sl st in each ch across. Fasten off. Sew to rnd 14 on front of Body. With black, overcast end of each foot.

Snout
Rnd 1: With G hook and lt. pink, ch 2, 6 sc in second ch from hook. *(6 sc made)*
Rnd 2: Working this rnd in **back lps** *(see Stitch Guide),* sc in each st around, join with sl st in first sc. Fasten off.
For **nostrils,** with black, embroider french knot *(see Stitch Guide)* on each side of Snout at edge of rnd 1. Sew Snout over rnds 5–7 on front of Body. Glue or sew eyes above Snout.

Ear (make 2)
Row 1: With G hook and lt. pink, ch 2, 2 sc in second ch from hook, turn. *(2 sc made)*
Row 2: Ch 1, sc in each st across, turn.
Row 3: Ch 1, 2 sc in each st across. Fasten off. *(4)*
Sew across rnds 2–3 on each side of Body.

Tail
With D hook and lt. pink, ch 10. Fasten off. Twist ch tight to form curl. Sew to rnd 14 at back of Body.

Corn
With D hook and yellow, ch 8, 3 sc in second ch from hook, 3 sc in each ch across, join with sl st in first sc. Fold corn lengthwise. Tack edges together.
For **shuck,** with D hook and lt. gold, ch 6, sl st in second ch from hook, sl st in each ch across, (ch 5, sl st in second ch from hook, sl st in next 3 chs) 2 times, sl st in first ch of beginning ch-6. Fasten off. Tack to one end of Corn. Sew to Arms.
Place egg inside Body, small end first. ●

Continued on page 38

Animal Egg-Stravaganza

Continued from page 37

Web F. Duck

Materials:
- Small amount each yellow, orange and green worsted yarn
- Small amount black 6-strand embroidery floss

Body
Rnds 1–14: With yellow, repeat rnds 1–14 of Basic Body. At end of rnd 14, fasten off.

Wings
With yellow, make Basic Wings.

Foot (make 2)
With D hook and orange, ch 3, sl st in second ch from hook, (ch 2, sl st in second ch from hook) 2 times, hdc in same ch as first sl st, sl st in first ch. Fasten off. Sew to rnd 14 on front of Body.

Bill
With D hook and orange, ch 4, sc in second ch from hook, ch 1, hdc in next ch, ch 1, sl st in last ch. Fasten off. Sew to rnd 5 on front of Body. Glue or sew eyes above Bill.

Topknot
Wrap 12" piece yellow yarn around finger three times, thread long end of yarn into needle, insert needle through all loops on finger, secure loops with slip knot, remove loops from finger. Sew to rnd 1 on Body.

Tail Feathers
With G hook and yellow, ch 4, sc in second ch from hook, (hdc, ch 1, hdc) in next ch, sl st in last ch. Fasten off. Sew to rnd 14 at back of Body.

Worm
With D hook and green, ch 10. Leaving 6" end for sewing, fasten off.
With 1-strand embroidery floss, using french knot *(see Stitch Guide)*, embroider eye at one end of Worm. Curving slightly, sew to Wings with green as shown in photo.
Place egg inside Body, small end first. ●

Eek A. Mouse

Materials:
- Small amount each gray, med. pink and lt. pink worsted yarn
- 1" square of yellow sponge

Body & Arms
With gray, make Basic Body & Arms.

Tail
With G hook and gray, ch 20, sl st in second ch from hook, sl st in each ch across. Fasten off. Sew to rnd 14 at back of Body.

Ear (make 2)
Rnd 1: With G hook and med. pink, ch 2, 6 sc in second ch from hook. *(6 sc made)*
Rnd 2: 2 sc in each st around, join with sl st in first sc. Fasten off. *(12)*
Rnd 3: Join gray with sc in first st, 2 sc in next st, (sc in next st, 2 sc in next st) around, join. Fasten off.
Sew to rnd 2 on each side of Body.

Pom-Pom (make 2)
Wrap gray around two fingers fifty times; slide loops off fingers. Tie separate 8" strand yarn around center; cut loops at each end. Trim smooth to ¾".

Face
For **nose,** with lt. pink, embroider french knot *(see Stitch Guide)* on rnd 5. Sew pom-poms under nose. Glue or sew eyes above nose.
For **whiskers,** tie 1" piece gray to each side of Face. Separate strands.

Cheese
Cut sponge to form triangle. Sew to Arms. Place egg inside Body, small end first. ●

Luck E. Rabbit

Materials:
- Small amount each white, lt. pink, med. pink, orange and green worsted yarn

Body & Arms
With white, make Basic Body & Arms.

Pom-Pom (make 3)
Wrap white around two fingers fifty times; slide loops off fingers. Tie separate 8" strand yarn around center; cut loops at each end. Trim two smooth to ¾" and one to 1".

Tail
Sew 1" pom-pom to rnd 14 at back of Body.

Ear (make 2)
Rnd 1: With G hook and med. pink, ch 8, sc in second ch from hook, sc in next ch, hdc in next 2 chs, sc in next ch, sl st in last 2 chs; working in remaining lps on opposite side of starting ch, sl st in next 2 chs, sc in next ch, hdc in next 2 chs, sc in last 2 chs, join with sl st in first sc. Fasten off.
Rnd 2: Join white with sc in first st, sc in each st around with 3 sc in tip of Ear, join. Fasten off. Sew across rnds 2–3 on each side of Body.

Face
For **nose,** with lt. pink, embroider french knot *(see Stitch Guide)* on rnd 5. Sew ¾" pom-poms under nose. Glue or sew eyes above nose.

Carrot
With D hook and orange, ch 8, 3 hdc in second ch from hook, sc in next 3 chs, sl st in last 3 chs. Fasten off.
For **top,** wrap 18" piece green yarn around finger six times, thread long end of yarn into needle, insert needle through all loops on finger, secure loops with slip knot, remove loops from finger. Sew to one end of Carrot. Sew Carrot to Arms.
Place egg inside Body, small end first. ●

Res Q. Rex

Materials:
- Small amount each white, black, red, lt. pink and tan worsted yarn
- Scrap gold felt
- Black permanent marker

Body & Arms
With white, make Basic Body & Arms.

Tail
With D hook and white, ch 10, sl st in second ch from hook, sl st in each ch across. Fasten off. Sew to rnd 14 at back of Body.
With permanent marker, paint spots at random over Body, Arms, Feet and Tail.

Ear (make 2)
With D hook and black, ch 8, tr in fourth ch from hook, tr in next ch, dc in next ch, hdc in next ch, sc in last ch. Fasten off. Sew to rnd 2 on each side of Body.

Pom-Pom (make 2)
Wrap white around two fingers fifty times; slide loops off fingers. Tie separate 8" strand yarn around center; cut loops at each end. Trim smooth to ¾".

Face
For **nose,** with lt. pink, embroider french knot *(see Stitch Guide)* on rnd 5. Sew pom-poms under nose. Glue or sew eyes above nose.

Bone
With D hook and tan, ch 8, (sl st, ch 2, sl st) in third ch from hook, sl st in next 4 chs, (sl st, ch 2, sl st, ch 2, sl st) in last ch. Fasten off. Sew to Arms.

Hat
Rnd 1: With G hook and red, ch 2, 6 sc in second ch from hook, **do not join rnds.** *(6 sc made)*
Rnd 2: 2 sc in each st around. *(12)*
Rnd 3: Sc in next 10 sts, 2 sc in last 2 sts. *(14)*
Rnd 4: 2 sc in next st, sc in next 3 sts, sc next 2 sts tog, sc in last 8 sts. *(14)*
Rnd 5: Sc in each st around.
Rnd 6: Working this rnd in **front lps** *(see Stitch Guide)*, 2 sc in each st around, join with sl st in first sc. Fasten off. *(28)*
Cut Badge from felt according to diagram. With permanent marker, write number "1" on Badge.

**Badge
Cut 1**

Sew Badge to front of Hat. Sew Hat in place on top of Head.
Place egg inside Body, small end first. ●

Red F. Rooster
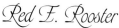

Materials:
- Small amount each white, red, yellow and tan worsted yarn
- Small amount black 6-strand embroidery floss

Body
Rnds 1–14: With white, repeat rnds 1–14 of Basic Body. At end of rnd 14, fasten off.

Wings
With white, make Basic Wings.

Foot (make 2)
With D hook and yellow, ch 4, sl st in second ch from hook, sl st in next ch, (ch 3, sl st in

Continued on page 40

Animal Egg-Stravaganza

Continued from page 39

second ch from hook, sl st in next ch) 2 times, sl st in first ch of starting ch. Fasten off.
Sew Feet evenly spaced to rnd 14 on front of Body.

Beak
Row 1: With D hook and yellow, ch 2, 2 sc in second ch from hook, turn. *(2 sc made)*
Row 2: Ch 1, sc in each st across. Fasten off.
Sew to front of Body on rnd 6. Glue or sew eyes above Beak.

Wattle (make 2)
With D hook and red, ch 2, (hdc, sl st) in second ch from hook. Fasten off. Sew under Beak.

Comb
Wrap 24" piece red around two fingers six times, thread long end of yarn into needle, insert needle through all loops on fingers, secure loops with slip knot, remove loops from fingers. Sew to rnd 1 on Body.

Tail Feathers
Wrap 24" piece white around two fingers eight times, thread long end of yarn into needle, insert needle through all loops on fingers, secure loops with slip knot, remove loops from fingers. Sew to rnd 14 on back of Body.

Worm
With D hook and tan, ch 10. Leaving 6" end for sewing, fasten off.
With 1-strand embroidery floss, using french knot *(see Stitch Guide),* embroider eye at one end of Worm. Curving slightly, sew to Wings with tan as shown in photo.
Place egg inside Body, small end first. ●

Rag Easter Basket

Designed by Maggie Weldon

Finished Size: 9" across x 4" deep.

Materials:
- 3"-wide lightweight fabric strips:
    27 yds. *(equivalent to 1½ yds. of 54"-wide fabric)* each of yellow, green, pink and purple
- Sewing thread and needle
- Q bulky crochet hook

Basic Stitches: Ch, sl st, sc.

Notes: To make strips uniform in width, cut or tear along the longest measurement of fabric piece.

Fold and press wrong side of each outer edge of strip to center *(see illustration 1),* fold in half *(see illustration 2).* Holding edges together in same manner, make a beginning slip knot. Fold edges in as you continue to crochet.

To sew ends of strips, hold end strips right sides together, then sew a ½" seam using a small running stitch *(see Stitch Guide).*

Basket

Rnd 1: With yellow, ch 2, 6 sc in second ch from hook, join with sl st in first sc. Fasten off. *(6 sc made)*

Rnd 2: Join green with sc in first st, sc in same st, 2 sc in each st around, join. Fasten off. *(12)*

Rnd 3: Join pink with sc in first st, 2 sc in next st, (sc in next st, 2 sc in next st) around, join. Fasten off. *(18)*

Rnd 4: Join purple with sc in first st, (2 sc in next st, sc in next 2 sts) 5 times, 2 sc in next st, sc in last st, join. Fasten off. *(24)*

Rnd 5: Join yellow with sc in first st, (2 sc in next st, sc in next 3 sts) 5 times, 2 sc in next st, sc in last 2 sts, join with sl st in **back lp** *(see Stitch Guide)* of first sc. *(30)*

Rnd 6: Working this rnd in **back lps**, for **side**, ch 1, sc in first st, ch 1, skip next st, (sc in next st, ch 1, skip next st) around, join with sl st in **both lps** of first sc. Fasten off. *(15 ch sps)*

Rnd 7: Join green with sc in any ch sp, ch 1, (sc in next ch sp, ch 1) around, join. Fasten off.

Rnd 8: Join pink with sc in any ch sp, ch 1, (sc in next ch sp, ch 1) around, join. Fasten off.

Rnd 9: Join purple with sc in any ch sp, ch 1, (sc in next ch sp, ch 1) around, join.

Row 10: For **handle**, ch 14, skip next 7 sts, drop lp from hook, insert hook in next ch sp, pick up dropped lp, yo, pull through dropped lp and ch sp, sl st in each ch across, sl st in same worked st on rnd 9, **turn,** sl st in ch sp between sc; working on opposite side of ch-14, sl st in each ch across, sl st in next sc on rnd 9. Fasten off. ●

Crochet Bunny

Designed by Mary Layfield

Finished Size: 13" tall.

Materials:
- Worsted yarn:
  - 3 oz. off-white
  - 3 oz. variegated
  - 2 oz. lt. pink
- 2 yds. black embroidery floss
- Scraps of white, lt. blue and black felt
- 4" pink ⅜" ribbon
- Polyester fiberfill
- 2 flat ¾" white buttons
- 2 flat ½" white buttons
- White 3mm pearl bead
- Small snap
- Fabric glue
- Pink sewing thread
- Sewing and tapestry needles
- F hook or hook needed to obtain gauge

Gauge: 9 sc = 2"; 9 sc rows = 2".

Basic Stitches: Ch, sl st, sc, hdc, dc, tr.

Body Side (make 2)
Row 1: Starting at neck edge, with off-white, ch 15, sc in second ch from hook, sc in each ch across, turn. *(14 sc made)*

Row 2: Ch 1, 2 sc in first st, sc in each st across with 2 sc in last st, turn. *(16)*

Row 3: Ch 1, sc in each st across, turn.

Row 4: Ch 1, 2 sc in first st, sc in each st across, turn. *(17)*

Rows 5–9: Ch 1, sc in each st across, turn.

Row 10: Ch 1, 2 sc in first st, sc in each st across, turn. *(18)*

Rows 11–13: Ch 1, sc in each st across, turn.

Row 14: Ch 1, sc in each st across leaving last st unworked, turn. *(17)*

Row 15: Ch 1, sc in each st across, turn.

Row 16: Ch 1, sc in each st across leaving last st unworked, turn. *(16)*

Row 17: Ch 1, sc in each st across, turn.

Rows 18–20: Sl st in first st, ch 1, sc in next st, sc in each st across leaving 2 sts unworked, turn. At end of last row, fasten off. *(13, 10, 7)*

Sew Body Sides together leaving neck edge unsewn. Stuff Body.

Head Side (make 2)
Row 1: Starting at neck edge, with off-white, ch 12, sc in second ch from hook, sc in next 4 sts, 2 sc in next st, sc in each st across, turn. *(12 sc made)*

Row 2: Ch 1, 2 sc in first st, sc in each st across, turn. *(13)*

Row 3: Ch 1, sc in each st across, turn.

Row 4: Ch 1, 2 sc in first st, sc in each st across, turn. *(14)*

Row 5: Ch 1, 2 sc in first st, sc in next 6 sts, 2 sc in next st, sc in each st across, turn. *(16 sc)*

Row 6: Ch 1, sc in each st across, turn.

Row 7: Ch 1, 2 sc in first st, sc in next 6 sts, 2 sc in next st, sc in each st across, turn. *(18)*

Row 8: Sl st in first st, ch 1, sc in next st, sc in each st across, turn. *Mark sl st at beginning of row 8 for Nose placement on front. (17)*

Row 9: Ch 1, sc in each st across, turn.

Row 10: Sl st in first st, ch 1, sc in next st, sc in each st across, turn. *(16)*

Row 11: Ch 1, sc in each st across leaving last st unworked, turn. *(15)*

Row 12: Ch 1, sc in each st across, turn.

Row 13: Ch 1, sc in each st across leaving last st unworked, turn. *(14)*

Row 14: Ch 1, sc in each st across, turn.

Rows 15-17: Sl st in first st, ch 1, sc in next st, sc in each st across leaving last 2 sts unworked, turn. At end of last row, fasten off. *(11, 8, 5)*

Head Center
Row 1: Starting at nose, with off-white, ch 2, 2 sc in second ch from hook, turn. *(2 sc made)*

Row 2: Ch 1, 2 sc in first st, 2 sc in last st, turn. *(4)*

Rows 3–5: Ch 1, sc in each st across, turn.

Row 6: Ch 1, 2 sc in first st, sc in each st across with 2 sc in last st, turn. *(6)*

Row 7: Ch 1, sc in each st across, turn.

Row 8: Ch 1, 2 sc in first st, sc in each st across with 2 sc in last st, turn. *(8)*

Rows 9–23: Ch 1, sc in each st across, turn.

Row 24: Sl st in first, ch 1, sc in next st, sc in each st across leaving last st unworked, turn. *(6)*

Rows 25–26: Ch 1, sc in each st across, turn.

Row 27: Sl st in first, ch 1, sc in next st, sc in each st across leaving last st unworked, turn. *(4)*

Rows 28–29: Ch 1, sc in each st across, turn. At end of last row, fasten off. *Row 29 is at back neck edge.*

Sew rows 1–7 of marked front edges on Head Sides together; matching row 1 of Head Center to ends of marked rows, sew rows 1-29 of Head Center to Head Sides across remainder of front, over top and down back leaving neck edges unsewn. Stuff Head.

Sew neck edges of Head and Body together.

Tail
Row 1: With pink, ch 22, sc in second ch from hook, (ch 3, sc in next ch) across, turn. *(21*

Continued on page 44

Crochet Bunny
Continued from page 43

Continued from page 43

ch-3 sps made)

Row 2: (Ch 6, sc) 3 times in each ch sp across. Fasten off.

Roll starting ch on Tail tightly and sew to rows 14 and 15 at center back of Body.

Facial Features

For **nose,** with pink, ch 3, 3 dc in third ch from hook. Fasten off.

Sew Nose centered over row 1 of Head Center.

For **eyes,** cut out the eye pieces from felt according to pattern pieces; glue together forming two Eyes *(see face illustration).* Glue eyes to Head centered over seams at ends of rows 3–6 of Head Center. With six strands black floss, embroider eyelashes above each eye.

CUT 2 EACH:

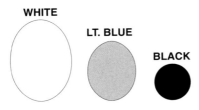

WHITE

LT. BLUE

BLACK

Legs

Leg & Foot Side (make 4)

Row 1: Starting at top, with off-white, ch 5, 2 sc in second ch from hook, sc in each ch across with 2 sc in last ch, turn. *(6 sc made)*

Row 2: Ch 1, sc in each st across, turn.

Row 3: Ch 1, 2 sc in first st, sc in each st across with 2 sc in last st, turn. *(8)*

Rows 4–19: Ch 1, sc in each st across, turn.

Row 20: Ch 1, sc in each st across; for **top of foot,** ch 8; turn. *(8 sc, 8 ch)*

Row 21: Ch 1, 2 sc in second ch from hook, sc in each ch and in each st across; for **heel,** ch 3; turn. *(16 sc, 3 ch)*

Row 22: Ch 1, 2 sc in second ch from hook, sc in next ch, sc in each st across with 2 sc in last st, turn. *(20 sc)*

Rows 23–24: Ch 1, sc in each st across, turn.

Row 25: Ch 1, 2 sc in first st, sc in each st across, turn. *(21)*

Row 26: Ch 1, sc in each st across. Fasten off.

Sole (make 2)

Row 1: With pink, ch 4, 2 sc in second ch from hook, sc in next ch, 2 sc in last ch, turn. *(5 sc)*

Rows 2–7: Ch 1, sc in each st across, turn.

Rows 8–10: Ch 1, 2 sc in first st, sc in each st across, turn. *(6, 7, 8)*

Rows 11–15: Ch 1, sc in each st across, turn.

Row 16: Sl st in first st, ch 1, sc in next st, sc in each st across leaving last st unworked, turn. *(6)*

Rows 17–18: Ch 1, sc in each st across, turn.

Rnd 19: Working around outer edge, ch 1, sc in each st and in end of each row around, join with sl st in first sc. Fasten off.

Foot Pads (make 8)

With off-white, ch 3, 2 sc in third ch from hook. Fasten off.

Sew four Foot Pads to each Sole *(see illustration).*

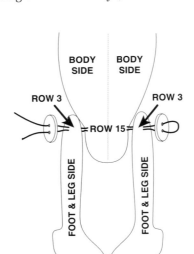

Leg Assembly & Finishing

With heels toward back, place row 3 of one Leg piece centered over row 15 on each side of Body, place one ¾" button centered over row 3 on each Leg piece; sew together through buttons, Leg pieces and Body, pulling slightly snug to indent Body *(see illustration).*

For each **Leg,** sew two Leg and Foot Sides together leaving stitches of row 26 unsewn. Stuff rows 1–19 of Leg.

Matching center of rnd 19 on Sole to seam at toe and row 1 on Sole to seam at Heel, sew one Sole to row 26 on each assembled Leg, stuffing before closing.

Arms

Outer Arm (make 2)

Row 1: Starting at top, with off-white, ch 8, sc in second ch from hook, sc in each ch across, turn. *(7 sc made)*

Rows 2–18: Ch 1, sc in each st across, turn.

Rows 19–22: Ch 1, sc in each st across leaving last st unworked, turn. At end of last row *(3)*, fasten off.

Inner Arm (make 2)

Rows 1–14: Repeat rows 1–14 of Outer Arm. At end of last row, fasten off.

Row 15: For **hand**, join pink with sc in first st, sc in each st across, turn.

Rows 16–22: Repeat rows 16–22 of Outer Arm.

Hand Pads (make 6)

With off-white, ch 3, 2 sc in third ch from hook. Fasten off.

Sew three Hand Pads to each hand *(see illustration)*.

Arm Assembly

With Hand Pads toward Body, place row 3 of one Inner Arm centered over row 2 on each side of Body, place one ¾" button centered over row 3 on each Arm piece; sew together through buttons, Arm pieces and Body.

For each **Arm,** matching ends of rows, sew Inner and Outer Arm pieces together stuffing before closing.

Ears

Pink Side (make 2)

Row 1: Beginning at top, with pink, ch 6, sc in second ch from hook, sc in each ch across, turn. *(5 sc made)*

Row 2: Ch 1, 2 sc in first st, sc in each st across with 2 sc in last st, turn. *(7)*

Row 3: Ch 1, sc in each st across, turn.

Rows 4–7: Repeat rows 2 and 3 alternately, ending with *(11)* sts in last row.

Rows 8–18: Ch 1, sc in each st across, turn.

Row 19: Ch 1, sc in each st across leaving last st unworked, turn. *(10)*

Row 20: Ch 1, sc in each st across, turn.

Rows 21–37: Repeat rows 19 and 20 alternately, ending with row 19 and *(1)*. Fasten off.

Off-White Side (make 2)

Rows 1–37: For **first ear,** with off-white, repeat rows 1–37 of Pink Ear Side; at end of last row, **do not turn or fasten off.**

Rnd 38: Hold one Pink Side in front of one Off-White Side with Pink piece facing you and curved edge on the left; matching ends of rows, sc in end of each row and in each st around with 3 sc in each corner and 3 sc in st of row 37, join with sl st in first sc. Fasten off.

Rows 1–37: For **second ear,** with off-white, repeat rows 1–37 of Pink Ear Side; at end of last row, **turn, do not fasten off.**

Rnd 38: Hold one Pink Side in front of one Off-White Side with Pink piece facing you and curved edge on the right; matching ends of rows, sc in each st across row 37, sc in end of each row and in each st around with 3 sc in st of row 37 and 3 sc in each corner, join with sl st in first sc. Fasten off.

To attach Ears, fold tops of Ears in half with Pink Sides on inside; with folds at back and straight edges on outside, sew tops of Ears to ends of rows 12 and 13 on Head Center.

Dress

Row 1: For **skirt,** with variegated, ch 45, sc in second ch from hook, sc in each ch across, turn. *(44 sts made)*

Row 2: Ch 1, sc in each st across, turn.

Row 3: Ch 3, 2 dc in each st across, turn. *(88)*

Row 4: Ch 3, dc in each st across, turn.

Row 5: (Ch 6, sc in next st) across to last st, ch 3, dc in last st, turn.

Row 6: (Sl st, ch 3, 3 dc) in first ch sp, 4 dc in each ch sp across. Fasten off.

Row 7: For **bib,** working in remaining lps on opposite side of starting ch on row 1, skip first 18 chs, join variegated with sc in next ch, sc in next 7 chs leaving last 18 chs unworked, turn. *(8)*

Rows 8–13: Ch 1, sc in each st across, turn. At end of last row, fasten off.

Shoulder Strap (make 2)

Row 1: With variegated, ch 20, sc in second ch from hook, sc in each ch across, turn. *(19 sc made)*

Row 2: (Ch 3, dc) in first st, 2 dc in each st across, turn. *(38)*

Row 3: (Ch 5, sc in next st) across to last st, ch 3, dc in last st, turn.

Row 4: (Ch 4, sc in next ch sp) across. Fasten off.

Dress Assembly & Finishing

Sew snap on ends of rows 1 and 2 on skirt.

With ruffles toward outside, sew four stitches of row 1 on each Strap behind top four rows on each side of bib. Sew other ends of Strap to row 1 on skirt next to snap.

Cut a 4" piece of ribbon, fold to form a ¾" bow and tie at center with sewing thread. Trim ends. Sew a pearl bead to center of bow. Glue bow to center front of Bib.

Place Dress on Bunny. ●

Bunny Hot Pad

Designed by Fran Mower

Finished Size: 7½" across x 12" long.

Materials:
- Cotton worsted yarn:
  3 oz. each white and yellow
  1 oz. pink
- Small amount each pink and blue 6-strand embroidery floss
- Embroidery and tapestry needles
- E hook or hook needed to obtain gauge

Gauge: Rnds 1–2 = 1"; 5 sc = 1".

Basic Stitches: Ch, sl st, sc, hdc, dc.

Head Front
Notes: *Work in continuous rnds; do not join or turn unless otherwise stated. Mark first st of each rnd.*
Rnd 1: With white, ch 2, 9 sc in second ch from hook. *(9 sc made)*
Rnd 2: 2 sc in each of next 8 sts, sc in next st. *(17)*
Rnd 3: (Sc in next st, 2 sc in next st) 7 times, sc in next 3 sts. *(24)*
Rnd 4: (2 sc in next st, sc in next 2 sts) around. *(32)*
Rnd 5: (2 sc in next st, sc in next 3 sts) around. *(40)*
Rnd 6: (2 sc in next st, sc in next 4 sts) around. *(48)*
Rnd 7: (2 sc in next st, sc in next 5 sts) around. *(56)*
Rnd 8: (2 sc in next st, sc in next 6 sts) around. *(64)*
Rnd 9: (2 sc in next st, sc in next 7 sts) around. *(72)*
Rnd 10: (2 sc in next st, sc in next 8 sts) around. *(80)*
Rnd 11: (2 sc in next st, sc in next 9 sts) around. *(88)*
Rnd 12: (2 sc in next st, sc in next 10 sts) around. *(96)*
Rnd 13: (2 sc in next st, sc in next 11 sts) around, join with sl st in first sc. Fasten off. *(104)*

Head Back
With yellow, work same as Head Front.

Ear Front (make 2)
Row 1: With pink, ch 16, sc in second ch from hook, sc in next 3 chs, hdc in next 4 chs, dc in last 7 chs, turn. *(15 sts made) Front of row 1 is right side of work.*
Row 2: Ch 1, sc in each st across, sc in end of row 1. Fasten off. *(16 sc)*
Row 3: With wrong side facing you, join white with sc in first sc on row 2, sc in next 14 sts, 2 sc in sc at end of row 1; working in remaining lps on opposite side of starting ch, 2 sc in first ch, sc in each ch across, turn. *(32 sc)*
Row 4: Ch 3, dc in next 14 sts, 2 dc in each of next 4 sts, dc in each st across. Fasten off. *(36 dc)*

Ear Back (make 2)
Rows 1–4: With white, repeat rows 1–4 of Ear Front.
Row 5: Holding one Ear Front and one Ear Back wrong sides together, with Ear Front facing you, working through both thicknesses, join white with sc in first st, sc in next 14 sts, 2 sc in each of next 7 sts, sc in last 14 sts. Fasten off.

Assembly
Hold wrong sides of Head Front and Back pieces together with Front facing you; working through both thicknesses, join white with sc in any st, sc in each st around leaving an opening large enough for Ears; with Ear Front facing you, place ends of Ears between Head Front and Back; working through all thicknesses, sl st in each st across Ears, join with sl st in first sc. Fasten off.

Bow Tie
Row 1: With yellow, ch 9, sc in second ch from hook, sc in each ch across, turn. *(8 sc made)*
Row 2: Ch 1, sc in each st across, turn.
Row 3: Ch 1, sc first 2 sts tog, sc in each st across to last 2 sts, sc last 2 sts tog, turn. *(6)*
Row 4: Ch 1, sc in each st across, turn.
Row 5: Ch 1, sc first 2 sts tog, sc in each st across to last 2 sts, sc last 2 sts tog, turn. *(4)*
Row 6: Ch 1, sc in each st across, turn.
Row 7: Ch 1, sc first 2 sts tog, sc last 2 sts tog, turn. *(2)*
Rows 8–9: Ch 1, sc in each st across, turn.
Row 10: Ch 1, 2 sc in first st, 2 sc in last st, turn. *(4)*
Row 11: Ch 1, sc in each st across, turn.
Row 12: Ch 1, 2 sc in first st, sc in each st across to last st, 2 sc in last st, turn. *(6)*
Row 13: Ch 1, sc in each st across, turn.
Row 14: Ch 1, 2 sc in first st, sc in each st across to last st, 2 sc in last st, turn. *(8)*
Rows 15–16: Ch 1, sc in each st across, turn. At end of last row, fasten off.
With tapestry needle and yellow, sew Bow Tie to Head Front *(see photo).*

Facial Features
1: For **nose,** with embroidery needle and pink thread, embroider satin stitch *(see Stitch Guide),* over rnd 1 on Head Front

(see illustration).

2: For **mouth,** with embroidery needle and pink, embroider straight stitches *(see Stitch Guide)* directly below nose over rnds 2–4 *(see illustration).*

3: For **eyes,** embroider straight stitches over rnds 5–6 above nose 1½" apart *(see Stitch Guide).* ●

Bunny Afghan
Continued from page 35

10, (sc, ch 4, sc) in ch-2 sp at corner, (ch 10, sc in next st, ch 4, sc in next st) across to next corner, skip loose ch-10 end, join. Fasten off. Lace ch-10 lps and connect last lp to first lp same as First Motif.

Second Motif
Rows 1–67: Repeat rows 1–67 of First Motif, using variegated background color and blue bunny color.

Rnd 68: With right side of work facing you, leaving 10" end, join pink with sc in ch-2 sp at top right-hand corner, work corner joining on this Row, sc in same ch sp as last sc, (ch 10, sc in next st, work side joining on this Row, sc in next st on this Motif) across to next ch-2 sp at corner, ch 10, (sc; for **inside corner joining, ch 2, drop lp from hook, insert hook from front to back through adjacent worked ch-4 sp on Motif of last Row, draw dropped lp through, ch 2;** sc) in ch-2 sp at corner, (ch 10, sc in next st, work side joining on last Row, sc in next st on this Motif) across to next ch-2 sp at corner, (sc, work corner joining, sc)

in ch-2 sp at corner, (ch 10, sc in next st, ch 4, sc in next st) across to next ch-2 sp at corner, ch 10, (sc, ch 4, sc) in ch-2 sp at corner, (ch 10, sc in next st, ch 4, sc in next st) across to next corner, skip loose ch-10 end and join. Fasten off. Lace ch-10 lps and connect last lp to first lp same as First Motif.

Third Motif
Work same as Second Motif of Second Row using variegated background color and pink bunny color.

Third Row
First Motif
Work same as First Motif on Second Row using white background color and blue bunny color.

Second Motif
Work same as Second Motif of Second Row

Continued on page 51

47

Victorian Cross Afghan

Designed by Marilyn Mezer

Finished Size: 55" x 63" not including Tassels.

Materials:
- 63 oz. off-white worsted yarn
- Sport yarn:
    - 400 yds. burgundy
    - 200 yds. blue
    - 200 yds. pink
    - 175 yds. rose
    - 175 yds. lt. green
    - 175 yds. med. green
    - 175 yds. dk. green
- 75 yds. metallic gold cord
- 6" square cardboard
- Tapestry needle
- G and H crochet hooks and I Afghan crochet hook or hook needed to obtain gauge

Gauge: Afghan hook and worsted yarn, 4 afghan sts = 1"; 7 afghan st rows = 2".

Basic Stitches: Ch, sl st, sc, dc.

Afghan
Panel (make 3)
Row 1: With afghan hook and off-white, ch 50, insert hook in second ch from hook, yo, pull through ch, (insert hook in next ch, yo, pull through ch) across leaving all lps on hook; to **work lps off hook, yo, pull through first lp on hook, (yo, pull through next 2 lps on hook—see illustration 1 on page 51)** across. Lp *(or vertical bar)* remaining on hook at end is first st on next row. *(50 sts made)*
Rows 2–207: For **afghan st, skip first vertical bar, (insert hook under next vertical bar, yo, pull through bar—see illustration 2) across to last vertical bar, insert hook under last vertical bar and lp directly behind it (see illustration 3), yo, pull through bar and lp;** work sts off hook.
Row 208: To bind off sts, (insert hook in next st, yo, pull through st and lp on hook) across. Fasten off.
Using cross stitch *(see Stitch Guide),* embroider Left and Right Panels according to graphs on pages 51-52. Embroider Center Panel design centered on last Panel according to graph.

Small Cross Panel (make 2)
Row 1: With afghan hook and off-white, ch 21, insert hook in second ch from hook, yo, pull through ch, (insert hook in next ch, yo, pull through ch) across leaving all lps on hook; work lps off hook. *(21 sts made)*
Rows 2–3: Work afghan st across, work off lps.
Row 4: Work afghan st across, work off 10 lps;

for **bead st,** ch 3, yo and pull through ch lp and next lp on hook, work off remaining lps.
Row 5: Work afghan st across, work off 9 lps, bead st, work off one lp, bead st, work off remaining lps.
Row 6: Work afghan st across, work off 8 lps, bead st, work off 3 lps, bead st, work off remaining lps.
Row 7: Work afghan st across, work off 7 lps, bead st, work off 5 lps, bead st, work off remaining lps.
Rows 8–9: Work afghan st across, work off 6 lps, bead st, work off 7 lps, bead st, work off remaining lps.
Row 10: Work afghan st across, work off 7 lps, bead st, work off 5 lps, bead st, work off remaining lps.
Row 11: Work afghan st across, work off 8 lps, bead st, work off 3 lps, bead st, work off remaining lps.
Row 12: Work afghan st across, work off 9 lps, bead st, work off one lp, bead st, work off remaining lps.
Row 13: Work afghan st across, work off 9 lps, bead st, work off remaining lps.
Rows 14–203: Repeat rows 4–13 consecutively.
Rows 204–207: Work afghan st across, work off lps.
Row 208: To bind off sts, (insert hook in next st, yo, pull through st and lp on hook) across. Fasten off.
Using cross stitch, embroider cross according to Small Cross graph in each diamond on Panel.

Edging
Row 1: With right side facing you, working in ends of rows across one long edge of one Small Cross Panel, with G crochet hook and off-white, join with sl st in first row, ch 3; (insert hook in same row as sl st, yo, pull up long lp through row) 3 times, yo, pull through all lps on hook, *ch 2, skip next row; for **puff st, (insert hook in next row, yo, pull up long lp through row) 3 times;** repeat from * across edge, ch 1, dc in last st, turn. *(104 puff sts, 103 ch sps made)*
Rows 2–3: Ch 4, puff st in next ch sp, (ch 2, puff st) in each ch sp across, ch 1, dc in last st, turn.
Row 4: To join Panels, with right sides tog, matching ends of rows on Center Panel to sts of row 3; working through both thicknesses, ch 1, sc in each st and in each ch sp across. Fasten off.
Repeat across other long edge of Small Cross Panel joining to Left Panel.
Repeat Edging on remaining Small Cross Panel

Continued on page 50

Victorian Cross Afghan
Continued from page 49

joining to remaining edge of Center Panel and to Right Panel.

Border

Row 1: Working across one short end of joined Panels, with G hook, join off-white with sc in first st at top of Right Panel, sc in each st across top edges of Panels with sc in each seam. Fasten off. *(193 sc made)*

Row 2: Repeat row 1 across remaining short end.

Rnd 3: Working around entire outer edge, join off-white with sl st in

first st of row 1, (puff st, ch 1, puff st, ch 1, puff st) in same st as sl st *(corner made),* ch 1, skip next st, (puff st in next st, ch 1, skip next st) across to last st at corner, (puff st, ch 1) 3 times in last st *(corner made);* *working in

RIGHT PANEL

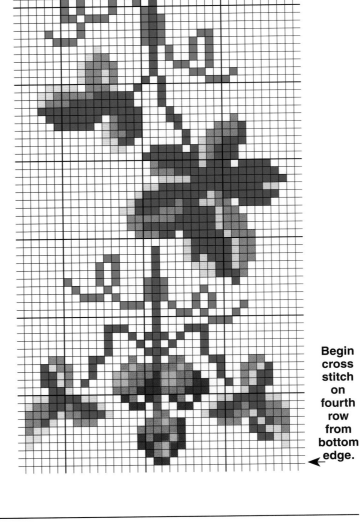

Skip next 3 rows; repeat graph leaving last 3 rows at top edge unworked.

Begin cross stitch on fourth row from bottom edge.

TASSEL

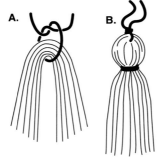

A.   B.

Afghan Stitch Illustrations

1.

2.

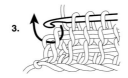

3.

SMALL CROSS

YARN/CORD:

☐ = OFF-WHITE
◼ = BURGUNDY
◼ = BLUE
☐ = PINK
◼ = ROSE
☐ = LT. GREEN
◼ = MED. GREEN
◼ = DK. GREEN
◼ = GOLD

ends of rows, skip next row, (puff st in next row, ch 1, skip next row) across long edge*, for **corner**, (puff st, ch 1) 3 times in next st on bottom edge, skip next st, (puff st in next st, ch 1, skip next st) across; repeat between first and second *, join with sl st in top of first puff st.

Rnds 4–5: (Sl st, puff st, ch 1, puff st, ch 1, puff st, ch 1) in first ch sp, (puff st, ch 1) 3 times in next ch sp, (puff st, ch 1) in each ch sp around with (puff st, ch 1) 3 times in second ch sp of each corner, join. At end of last rnd, fasten off.

Rnd 6: With H hook, join burgundy with sc in first ch sp at any corner, 2 sc in same ch sp as first sc, 2 sc in each ch sp around with 3 sc in first ch sp of each corner, join with sl st in

first sc, **turn.**

Rnd 7: Ch 1, sc in each st around with 3 sc in each center corner st, join. Fasten off.

Tassel (make 24)
Wrap off-white around cardboard 20 times. Tie all strands together with separate strand of yarn *(see illustration A);* cut all strands at bottom and slip off cardboard. Wrap separate strand of yarn several times around all strands ¾" from fold *(see illustration B)* and tie ends securely. Trim ends.

Aligning Tassels with corners of Panels and spacing 1½" apart, attach Tassels in pairs across each short end of Afghan as shown in photo. ●

Graphs continued on page 52

Bunny Afghan
Continued from page 47

using variegated background color and pink bunny color.

Third Motif
Work same as Third Motif of Second Row using white background color and blue bunny color. ●

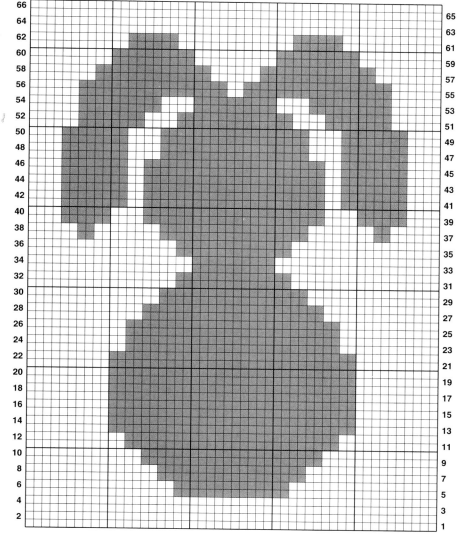

Key:

■ = Sc Bunny Color

□ = Sc Background Color

Victorian Cross Afghan

Continued from page 51

LEFT PANEL

CENTER PANEL

Skip next 3 rows; repeat graph leaving last 3 rows at top edge unworked.

Begin cross stitch on fourth row from bottom edge. ←

chapter 4

Parent's Pride

Edible blossoms add a flourish when conveying messages of friendship and appreciation.

Mini Veggie Bouquet

Large baking potato, for base
Bunch of green onions
3 medium carrots
1 cup cauliflower florets
1 cup broccoli florets
Cherry tomatoes
Bamboo skewers

Microwave potato for 2 to 2½ minutes. Allow to cool. Can be wrapped in plastic wrap and stored in refrigerator until ready to use. Place potato in center of plate. Cut each carrot into four equal lengths. Affix tomatoes, carrots, broccoli and cauliflower florets to skewers. Trim skewers to various lengths and arrange on potato base as desired. Trim onions and place around bottom of potato base. Serve immediately, or mist with water, wrap lightly and store in refrigerator until time to serve.

Football Afghan

Designed by Eleanor Albano-Miles

Finished Size: 44" x 64".

Materials:
- Worsted yarn:
    17½ oz. brown
    14 oz. gold
    14 oz. green
    3 oz. off-white
- Safety pins
- Tapestry needle
- J hook or hook needed to obtain gauge

Gauge: 3 sc = 1"; 4 sc rows = 1".

Basic Stitches: Ch, sl st, sc, hdc, dc.

Football (make 60)

Row 1: With brown, ch 2, 3 sc in second ch from hook, turn. *(3 sc made)*

Row 2: Ch 1, 2 sc in first st, sc in next st, 2 sc in last st, turn. *(5)*

Row 3: Ch 1, 2 sc in first st, sc in each st across to last st, 2 sc in last st, turn. Fasten off. *(7)*

Row 4: Join aran with sc in first st, sc in same st as first sc, sc in each st across to last st, 2 sc in last st, turn. Fasten off. *(9)*

Row 5: Join brown with sc in first st, sc in same st as first sc, sc in each st across to last st, 2 sc in last st, turn. *(11)*

Rows 6–13: Ch 1, sc in each st across, turn. At end of last row, fasten off.

Row 14: Join off-white with sl st in first st, sc in next st, sc in each st across to last 2 sts, sc last 2 sts tog, turn. Fasten off. *(10 sts)*

Row 15: Join brown with sl st in first st, sc in each st across to last 3 sts, sc next 2 sts tog leaving sl st unworked, turn. *(8 sts)*

Row 16: Ch 1, sc first 2 sts tog, sc in each st across to last 3 sts, sc next 2 sts tog leaving sl st unworked, turn. *(5)*

Row 17: Ch 1, sc first 2 sts tog, sc in next st, sc last 2 sts tog, turn. *(3)*

Row 18: Ch 1, sc 3 sts tog, turn.

Rnd 19: For edging, ch 1, (sc, ch 2, sc) in st, sc in end of each row around with (sc, ch 2, sc) in remaining lp on opposite side of starting ch-2 on row 1, join with sl st in first sc. Fasten off. *(40)*

For lacing, with off-white, using Straight Stitch *(see Stitch Guide)*, embroider lines *(see illustration)* centered between rows 7–12 on front of each Football *(see photo)*.

Center Strip (make 6)

With brown, sew ends of Footballs together forming a Strip of ten Footballs.

Panel (make 6)

Rnd 1: Working around outer edges of one Strip, with right side facing you, join gold with sc in ch-2 sp at one end of Footballs, (sc, ch 2, 2 sc) in same ch sp as joining sc, sc in each st across to ch-2 sp at opposite end of Strip, (2 sc, ch 2, 2 sc) in ch-2 sp, sc in each st around, join with sl st in first sc, **turn.** *(408 sc, 2 ch-2 sps made)*

Rnd 2: Ch 3, dc in next 8 sts, *2 dc in each of next 4 sts, (dc in next 16 sts, 2 dc in each of next 4 sts) 9 times, dc in next 10 sts, (2 dc, ch 2, 2 dc) in next ch-2 sp*, dc in next 10 sts; repeat between first and second *, dc in last st, join with sl st in top of ch-3, **turn.** Fasten off.

Rnd 3: Join green with sc in any ch-2 sp at one end, (sc, ch 2, 2 sc) in same sp as joining sc; *working in **back lps** *(see Stitch Guide)*, sc in next 27 sts, skip next 2 sts, (sc in next 22 sts, skip next 2 sts) 8 times, sc in next 27 sts*, (2 sc, ch 2, 2 sc) in ch sp at end; repeat between first and second *, join with sl st in first sc, **turn.**

Rnd 4: Ch 3, dc in next 14 sts, *2 dc in each of next 5 sts, dc in next 7 sts, (skip next 2 sts, dc in next 7 sts, 2 dc in each of next 5 sts, dc in next 8 sts) 9 times, dc in next 8 sts, (2 dc, ch 2, 2 dc) in next ch-2 sp*, dc in next 16 sts; repeat between first and second *, dc in next 8 sts, (2 dc, ch 2, 2 dc) in last ch-2 sp, dc in last st, join with sl st in top of ch-3, **turn.** Fasten off.

Rnd 5: Working this rnd in **back lps,** join gold with sc in any ch sp at one end, (sc, ch 2, 2 sc) in same ch sp as joining sc, *sc in next 34 sts, skip next 2 sts, (sc in next 23 sts, skip next 2 sts) 8 times, sc in next 34 sts*, (2 sc, ch 2, 2 sc) in ch-2 sp at end; repeat between first and second *, join with sl st in first sc. Fasten off.

Rnd 6: With right side facing you, working this rnd in **back lps,** join green with sc in any ch sp at one end, (sc, ch 2, 2 sc) in same ch sp as joining sc, *sc in next 35 sts, skip next 2 sts, (sc in next 21 sts, skip next 2 sts) 8 times, sc in next 35 sts*, (2 sc, ch 2, 2 sc) in ch sp at end; repeat between first and second *, join with sl st in first sc. Fasten off.

Assembly

Holding two Panels wrong sides together, mark sts with pins according to illustration below.

Working through **back bar of sc** *(see illustration)*, beginning and ending in marked sts, with matching yarn, sew Panels together removing pins as you work.

Border

Rnd 1: Working in **back lps** around outer edges of joined Panels, with right side facing you, join brown with sl st in any st, ch 2, hdc in each st and in each seam around with 3 hdc in each ch sp of each Panel, join with sl st in top of ch-2.

Rnd 2: Ch 1, **reverse sc** *(see Stitch Guide)* in each st around, join with sl st in first sc. Fasten off. ●

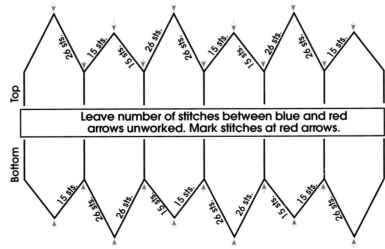

Leave number of stitches between blue and red arrows unworked. Mark stitches at red arrows.

Loving Gifts

Designed by Ann Parnell

Shell Lapghan

Finished Size: 42" x 57".

Materials:
- Sport yarn:
    - 12 oz. green
    - 6 oz. each of dk. rose and pale rose
    - 3 oz. ecru
- G hook or hook needed to obtain gauge

Gauge: 3 shells and 2 sc = 3"; 7 shell rows = 3".

Basic Stitches: Ch, sl st, sc, hdc, dc.

Note: When **changing colors** (see Stitch Guide), do not fasten off yarn, pick up again as needed.

Lapghan
Row 1: With green, ch 171, 3 dc in fourth ch from hook, skip next ch, sc in next ch, (ch 2, skip 2 chs; for **shell**, 3 dc in next ch; skip next ch, sc in next ch) across, changing to dk. rose in last sc made, turn. *(34 shells made) Row 1 is wrong side of work.*
Note: *Always change to next color in last st made.*
Row 2: With dk. rose, ch 3, 3 dc in first sc, skip shell, sc in ch-2 sp, (ch 2, 3 dc in next sc, skip shell, sc in ch-2 sp) across to last sc, ch 2, 3 dc in next sc, skip shell, sc in ch-3 sp at end of row, changing to pale rose, turn.
Row 3: With pale rose, repeat row 2 changing to green.
Row 4: With green, repeat row 2 changing to dk. rose.
Rows 5–133: Repeat rows 2–4 consecutively 43 times. At end of last row, do not change to dk. rose, fasten off pale rose and dk. rose.

Border
Rnd 1: With green and right side facing you, ch 1, (2 hdc in sc, skip next dc, sc in next 2 dc, sc in sp) across to last sc, 2 hdc in sc, skip next dc, sc in next 2 dc; working down side, 3 hdc in each ch-3 sp across, ending with 6 hdc in last sp; working across bottom, (sc in base of shell, sc and hdc in ch-1 sp, hdc and sc in ch-2 sp) across, ending with sc in base of last shell, 3 hdc in last st; working across side, 3 hdc in each ch-3 sp across, ending with hdc in last st, join with sl st in first st. Fasten off.
Rnd 2: With ecru, join with sc in third st of any 6 hdc in corner, *(ch 2, sc in next st) 2 times, (ch 2, skip next st, sc in next st) across to corner; repeat from * around, ending with ch 2, skip next st, join.
Rnd 3: Sl st in next sp, ch 6; working behind ch, dc back into first sp to right, (ch 1, dc in next empty sp to left, ch 3; holding sts forward, dc in first sp to right) around, join with sl st in third ch of ch-6. Fasten off.

Shell Shawl

Finished Size: 25" x 60".

Materials:
- Sport yarn:
    - 9 oz. green
    - 6 oz. each of dk. rose and pale rose
    - 3 oz. ecru
- G hook or hook needed to obtain gauge

Gauge: 3 shells and 2 sc = 3"; 7 shell rows = 3".

Basic Stitches: Ch, sl st, sc, hdc, dc.

Note: When **changing colors** (see Stitch Guide), do not fasten off yarn, pick up again as needed.

Shawl
Row 1: With green, ch 256, 3 dc in fourth ch from hook, skip next ch, sc in next ch, (ch 2, skip 2 chs; for **shell**, 3 dc in next ch; skip next ch, sc in next ch) across, changing to dk. rose in last st, turn. *(51 shells made)*
Note: *Always change to next color in last st made.*
Rows 2–67: Work rows 2–4 of Lapghan consecutively 22 times. At end of last row, do not change to dk. rose, fasten off dk. rose and pale rose, turn.

Border
Rnds 1–3: Work rnds 1–3 of Lapghan Border.

Shell Slippers

Finished Sizes: Small = 8" sole, Medium = 9" sole and Large = 10" sole.

Materials:
- Sport yarn:
    - 3 oz. green
    - 1 oz. each dk. rose, pale rose, and ecru
- Tapestry needle
- G hook or hook needed to obtain gauge

Gauges: For **Soles (2 strands held tog),** 3 sc = 1"; 4 sc rows = 1". For **Sides (1 strand yarn),** 3 shells and 2 sc = 3"; 7 shell rows = 3".

Basic Stitches: Ch, sl st, sc, hdc, dc.

Notes: Instructions are for small size; changes for medium and large are in [ ].
When **changing colors** (see Stitch Guide), do not fasten off yarn, pick up again when needed.

Slipper (make 2)
Sole
Row 1: With green, holding 2 strands tog, ch 3, 2 sc in second ch from hook, 2 sc in last ch, turn. *(4 sc made)*

Continued on page 58

Row 2: Ch 1, 2 sc in first st, sc in each st across with 2 sc in last st, turn. *(6.*

Rows 3–13 [3–14, 3–15]: Ch 1, sc in each st across, turn.

Rows 14–15 [15–16, 16–17]: Ch 1, 2 sc in first st, sc in each st across, turn. *(8)*

Row 16 [17, 18]: Ch 1, sc in each st across, turn.

Rows 17–19 [18–21, 19–25]: Repeat rows 14–16 [15–17, 16–18] consecutively, ending with row 16 [15, 16] and *(10 sts) [11 sts, 13 sts].*

Rows 20–24 [22–28, 26–32]: Ch 1, sc in each st across, turn.

Row 25 [29, 33]: Ch 1, skip first st, sc in each st across to last 2 sts, sc last 2 sts tog, turn. *(8) [9, 11]*

Rows 26–29 [30–33, 34–37]: Repeat rows 20 and 25 [22 and 29, 26 and 33] alternately. At end of last row *(4) [5, 7]* sc.

Row 30 [34, 38]: Ch 1, skip first st, sc in each of next 2 [3, 5] sts, sl st in last st, turn.

Rnd 31 [35, 39]: Ch 1, sc around outer edge, working 3 [5, 7] sts across toe, 30 [34, 37] sts on side, 5 [3, 3] sts across heel, 30 [34, 37] sts on opposite side, sl st in first st, ending with *(68) [76, 84]* sc. Fasten off. Mark this rnd as right side.

Side
(Use only 1 strand of yarn)

Row 1: With wrong side facing you, working this row in **front lps** *(see Stitch Guide),* join green with sl st in st at center back, ch 3, 3 dc in next st, skip next st, (sc in next st, ch 2, skip next st; for **shell,** 3 dc in next st, skip next st) around, ending with sc in last st and changing to dk. rose, turn. *(17 shells made) [19 shells made, 21 shells made]*

Note: *Always change to next color in last st made.*

Rows 2–4: Repeat rows 2–4 of Lapghan.

Row 5: With dk. rose, ch 3, 3 dc in sc, (sc in next sp, ch 2, 3 dc in next sc) 4 [5, 6] times, (sc in next sp, ch 1) 7 times; repeat between first ( ) 5 [6, 7] times, sc in last sp changing to pale rose, turn.

Row 6: With pale rose, ch 3, 3 dc in sc, (sc in next sp, ch 2, 3 dc in next sc) 4 [5, 6] times, (sc in next sp) 7 times; repeat between first ( ) 5 [6, 7] times, sc in last sp changing to green, turn.

Row 7: With green, ch 3, 3 dc in sc, (sc in next sp, ch 2, 3 dc in next sc) 3 [4, 5] times, sc in next sp, yo, skip shell, pull lp up in next sp, (yo, skip next st, pull lp up in next st) 4 times, yo, pull lp up in next ch-2 sp, yo, pull through all 13 lps on hook, ch 1, 3 dc in next sc, (sc in next sp, ch 2, 3 dc in next sc) 3 [4, 5] times, sc in last sp. Fasten off. Sew back seam.

Rnd 8: Working in rnds, with ecru and right side facing, join with sc at center back, 2 hdc in next sc, (sc in next sp, 2 hdc in next sc) around to center front, 3 dc in center st, 2 hdc

in next sc; repeat between ( ) around, join sl st in first st, **turn.** *(26) [32, 38]*

Rnd 9: Ch 1, sc in each st around, join, **do not turn.**

Rnd 10: Ch 6; working behind ch, (dc back into first st to the right, ch 1, dc in next unworked st to the left, ch 3) around, ending with ch 1, join with sl st in third ch of ch-6. Fasten off.

Shell Tissue Box Cover

Finished Size: 3½" x 4½" x 6" tall.

Materials:
- 1 oz. each green, dk. rose, pale rose and ecru sport yarn
- Tapestry needle
- G hook or hook needed to obtain gauge

Gauge: 3 shells and 2 sc = 3", 7 shell rows = 3".

Basic Stitches: Ch, sl st, sc, hdc, dc.

Note: When **changing colors** *(see Stitch Guide),* do not fasten off yarn, pick up again as needed.

Top

Row 1: With green, ch 21, 3 dc in fourth ch from hook, skip next ch, sc in next ch, (ch 2, skip 2 chs; for **shell,** 3 dc in next ch; skip next ch, sc in next ch) across changing to dk. rose in last sc made, turn *(4 shells made) Row 1 is wrong side of work.*

Note: *Always change to next color in last stitch made.*

Rows 2–3: Work rows 2–3 of Lapghan, turn. Fasten off dk. rose.

Row 4: For **first side,** with green, ch 3, 3 dc in sc, skip shell, sc in ch-2 sp changing to dk. rose, turn. *(1 shell)*

Rows 5–6: Repeat row 4 with dk. rose, then with pale rose.

Rows 7–9: Repeat rows 4–6.

Row 10: With green, ch 3, 3 dc in sc, skip shell, sc in ch-2 sp, ch 9, **do not turn,** drop yarn, **do not fasten off.**

Row 4: For **second side,** with separate strand of green, skip 2 shells on row 3, join with sc in next ch-2 sp, ch 2, 3 dc in sc, skip shell, sc in ch-3 sp, turn.

Rows 5–9: Repeat rows 5–9 of first side. Fasten off green and pale rose.

Row 10: For **second side,** pick up dropped yarn from row 10 on first side, sl st in first sc, ch 3, 3 dc in same st, skip shell, sc in ch-3 sp changing to dk. rose, turn.

Row 11: With dk. rose, ch 3, 3 dc in sc, skip shell, sc in ch-3 sp, ch 2; working on ch-9, skip next ch, (3 dc in next ch, skip next ch, sc in next ch, ch 2, skip next ch) 2 times 3 dc in next sc, skip shell, sc in ch-3 sp changing to pale rose, turn. Fasten off dk. rose. *(4 shells)*

Rows 12–13: Work row 2 with pale rose and green consecutively. Fasten off pale rose.

Border

With green and right side facing, ch 1, (2 hdc in sc, skip next dc, sc in next 2 dc, sc in sp) across with last sc in ch-3 sp; working across side, 3 sc in each ch-3 sp; working across bottom, sc in same sp, sc in base of shell, sc and hdc in ch-1 sp, (hdc and sc in ch-2 sp, sc in base of shell, sc and hdc in ch-1 sp) across; working across side, sc in same st, 3 sc in each ch-3 sp, sc in last st, join with sl st in first st. Fasten off. *(80 sts made)*

Top Opening

Rnd 1: With ecru and right side facing you, join with sc in first st after any corner, 5 sc across side, (6 sc across next side) 3 times, join with sl st in first st. *(24 sts made)*

Rnd 2: Ch 6; working behind ch, dc back into first st to the right, (ch 1, skip one st to the left, dc in next st, ch 3; working behind sts, dc back into skipped st) around, ch 1, join sl st in third of ch-6. Fasten off.

Lower Section

Row 1: With green, ch 81, 3 dc in fourth ch from hook, skip next ch, sc in next ch, (ch 2, skip 2 chs, 3 dc in next ch, skip next ch, sc in next ch) across, changing to dk. rose in last st made, turn. *(16 shells made) Row 1 is wrong side of work.*

Rows 2–16: Repeat rows 2–4 of Lapghan 5 times. At end of last row, fasten off. Sew ends of rows together.

Top Edge

Rnd 1: With green and right side facing, join with sc in any ch-2 sp, (sc in next 2 dc, skip next dc, 2 hdc in next sc, sc in ch-2 sp) around, omitting sc on last repeat and ending with sl st in first sc. Fasten off. *(80 sts made)*

Rnd 2: For joining row, with wrong sides together and top section facing you, working through both thicknesses, join ecru with sc in corner st of top and in any st on lower section, (ch 2, skip next st, sc in next) around, join.

Rnd 3: Work rnd 3 of Lapghan Border.

Bottom Edge

Rnd 1: With green and right side facing, join with sc in base of any shell, (sc, hdc) in next sp, (hdc, sc) in next sp, *sc in next shell, (sc, hdc) in next sp, (hdc, sc) in next sp; repeat from * around, ending with sl st in first sc. Fasten off. *(80 sts made)*

Rnd 2: With ecru, join with sc in any st, (ch 2, skip next st, sc in next st) around, ending with sl st in first sc.

Rnd 3: Work rnd 3 of Lapghan Border.

Pillow Corsage/Doorknob Cover

Finished Size: 6" diameter.

Materials:
- ½ oz. each green, dk. rose, pale rose and ecru sport yarn
- 1 yd. ecru ⅜" ribbon
- Tapestry needle
- G hook or hook needed to obtain gauge

Gauge: 3 sc = 1"; 4 rows = 1".

Basic Stitches: Ch, sl st, sc, hdc, dc, tr.

Doily Base

Rnd 1: With ecru, ch 6, sl st in first ch to form a ring, ch 5 *(counts as first dc and ch-2)*, (dc, ch 2) 9 times in ring, join with sl st in third ch of ch-5. *(10 dc made)*

Rnd 2: (Sl st, ch 5, dc) in next sp, (dc, ch 2, dc) in each sp around, join. *(20 dc)*

Rnd 3: (Sl st, ch 5, dc, ch 2, dc) in next sp, (dc, ch 2, dc, ch 2, dc) in each ch-2 sp around, join. *(30 dc)*

Rnd 4: (Sl st, ch 5, dc) in next sp, (dc, ch 2, dc) in each ch-2 sp around, join. *(40 dc)*

Rnd 5: Ch 1, sc in first st, *ch 1, skip next dc, (dc, ch 1) 5 times in next dc, skip next dc, sc in next dc; repeat from * around, join. Fasten off. *(10 shells)*

Large Rose (make 1 dk. rose and 1 pale rose)

Rnd 1: Ch 4, sl st in first ch to form ring, (sc, 3 dc) 3 times in ring, **do not join rnds.**

Rnd 2: Working behind rnd 1 between sts, (sc, ch 2) 4 times spaced evenly in ring.

Rnd 3: For **petals**, (sc, dc, 3 tr, dc, sc) in each ch-2 sp. *(4 petals)*

Rnd 4: Working behind rnd 3 between sts, (sc, ch 2) 2 times in first ch-2 sp of rnd 2, (sc, ch 2) in next ch-2 sp, (sc, ch 2) 2 times in next ch-2 sp, (sc, ch 2) in next ch-2 sp. *(6 lps)*

Rnd 5: Repeat rnd 3. Fasten off. *(6 petals)*

Small Rose (make 1 dk. rose and 1 pale rose)

Rnds 1–3: Work same as Large Rose, except work between ( ) 5 times in rnd 2, fasten off at end of rnd 3. *(5 petals)*

Bud (make 1 dk. rose and 1 pale rose)

Ch 4, 8 tr in fourth ch from hook, dc in same ch, ch 1, roll up bud, sl st in same st behind work between the third and fourth trs. Fasten off.

Leaf (make 12)

With green, ch 10, sl st in second ch from hook; (working in each ch to end, sc, hdc, dc, dc, dc, hdc, sc), 3 sc in last ch; repeat between ( ) in remaining lps on opposite side of ch, join with sl st in sl st. Fasten off.

Sew three Leaves under each Large Rose, two Leaves under each Small Rose, and one under each Bud. Sew flowers to Doily. Tie a lp in center of ribbon, tie to Doily edge with a bow.

Parent's Pride

Continued on page 60

Loving Gifts
Continued from page 59

Loving Rose

Finished Size: Rose is 2¾".

Materials:
- Small amount each green and pale rose sport yarn
- Tapestry needle
- E hook or hook to obtain gauge

Gauge: 3 sc = 1"; 4 rows = 1".

Basic Stitches: Ch, sl st, sc, hdc, dc, tr.

Large Rose & Leaf
Work one Large Rose and three Leaves of Pillow Corsage/Doorknob Cover on page 59.

Plaid Lapghan

Finished Size: 40" x 50".

Materials:
- Sport yarn:
  18 oz. grey
  9 oz. white
  6 oz. each red and black
- G and H hooks or hook needed to obtain gauge

Gauge: With **H hook,** 5 sts = 1"; 4 rows = 1".

Basic Stitches: Ch, sl st, sc.

Notes:
1: To make "woven" pattern, chains of contrasting colors will be covered *(not worked into)* on every other row.
2: Make chains the same number of sts as row being worked, leaving a 3" length of yarn at each end to become part of fringe.
3: Always secure chain in first st so that it will be easier to adjust length at end of row if necessary.
4: When covered, chain should be loose enough to allow fabric to stretch slightly, yet tight enough not to buckle.

Lapghan
Row 1: With H hook and grey, ch 250, sc in second ch from hook, (ch 1, skip next ch, sc in next ch) across, turn. *(249 sts and chs)* Make red chain *(see Note 2).*
Row 2: With grey, covering red ch, insert hook in first st of ch *(see Note 3),* yo, pull through both lps; holding ch across top of row and working around it, sc in first sc, (ch 1, skip next ch, sc in next sc) across to last 2 sts; adjust length of ch to correct tension *(see Note 4),* ch 1, skip next ch, pull up a lp in last sc, insert hook in last st of ch, yo, pull through all lps, turn. *Mark this row as right side.*

Row 3: With grey, ch 1, sc in first sc, (ch 1, skip next ch, sc in next sc) across, turn.
Row 4: Repeat row 2, covering white ch. All even-numbered rows will repeat row 2.
Row 5: Repeat row 3. All odd-numbered rows will repeat row 3.
Row 6: Grey, covering black ch.
Row 7: Grey.
Row 8: Grey, covering white ch.
Row 9: Grey.
Row 10: Grey, covering red ch.
Row 11: Grey. Fasten off at end of row.
Row 12: With black, join with sl st in first st, covering white ch.
Row 13: Black.
Row 14: Black, covering red ch.
Row 15: Black. Fasten off.
Row 16: Join with grey, covering white ch.
Row 17: Grey.
Row 18: Grey, covering black ch.
Row 19: Grey. Fasten off.
Row 20: Join with red, covering white ch.
Row 21: Red.
Row 22: Red, covering grey ch.
Row 23: Red. Fasten off.
Row 24: Join with grey, covering white ch.
Row 25: Grey.
Row 26: Grey, covering red ch.
Row 27: Grey. Fasten off.
Row 28: Join with white, covering black ch.
Row 29: White.
Row 30: White, covering red ch.
Row 31: White. Fasten off.
Row 32: Join with grey, covering black ch.

Row 33: Grey.

Row 34: Grey, covering white ch.

Row 35: Grey.

Row 36: Grey, covering red ch.

Row 37: Grey.

Row 38: Grey, covering white ch.

Row 39: Grey.

Rows 40–63: Repeat color pattern of rows 32–39 three times. Fasten off at end of last row.

Rows 64–69: Repeat rows 28–33.

Row 70: Grey, covering red ch.

Row 71: Grey. Fasten off.

Rows 72–77: Repeat rows 20–25.

Row 78: Grey, covering black ch.

Row 79: Grey.

Rows 80–147: Repeat rows 12–79.

Rows 148–153: Repeat rows 12–17.

Rows 154–163: Repeat rows 2–11. **Do not fasten off.**

Row 164: With **G hook** and grey, ch 1, sl st in first sc, (ch 1, skip next ch, sl st in next sc) across. Fasten off.

Border

With wrong side facing you, working into opposite side of beginning ch, with G hook and grey, sl st in first sc, ch 1, skip next ch and next sc, sl st in next ch, (ch 1, skip next sc, sl st in next ch) across, join with sl st in last st. Fasten off.

Fringe

For each fringe, cut three strands 5" long using color of the ch. With all strands held together, fold in half, insert hook in st, pull fold through st, pull ends through fold, tighten. Fringe at each end of each ch, trim evenly.

Plaid Shoulder Wrap

Finished Size: 25" x 60".

Materials:

- Sport yarn:
    - 12 oz. grey
    - 6 oz. white
    - 3 oz. each of red and black
- G and H hooks or hook needed to obtain gauge

Gauge: With **H hook,** 5 sts = 1"; 4 rows = 1".

Basic Stitches: Ch, sl st, sc.

Notes: See Notes on Lapghan.

Shoulder Wrap

Row 1: With H hook and grey, ch 300, sc in second ch from hook, (ch 1, skip next ch, sc in next ch) across, turn. *(299 sts made)*

Rows 2–79: Repeat rows 2–79 Lapghan.

Rows 80–85: Work rows 12–17 of Lapghan.

Rows 86–95: Work rows 2–11 of Lapghan.

Row 96: Work row 164 of Lapghan.

Border & Fringe

Work same as Lapghan.

Plaid Slippers

Finished Sizes: Instructions are for 10" soles, changes for 11" and 12" are in [ ].

Materials:

- Sport yarn:
    - 2 oz. grey
    - 40 yds. red
    - 30 yds. black
    - 20 yds. white
- Tapestry needle
- G and H hooks or hook needed to obtain gauges

Gauge: H hook (2 strands held together), 11 sts = 1", 4 rows = 1".

Basic Stitches: Ch, sl st, sc.

Note: Use two strands of yarn held together throughout. Chains will be single strand *(see Notes at beginning of Lapghan).*

Sole

Row 1: With H hook and grey *(two strands),* ch 3, 2 sc in second ch from hook, 2 sc in last ch, turn. *(4 sc made)*

Row 2: Ch 1, 2 sc in first st, sc in each st across with 2 sc in last st, turn. *(6)*

Rows 3–15 [3–16, 3–17]: Ch 1, sc in each st across, turn.

Rows 16–17 [17–18, 18–19]: Ch 1, 2 sc in first st, sc in each st across, turn. *(7, 8)*

Row 18 [19, 20]: Ch 1, sc in each st across, turn.

Rows 19–25 [20–27, 21–30]: Repeat rows 16–18 [17–19, 18–20] consecutively, ending with row 16 [18, 18] and *(13) [14, 15] sc.*

Rows 26–32 [28–36, 31–40]: Ch 1, sc in each st across, turn.

Row 33 [37, 41]: Ch 1, skip first st, sc in each st across to last 2 sts, sc last 2 sts tog, turn. *(11) [12, 13]*

Rows 34–37 [38–41, 42–45]: Repeat rows 26 and 33 [28 and 37, 31 and 41] alternately. At end of last row *(7) [8, 9] sc.*

Row 38 [42, 46]: Ch 1, skip first st, sc in next 6 [7, 8] sts, sl st in last st, turn.

Row 39 [43, 47]: Ch 1, sc in each st across. Fasten off.

Top

Row 1: With H hook and grey *(two strands),* ch 8 [10, 10], (sc, ch 1, sc) in second ch from hook, (ch 1, skip next ch, sc in next ch) across, ch 1, sc in last ch again, turn. *(11 sts and chs made) [13 sts and chs made, 13 sts and ch made]*

Note: Read all Notes at beginning of Lapghan before proceeding.

Row 2: Make red chain. Repeat row 2 of Lapghan.

Continued on page 62

Loving Gifts

Continued from page 61

Row 3: With grey, ch 1, (sc, ch 1, sc) in first sc, (ch 1, skip 1 ch, sc in next sc) across, ending with ch 1, sc in last sc again, turn. *(15) [17, 17]*

Row 4: Repeat row 4 of Lapghan.

Row 5: Repeat row 3 of Top. *(19) [21, 21]*

Row 6: Repeat row 6 of Lapghan.

Row 7: With grey, ch 1, sc in first st, (ch 1, skip next ch, sc in next sc) across, turn.

Note: When repeating rows from Lapghan, all even-numbered rows will repeat row 2 of Lapghan, all odd-numbered rows will repeat row 3 of Lapghan.

Rows 8–13: Repeat rows 20–25 of Lapghan.

Rows 14–17: Repeat rows 6–9 of Lapghan.

Rows [18–19, 18–21]: For Medium and Large only, repeat rows [36–37, 36–39] of Lapghan.

Row 18 [20, 22]: For first side, ch 1, sc in first st, (ch 1, skip next ch, sc in next sc) 3 times, leave remaining 12 [14, 14] sts unworked, turn. *(7 sc)*

Rows 19–27 [21–31, 23–35]: Repeat row 7.

Row 28 [32, 36]: Ch 1, (sc, ch 1, sc) in first sc, (ch 1, skip next ch, sc in next sc) across, turn. *(9)*

Rows 29–31 [33–35, 37–39]: Repeat row 7.

Row 32 [36, 40]: Repeat row 28 [32, 36] ending with *(11 sc)*.

Rows 33–39 [37–41, 43–47]: Repeat row 7. Fasten off at end of last row.

Row 18 [20, 22]: For **second side**, with right side facing, skip 5 [7, 7] sts on row 17 [19, 21], join with grey, sc in next sc, (ch 1, skip next ch, sc in next sc) across, turn. *(7 sts)*

Rows 19–27 [21–31, 23–35]: Repeat row 7.

Row 28 [32, 36]: Ch 1, sc in first sc, (ch 1, skip next ch, sc in next sc) across to last 2 sts, ch 1, skip next ch, (sc, ch 1, sc) in last st, turn. *(9)*

Rows 29–31 [33–35, 37–39]: Repeat row 7.

Row 32 [36, 40]: Repeat row 28 [32, 36] ending with *(11 sc)*.

Rows 33–39 [37–43, 41–47]: Repeat row 7. At end of last row, fasten off.

Sew back seam with wrong sides together. Matching fronts and center backs, whipstitch Top to Sole, working through outside lp only on last row of sole.

Top Edging

Rnd 1: With G hook and single strand of grey, with right side facing you, join at center back with sc, sc in each st and in each row around, join with sl st in first st.

Rnd 2: Ch 1, sc in each st around, join. Fasten off.

Tie (make 2)

With G hook and black, ch 90 [98, 106]. Leaving 3" of yarn on both ends, fasten off. Weave under every other st on row 1 of Top Edging, beginning at center front. Make a fringe of six strands (5" long) in first and last ch for tassel.

Plaid Tissue Box Cover

Finished Size: 5" x 5" x 5½" tall.

Materials:
- Sport yarn:
    - 2 oz. grey
    - 1 oz. each red, white and black
- Tapestry needle
- G and H hooks or hook needed to obtain gauge

Gauge: With **H hook,** 5 sts = 1"; 4 rows = 1".

Basic Stitches: Ch, sl st, sc.

Notes: See Notes on Lapghan.

Top

Rnd 1: With H hook and grey, ch 36, sl st in first ch to form ring, ch 1, sc in each ch around, join with sl st in first sc. *(36 sc made)* Mark this rnd as right side.

Rnd 2: Ch 1, working this and following rnds in **back lps** *(see Stitch Guide)*, 3 sc in same st *(corner made)*, (sc in next 8 sts, 3 sc in next st) 3 times, sc in last 8 sts, join. *(44)*

Rnds 3–5: Ch 1, sc in each st around with 3 sc in center st of each corner, join *(8 sts added each rnd)*. At end of last row, fasten off. *(68)*

Lower Section

Row 1: With H hook and grey, ch 28, sc in second ch from hook, (ch 1, skip next ch, sc in next ch) across, turn. *(27 sc made)*

Notes: Read all Notes at beginning of Lapghan before proceeding.

Row 2: Make red chain *(see Note 2)*. With grey, covering red ch, insert hook in first st of ch *(see Note 3)*, yo, pull through both lps; holding ch across top of row and working around it, sc in first sc, (ch 1, skip next ch, sc in next sc) across to last 2 sts; adjust length of ch to correct tension *(see Note 4)*, ch 1, skip next ch, pull up a lp in last sc, insert hook in last st of ch, yo, pull through all lps, turn. *Mark this row as right side.*

Row 3: With grey, ch 1, sc in first sc, (ch 1, skip next ch, sc in next sc) across, turn.

Row 4: With black, covering white ch, join with sl st in first st, repeat row 2. All even numbered rows will repeat row 2.

Row 5: Repeat row 3. **Do not fasten off.** All odd numbered rows will repeat row 3. **Do not fasten off** unless stated for that row.

Rows 6–25: Work rows 14–33 of Lapghan.

Rows 34–35: Repeat rows 2 and 3 of Tissue Cover.

Rows 36–57: Work rows 12–33 of Lapghan.

Rows 58–64: Work rows 70–76 of Lapghan. Fasten off at end of last row.

Fringe

Make Fringe same as Lapghan on one of the long ends. Sew the two short ends together.

Top Edging & Joining

Rnd 1: With G hook and grey, join with sc at seam on Lower Section, work 67 more sc evenly spaced around top edge, join with sl st in first sc. *(68 sc made)*

Rnd 2: With wrong sides together and Lower Section facing you, hold Top to Lower Section; working through both thicknesses, ch 1, sc in each st around, join. Fasten off.

Tie

With G hook and black, ch 60. Leaving 3" yarn on both ends, fasten off. Weave through sts around opening on Top, beginning at one corner. Tie in a bow.

Plaid Glasses Case

Finished Size: 3½" x 6½" tall.

Materials:

- Sport yarn:
    - 1 oz. grey
    - 20 yds. red
    - 10 yds. each black and white
- G and H hooks or hook needed to obtain gauge

Gauge: **H hook (two strands held together),** 11 sts = 3"; 4 rows = 1".

Basic Stitches: Ch, sl st, sc.

Note: Use two strands of yarn held together throughout. Chains will be single strand *(see all Notes at beginning of Lapghan).*

Case

Row 1: With H hook and grey *(two strands),* ch 22, (sc, ch 1, sc) in second ch from hook, (ch 1, skip next ch, sc in next ch) across, turn. *(23 sts and chains made)*

Row 2: With grey, covering black ch *(see Note 2),* insert hook in first st of ch, yo, pull through both lps; holding ch across top of row and working around it, sc in first sc, (ch 1, skip next ch, sc in next sc) across to last 2 sts; adjust length of ch to correct tension *(see Note of Lapghan),* ch 1, skip next ch, pull up a lp in last sc, insert hook in last st of ch, yo through all lps, turn. *Mark this row as right side.*

Row 3: With grey, ch 1, (sc, ch 1, sc) in first sc, (ch 1, skip next ch, sc in next sc) across, turn. *(25)*

Row 4: With red, join with sl st in first sc, covering white ch, repeat row 2.

Row 5: With red, repeat row 3. *(27)*

Note: When repeating rows of Lapghan, all even-numbered rows repeat row 2 of Lapghan, all odd-numbered rows repeat row 3 of Lapghan.

Rows 6–11: Repeat rows 74–79 of Lapghan.

Rows 12–13: With grey, ch 1, sc in first st, (ch 1, skip next ch, sc in next sc) across, turn.

Rows 14–18: Repeat rows 18–22 of Lapghan.

Row 19: With red, ch 1, skip first sc and ch, (sc in next sc, skip next ch, sc in next sc) across, turn. Fasten off. *(25)*

Row 20: With grey, join, covering white ch, ch 1, sc in first sc, (ch 1, skip 1 ch, sc in next sc) across, turn.

Row 21: With grey, repeat row 17. *(23)*

Row 22: With grey, covering black ch, repeat row 20.

Row 23: With grey, repeat row 21, fasten off. Weave in ends.

Finishing

With G hook and grey *(two strands),* with right side facing, join with sl st in last st before rounded end, sc evenly across rounded end. Fold in half with first and last rows together; working through both thicknesses, sl st down side, ch 1, sc across bottom. Fasten off. ●

Football Caddy

An Original by Annie

Finished Size: Base is 7" wide x 25½" long.

Materials:
- Worsted yarn:
  5 oz. brown
  3 oz. blue
  Small amount each gray and white
- ¼ cup aquarium gravel
- Self-seal pint-size plastic bag
- 1⅛"-tall x 3¼"-across container *(we used a 6½ oz. tuna can)*
- 2 Velcro® ⅝" circles or 2 curtain weights
- Polyester fiberfill
- Tapestry needle
- G hook or hook needed to obtain gauge

Gauge: 4 sts = 1"; 4 sc rows = 1"; 13 dc rows = 6".

Basic Stitches: Ch, sl st, sc, dc.

Base
Row 1: With blue, ch 27, sc in second ch from hook, sc in each ch across, turn. *(26 sc made)*
Rows 2–9: Ch 1, sc in each st across, turn. At end of last row, fasten off.
Row 10: Join gray with sc in first st, sc in each st across, turn.
Rows 11–17: Ch 1, sc in each st across, turn. At end of last row, fasten off.
Row 18: Join blue with sc in first st, sc in each st across, turn.
Rows 19–100: Ch 1, sc in each st across, turn. At end of last row, **do not turn.**
Row 101: Working around outer edge, changing colors *(see Stitch Guide)* to match, ch 1, sc in end of each row, in each ch and in each st around with 3 sc in each corner, join with sl st in first sc. Fasten off.

Large Pocket
Row 1: With blue, ch 25, sc in second ch from hook, sc in each ch across, turn. *(24 sc made)*
Rows 2-7: Ch 1, sc in each st across, turn. At

end of last row, fasten off.
Row 8: Join gray with sc in first st, sc in each st across, turn.
Rows 9–15: Ch 1, sc in each st across, turn. At end of last row, **do not turn.**
Row 16: With blue, repeat row 8.
Rows 17–25: Ch 1, sc in each st across, turn. At end of last row, **do not turn.**
Row 26: Working around 3 outer edges, changing colors to match, ch 1, sc in end of each row and in each ch around to opposite end of row 25 with 3 sc in each corner. Fasten off.

Small Pocket
Row 1: With blue, ch 21, sc in second ch from hook, sc in each ch across, turn. *(20 sc made)*
Rows 2–5: Ch 1, sc in each st across, turn. At end of last row, fasten off.
Row 6: Join gray with sc in first st, sc in each st across, turn.
Rows 7–13: Ch 1, sc in each st across, turn. At end of last row, fasten off.
Row 14: Join blue with sc in first st, sc in each st across, turn.
Rows 15–20: Ch 1, sc in each st across, turn. At end of last row, **do not turn.**
Row 21: Working around 3 outer edges, changing colors to match, ch 1, sc in end of each row and in each ch around to opposite end of row 20 with 3 sc in each corner. Fasten off.

Cup & Ball
Note: *Work in continuous rnds, do not join or turn unless otherwise stated. Mark first st of each rnd.*
Rnd 1: For **cup,** with brown, ch 2, 6 sc in second ch from hook. *(6 sc made)*
Rnd 2: 2 sc in each st around. *(12)*
Rnd 3: (Sc in next st, 2 sc in next st) around. *(18)*
Rnd 4: (Sc in next 2 sts, 2 sc in next st) around. *(24)*
Rnd 5: (Sc in next 3 sts, 2 sc in next st) around. *(30)*

Rnd 6: (Sc in next 4 sts, 2 sc in next st) around. *(36)*

Rnd 7: (Sc in next 5 sts, 2 sc in next st) around. *(42)*

Rnd 8: Working in **front lps** *(see Stitch Guide)*, sc in each st around.

Rnds 9–21: Sc in each st around. At end of last rnd, join with sl st in first sc.

Rnd 22: For **ball,** working in **back lps,** ch 1, sc in each st around.

Rnd 23: (Sc in next 6 sts, 2 sc in next st) around. *(48)*

Rnd 24: Sc in next 4 sts, 2 sc in next st, (sc in next 7 sts, 2 sc in next st) 5 times, sc in last 3 sts. *(54)*

Rnd 25: (Sc in next 8 sts, 2 sc in next st) around. *(60)*

Rnd 26: Sc in next 5 sts, 2 sc in next st, (sc in next 9 sts, 2 sc in next st) 5 times, sc in last 4 sts. *(66)*

Rnd 27: (Sc in next 10 sts, 2 sc in next st) around. *(72)*

Rnd 28: Sc in next 6 sts, 2 sc in next st, (sc in next 9 sts, 2 sc in next st) 5 times, sc in last 5 sts. *(78)*

Rnds 29–33: Sc in each st around. At end of last rnd, join with sl st in first sc.

Rnd 34: (3 sc in next st, sc in next 38 sts) around. *(82)*

Rnd 35: Sc in next st, 3 sc in next st, sc in next 40 sts, 3 sc in next st, sc in last 39 sts. *(86)*

Rnd 36: Sc in next 2 sts, 3 sc in next st, sc in next 42 sts, 3 sc in next st, sc in last 40 sts. *(90)*

Rnd 37: Sc in next 3 sts, 3 sc in next st, sc in next 44 sts, 3 sc in next st, sc in last 41 sts. *(94)*

Rnd 38: Sc in next 4 sts, 3 sc in next st, sc in next 46 sts, 3 sc in next st, sc in last 42 sts. *(98)*

Rnd 39: Sc in next 5 sts, 3 sc in next st, sc in next 48 sts, 3 sc in next st, sc in last 43 sts. *(102)*

Rnd 40: Sc in next 6 sts, 3 sc in next st, sc in next 50 sts, 3 sc in next st, sc in last 44 sts. *(106)*

Rnd 41: Sc in next 6 sts, sc next 3 sts tog, sc in next 50 sts, sc next 3 sts tog, sc in last 44 sts. *(102)*

Rnd 42: Sc in next 5 sts, sc next 3 sts tog, sc in next 48 sts, sc next 3 sts tog, sc in last 43 sts. *(98)*

Rnd 43: Sc in next 4 sts, sc next 3 sts tog, sc in next 46 sts, sc next 3 sts tog, sc in last 42 sts. *(94)*

Rnd 44: Sc in next 3 sts, sc next 3 sts tog, sc in next 44 sts, sc next 3 sts tog, sc in last 41 sts. *(90)*

Rnd 45: Sc in next 2 sts, sc next 3 sts tog, sc in next 42 sts, sc next 3 sts tog, sc in last 40 sts. *(86)*

Rnd 46: Sc in next st, sc next 3 sts tog, sc in next 40 sts, sc next 3 sts tog, sc in last 39 sts. *(82)*

Rnd 47: (Sc next 3 sts tog, sc in next 38 sts) around. *(78)*

Rnd 48: (Sc in next 11 sts, sc next 2 sts tog) around. *(72)*

Rnd 49: Sc in next 5 sts, sc next 2 sts tog, (sc in next 10 sts, sc next 2 sts tog) 5 times, sc in last 5 sts. *(66)*

Rnd 50: (Sc in next 9 sts, sc next 2 sts tog) around. *(60)*

Rnd 51: Sc in next 4 sts, sc next 2 sts tog, (sc in next 8 sts, sc next 2 sts tog) 5 times, sc in last 4 sts. *(54)*

Rnd 52: (Sc in next 7 sts, sc next 2 sts tog) around. *(48)*

Rnd 53: Sc in next 3 sts, sc next 2 sts tog, (sc in next 6 sts, sc next 2 sts tog) 5 times, sc in last 3 sts, join with sl st in first sc. Fasten off. Stuff. *(42)*

Strip *(make 2)*

Rnd 1: With white, ch 55, sl st in first ch to form ring, ch 1; working in **back bar of ch** *(see Stitch Guide),* sc in each ch around. *(55 sc made)*

Rnds 2–3: Sc in each st around. At end of last rnd, join with sl st in first sc. Fasten off.

Sew one Stripe 2¼" from tip on each end of Ball.

Lacing Strip

Row 1: With white, ch 23; working in **back bar of ch,** sc in second ch from hook, sc in each ch across, turn. *(20 sc made)*

Row 2: Ch 1, sc in each st across. Fasten off.

Sew to one side of Ball centered over rnds 30–32.

Lace *(make 7)*

With white, ch 6. Fasten off.

Sew two sts apart centered over rnds 28–34 on Lacing Strip.

Finishing

1: Matching colors, sew sides and bottom of Small Pocket centered over rows 1–21 on Large Pocket.

2: With Small Pocket on outside, sew sides and bottom of Large Pocket centered over rows 1–26 of Base.

3: Place gravel in plastic bag and seal. With gravel in one corner, fold bag to measure 3" square.

4: With Lacing Strip toward Pockets, sew bottom of Ball centered over rnds 55–68 on Base, inserting plastic bag before closing.

5: Using loopy side, attach Velcro to end of row 63 on wrong side of Base, or sew one curtain weight to each corner opposite Pockets on wrong side of Base.

6: Place container in Cup.

7: For each fringe, cut one strand blue 6" long. Fold in half, insert hook in st, pull fold through st, pull ends through fold, tighten. Working in sts on rnd 101, fringe in each st across bottom edge below pockets. ●

Mother's Love Angel

An Original by Annie

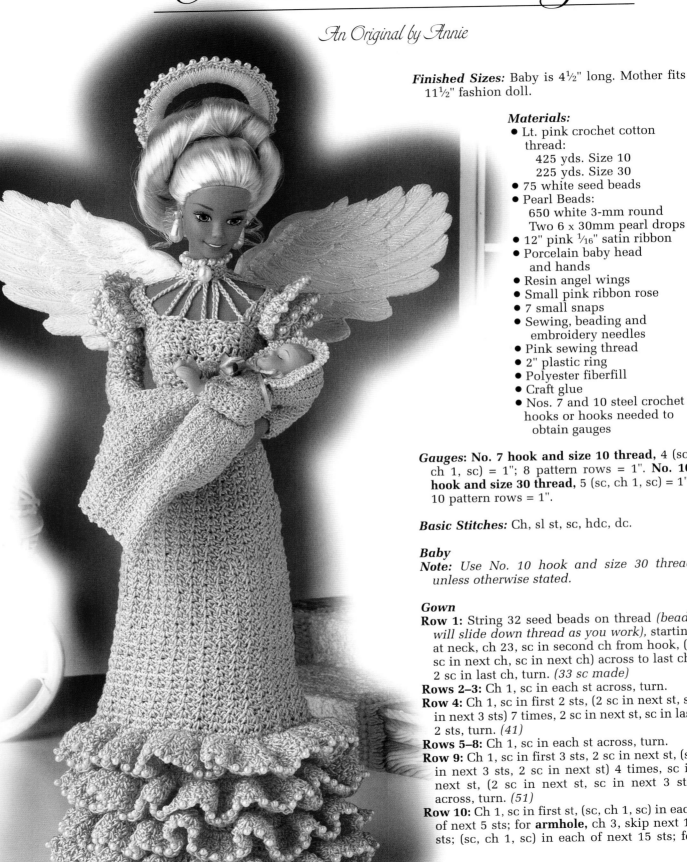

Finished Sizes: Baby is 4½" long. Mother fits 11½" fashion doll.

Materials:
- Lt. pink crochet cotton thread:
  - 425 yds. Size 10
  - 225 yds. Size 30
- 75 white seed beads
- Pearl Beads:
  - 650 white 3-mm round
  - Two 6 x 30mm pearl drops
- 12" pink ¹⁄₁₆" satin ribbon
- Porcelain baby head and hands
- Resin angel wings
- Small pink ribbon rose
- 7 small snaps
- Sewing, beading and embroidery needles
- Pink sewing thread
- 2" plastic ring
- Polyester fiberfill
- Craft glue
- Nos. 7 and 10 steel crochet hooks or hooks needed to obtain gauges

Gauges: No. 7 hook and size 10 thread, 4 (sc, ch 1, sc) = 1"; 8 pattern rows = 1". **No. 10 hook and size 30 thread,** 5 (sc, ch 1, sc) = 1"; 10 pattern rows = 1".

Basic Stitches: Ch, sl st, sc, hdc, dc.

Baby
Note: *Use No. 10 hook and size 30 thread unless otherwise stated.*

Gown
Row 1: String 32 seed beads on thread *(beads will slide down thread as you work)*, starting at neck, ch 23, sc in second ch from hook, (2 sc in next ch, sc in next ch) across to last ch, 2 sc in last ch, turn. *(33 sc made)*

Rows 2–3: Ch 1, sc in each st across, turn.

Row 4: Ch 1, sc in first 2 sts, (2 sc in next st, sc in next 3 sts) 7 times, 2 sc in next st, sc in last 2 sts, turn. *(41)*

Rows 5–8: Ch 1, sc in each st across, turn.

Row 9: Ch 1, sc in first 3 sts, 2 sc in next st, (sc in next 3 sts, 2 sc in next st) 4 times, sc in next st, (2 sc in next st, sc in next 3 sts) across, turn. *(51)*

Row 10: Ch 1, sc in first st, (sc, ch 1, sc) in each of next 5 sts; for **armhole,** ch 3, skip next 12 sts; (sc, ch 1, sc) in each of next 15 sts; for

armhole, ch 3, skip next 12 sts; (sc, ch 1, sc) in each of next 5 sts, sc in last st, turn. *(25 ch-1 sps, 2 sc)*

Row 11: Ch 1, sc in first st, (sc, ch 1, sc) in each of next 5 ch-1 sps, (sc, ch 1, sc) in each of next 3 chs, (sc, ch 1, sc) in each of next 15 ch-1 sps, (sc, ch 1, sc) in each of next 3 chs, (sc, ch 1, sc) in each ch-1 sp across to last st, sc in last st, turn. *(31 ch-1 sps, 2 sc)*

Rows 12–15: Ch 1, sc in first st, (sc, ch 1, sc) in each ch sp across to last st, sc in last st, turn.

Rnd 16: Working in rnds, ch 1, (sc, ch 1, sc) in first st, (sc, ch 1, sc) in each ch sp around, skip last st, join with sl st in first sc, turn. *(32 ch-1 sps)*

Rnds 17–44: Ch 1, (sc, ch 1, sc) in each ch sp around, join, **turn.** At end of last rnd, **do not turn.**

Rnd 45: Ch 1, (sc, pull up one bead, ch 1, sc) in each ch sp around, join. Fasten off.

Sleeves

Rnd 1: Working on opposite side of ch-3 on armhole, join with sc in center ch of ch-3, ch 1, sc in same ch as first sc, skip next ch, *(sc, ch 1, sc) in next st, skip next st or ch; repeat from * around to last ch of ch-3, (sc, ch 1, sc) in last ch, join with sl st in first sc, turn. *(8 ch-1 sps)*

Rnds 2–6: Ch 1, (sc, ch 1, sc) in each ch-1 sp around, join, **turn.**

Rnds 7–9: Ch 1, (sc, ch 1, sc) in each ch-1 sp around to last 2 ch sps, sc in next ch sp, ch 1, sc in last ch sp, join, **turn.**

Rnds 10–11: Ch 1, (sc, ch 1, sc) in each ch-1 sp around, join. At end of last rnd, leaving 8" end for weaving, fasten off.

Insert hand, weave end through sts of rnd 11, pull tight, secure end.

Repeat on remaining armhole.

Bonnet

Row 1: String 35 seed beads on thread, ch 7, sc in second ch from hook, sc in next 4 chs, 3 sc in last ch; working on opposite side of ch, sc in next 5 chs, turn. *(13 sc made)*

Row 2: Ch 1, sc in first 5 sts, 2 sc in next st, sc in next st, 2 sc in next st, sc in last 5 sts, turn. *(15)*

Row 3: Ch 1, sc in first 5 sts, 2 sc in next st, (sc in next st, 2 sc in next st) 2 times, sc in last 5 sts, turn. *(18)*

Row 4: Ch 1, 2 sc in first st, sc in next 3 sts, (2 sc in next st, sc in next st) 2 times, sc in next 2 sts, (sc in next st, 2 sc in next st) 2 times, sc in next 3 sts, 2 sc in last st, turn. *(24 sc)*

Row 5: Ch 1, sc in first 4 sts, hdc in each st across to last 4 sts, sc in last 4 sts, turn.

Row 6: Ch 1, sc in first 4 sts, (2 hdc in next st, hdc in next 2 sts) 5 times, 2 hdc in next st, sc in last 4 sts, turn. *(30)*

Rows 7–11: Ch 1, sc in first 3 sts, hdc in each st across to last 3 sts, sc in last 3 sts, turn. At end of last row, **do not turn.**

Rnd 12: Working around outer edge in ends of rows and in sts, ch 1, skip first row, (sc next 2 rows tog) across, ch 1, working in **back lps** *(see Stitch Guide),* sc in each st across, join with sl st in first sc, **turn.**

Row 13: Ch 1, (sc, pull up bead, ch 1, sc) in each st across to ch-1. Fasten off.

Finishing

1: Place Gown over porcelain head, sew back opening closed. Tack Sleeves together and to Gown in front as shown in photo.

2: Glue ribbon rose to center front of Gown.

3: Stuff head and upper part of body slightly with fiberfill.

4: Cut ribbon in half. Turn under ¼" on one end of each piece and sew one to the first and one to the last unworked **front lp** on rnd 12 of Bonnet. Place Bonnet on head and tie ribbon in bow under chin.

Mother Angel

Note: *Use No. 7 hook and size 10 thread unless otherwise stated.*

Bodice

Row 1: Ch 26, sc in second ch from hook, sc in each ch across, turn. *(25 sc made)*

Row 2: Ch 1, (sc, ch 1, sc) in first st, *skip next st, (sc, ch 1, sc) in next st; repeat from * across, turn. *(13 ch sps)*

Row 3: Ch 1, (sc, ch 1, sc) in each of first 2 ch-1 sps; for **increase (inc), (sc, ch 1, sc, ch 1, sc) in next ch-1 sp;** (sc, ch 1, sc) in each of next 7 ch-1 sps, inc, (sc, ch 1, sc) in each of last 2 ch-1 sps, turn. *(15 ch sps)*

Row 4: Ch 1, (sc, ch 1, sc) in each of first 5 ch sps, inc, (sc, ch 1, sc) in each of next 3 ch sps, inc, (sc, ch 1, sc) in each of last 5 ch sps, turn. *(17 ch sps)*

Rows 5–9: Ch 1, (sc, ch 1, sc) in each ch sp across, turn.

Row 10: Ch 1, (sc, ch 1, sc) in each of first 7 ch sps, 7 dc in next ch sp, sc in next ch sp, 7 dc in next ch sp, (sc, ch 1, sc) in each of last 7 ch sps, turn.

Row 11: Ch 1, (sc, ch 1, sc) in each of first 6 ch sps, skip next ch sp, 2 dc in next dc, dc in next 4 dc, 3 dc in next dc, skip next dc, sc in next sc, skip next dc, 3 dc in next dc, dc in next 4 dc, 2 dc in next dc, skip next ch sp, (sc, ch 1, sc) in each of last 6 ch sps, turn.

Row 12: Ch 1, (sc, ch 1, sc) in each of first 6 ch sps, *skip next dc, (sc, ch 1, sc) in next dc*; repeat between * 3 more times, skip next dc, sc in next sc; repeat between first and second * 4 more times, skip next ch sp, (sc, ch 1, sc) in each of last 6 ch sps, turn. *(20 ch sps)*

Row 13: Ch 1, (sc, ch 1, sc) in each ch sp across, turn.

Row 14: Ch 1, inc, (sc, ch 1, sc) in each ch sp across to last ch sp, inc, turn. *(22 ch sps)*

Row 15: Ch 1, skipping ch sps, sc in each st across, turn. *(44 sc)*

Row 16: For **first shoulder,** ch 1, sc in first 8 sts; for **armhole,** ch 13, skip next 5 sts; sc in next

Continued on page 68

2 sts leaving remaining sts unworked, turn. *(10 sc)*

Row 17: Sl st in first 2 sts, sc in next 12 chs, sc next ch and next st tog, sc in last 7 sts, turn. *(22 sts)*

Row 18: Ch 1, sc in first 6 sts, sc next 2 sts tog; working in **front lps**, sc in next 12 sts; working in **both lps**, ch 1, skip next sl st, sl st in next sl st, sl st in next 2 sts on row 15, turn.

Row 19: Ch 1, skip first sl st, sl st in next 2 sl sts, sc in each sc across. Fasten off.

Row 16: For **second shoulder**, skip next 12 sts on row 15, join with sc in next st, sc in next st; for **armhole**, ch 13, skip next 5 sts; sc in last 8 sts, turn. *(10 sc)*

Row 17: Ch 1, sc in first 7 sts, sc next st and next ch tog, sc in next 12 chs, sl st in last 2 sts, sl st in next st on row 15, turn. *(23 sts)*

Row 18: Sl st in first 2 sts, ch 1, skip next sl st; working in **front lps**, sc in next 12 sts; working in **both lps**, sc next 2 sts tog, sc in last 6 sts, turn. *(21 sts)*

Row 19: Ch 1, sc in each sc across to sl sts, ch 1, skip next sl st, sl st in next sl st, sl st in next st on row 15. Fasten off.

Collar

Row 1: String sixteen 3mm pearls on thread, ch 20, sc in second ch from hook, sc in each ch across, turn. *(19 sc made)*

Row 2: Ch 1, sc in each st across, turn.

Row 3: Ch 1, sc in first 2 sts, (sc, pull up bead) in each st across to last st, sc in last st, **do not turn.**

Row 4: Working in ends of rows, sc in each row; working in remaining lps of starting ch on opposite side of row 1, sc in first ch, ch 7, sl st in first st at top of left back on Bodice, ch 7, skip next 4 sts on Collar, sl st in next st, ch 8, skip next 5 sts on Bodice, sl st in next 5 sts, ch 6, sl st in each of next 2 sts on Collar, ch 8, skip next 4 sts on Bodice, sl st in next 5 sts, ch 9, sl st in next st on Collar, ch 9, skip next 2 sts on Bodice, sl st in next 3 sts, ch 9, sl st in next 2 sts on Collar, ch 9, skip next st on Bodice, sl st in next 4 sts, ch 9, skip next st on Collar, sl st in next 2 sts, ch 8, skip next 3 sts on Bodice, sl st in next 6 sts, ch 6, sl st in next 2 sts on Collar, ch 7, skip next 5 sts on Bodice, sl st in next 6 sts, ch 7, skip next 2 sts on Collar, sl st in last st; working in ends of rows, sc in each row across, join with sl st in first sc on row 3. Fasten off.

Sleeve

Rnd 1: Join with sc in center st of skipped sts on row 15 of one armhole, sc in next st; working on opposite side of ch-13, hdc next st and next ch tog, sc in next 11 chs, hdc next ch and st tog, sc in last st, join with sl st in first sc. Fasten off. *(16 sts made)*

Row 2: Working in **back lps**, skip first 4 sts, join with sc in fifth st, (2 sc in next st, sc in next 2 sts) 3 times leaving remaining sts unworked, turn.

Row 3: Working in **back lps**, ch 1, skip first st, sc in next 11 sts, skip next st, sc in end of row 2, sc in next 4 sts on rnd 1, turn. *(16 sc)*

Rnd 4: Working in rnds, ch 1, sc in first 16 sts, sc in end of next row, 2 sc in end st on row 2, sc in each of remaining sts on rnd 1, join with sl st in first sc, **turn.** *(21 sc)*

Rnd 5: Ch 1, skip first st, *(sc, ch 1, sc) in next st, skip next st; repeat from * around, join, **turn.** *(10 ch sps)*

Rnds 6–9: Ch 1, (sc, ch 1, sc) in each ch sp around to last 2 ch sps, sc in next ch sp, ch 1, sc in last ch sp, join, **turn.** At end of last rnd *(6 ch sps)*.

Rnds 10–23: Ch 1, (sc, ch 1, sc) in each ch sp around, join. **turn.** At end of last rnd, fasten off.

First Ruffle

Row 1: String twelve 3mm beads on thread; working in **remaining lps** of sts on rnd 1 of Sleeve, join with sc in first st, sc in next 12 sts, turn. *(13 sc made)*

Row 2: Working in **back lps**, ch 1, (sc, ch 1, sc) in each st across, turn.

Rows 3–4: Ch 1, (sc, ch 1, sc) in each ch sp across, turn.

Row 5: Ch 1, (sc, pull up bead, ch 1, sc) in each ch sp across. Fasten off.

Second Ruffle

Rows 1–5: Working in **remaining lps** of row 1 on First Ruffle, repeat rows 1–5 of First Ruffle.

Third Ruffle

Rows 1–5: Working in **remaining lps** of sts on row 17 of Bodice, repeat rows 1–5 of First Ruffle.

Repeat Sleeve and Ruffles on remaining armhole.

Skirt

Row 1: Working in remaining lps of starting ch on row 1 of Bodice, join with sc in first ch, ch 1, sc in same ch as first sc, (sc, ch 1, sc) in each ch across, turn. *(26 ch sps made)*

Rows 2–9: Ch 1, (sc, ch 1, sc) in each ch sp across, turn.

Row 10: Ch 1, (sc, ch 1, sc) in each of first 4 ch sps, *inc, (sc, ch 1, sc) in each of next 8 ch sps; repeat from *, inc, (sc, ch 1, sc) in each of last 3 ch sps, turn. *(29 ch sps)*

Rows 11–17: Ch 1, (sc, ch 1, sc) in each ch sp across, turn.

Row 18: Ch 1, (sc, ch 1, sc) in first ch sp, *inc, (sc, ch 1, sc) in each of next 3 ch sps*; repeat between first and second * 2 more times, (sc, ch 1, sc) in each of next 4 ch sps; repeat between first and second * 3 more times, turn. *(35 ch sps)*

Rnds 19–39: Working in rnds, ch 1, (sc, ch 1, sc) in each ch sp around, join with sl st in first sc, **turn.**

Rnd 40: Ch 1, inc, *(sc, ch 1, sc) in each of next

10 ch sps, inc; repeat from *, (sc, ch 1, sc) in each of last 12 ch sps, join, **turn**. *(38 ch sps)*

Rnds 41–42: Ch 1, (sc, ch 1, sc) in each ch sp around, join, **turn**. At end of last rnd, **do not turn.**

Rnd 43: Ch 1, sc in each st and in each ch sp around, join. *(114 sc)*

Rnd 44: Working in **back lps,** ch 1, (sc, ch 1, sc) in first st, skip next 2 sts, *(sc, ch 1, sc) in next st, skip next 2 sts; repeat from * around, join, **turn**.

Rnds 45–48: Ch 1, (sc, ch 1, sc) in each ch sp around, join, **turn**. At end of last rnd, **do not turn.**

Rnd 49: Ch 1, sc in each st and in each ch sp around, join. *(114 sc)*

Rnd 50: Working in **back lps,** ch 1, (sc, ch 1, sc) in first st, skip next 2 sts, *(sc, ch 1, sc) in next st, skip next 2 sts; repeat from * around, join, **turn**.

Rnds 51–54: Ch 1, (sc, ch 1, sc) in each ch sp around, join, **turn**. At end of last rnd, **do not turn.**

Rnd 55: Ch 1, sc in each st and in each ch sp around, join. *(114 sc)*

Rnd 56: Working in **back lps,** ch 1, (sc, ch 1, sc) in first st, skip next 2 sts, *(sc, ch 1, sc) in next st, skip next 2 sts; repeat from * around, join, **turn**.

Rnds 57–60: Ch 1, (sc, ch 1, sc) in each ch sp around, join, **turn**. At end of last rnd, **do not turn.**

Rnd 61: Ch 1, sc in each st and in each ch sp around, join. *(114 sc)*

Rnd 62: Working in **back lps,** ch 1, (sc, ch 1, sc) in first st, skip next 2 sts, *(sc, ch 1, sc) in next st, skip next 2 sts; repeat from * around, join, **turn**.

Rnds 63–66: Ch 1, (sc, ch 1, sc) in each ch sp around, join, **turn**. At end of last rnd, fasten off.

First Ruffle
Rnd 1: String 114 beads on thread, working in **remaining lps** of rnd 43, join with sl st in first st, ch 3, dc in each st around, join with sl st in top of ch-3. *(114 dc made)*

Rnd 2: Ch 1, (sc, ch 1, sc) in each st around, join with sl st in first sc, **turn**. *(114 ch sps)*

Rnds 3–5: Ch 1, (sc, ch 1, sc) in each ch sp around, join, **turn**.

Rnd 6: Ch 1, (sc, pull up bead, ch 1, sc) in each ch sp around, join. Fasten off.

Second Ruffle
Rnd 1: String 114 beads on thread, working in

remaining lps of rnd 49, join with sl st in first st, ch 3, dc in each st around, join with sl st in top of ch-3. *(114 dc made)*

Rnd 2: Ch 1, (sc, ch 1, sc) in each st around, join with sl st in first sc, **turn**. *(114 ch sps)*

Rnds 3–5: Ch 1, (sc, ch 1, sc) in each ch sp around, join, **turn**.

Rnd 6: Ch 1, (sc, pull up bead, ch 1, sc) in each ch sp around, join. Fasten off.

Third Ruffle
Rnd 1: String 114 beads on thread, working in **remaining lps** of rnd 55, join with sl st in first st, ch 3, dc in each st around, join with sl st in top of ch-3. *(114 dc made)*

Rnd 2: Ch 1, (sc, ch 1, sc) in each st around, join with sl st in first sc, **turn**. *(114 ch sps)*

Rnds 3–5: Ch 1, (sc, ch 1, sc) in each ch sp around, join, **turn**.

Rnd 6: Ch 1, (sc, pull up bead, ch 1, sc) in each ch sp around, join. Fasten off.

Fourth Ruffle
Rnd 1: String 114 beads on thread, working in **remaining lps** of rnd 61, join with sl st in first st, ch 3, dc in each st around, join with sl st in top of ch-3. *(114 dc made)*

Rnd 2: Ch 1, (sc, ch 1, sc) in each st around, join with sl st in first sc, **turn**. *(114 ch sps)*

Rnds 3–5: Ch 1, (sc, ch 1, sc) in each ch sp around, join, **turn**.

Rnd 6: Ch 1, (sc, pull up bead, ch 1, sc) in each ch sp around, join. Fasten off.

Halo
String 37 beads onto thread.

Rnd 1: Working around plastic ring *(see Stitch Guide),* work 111 sc, covering ring completely, join with sl st in first sc.

Rnd 2: Sl st in first st, pull up bead, skip next 2 sts, (sl st in next st, pull up bead, skip next 2 sts) around, join with sl st in first sl st. Fasten off.

Finishing
1: With sewing thread and needle, sew one snap to ends of Collar and remaining snaps evenly spaced down back opening on Bodice and Skirt.

2: For **earring** *(make 2),* place one 3mm bead and one teardrop bead on each straight pin. Insert in ears.

3: Tack or glue wings to back of Bodice.

4: Place Gown on doll and Halo on head. ●

Golf Afghan

Designed by Penny Thompson

Finished Size: 55" x 59½".

Materials:
- Worsted yarn:
  - 32 oz. med. green
  - 24 oz. dk. green
  - 6 oz. brown
  - 3 oz. red
  - 2 oz. tan
  - 2 oz. white
- 2" square cardboard
- Tapestry needle
- H hook or hook needed to obtain gauge

Gauge: 3 sc = 1"; 7 sc rows = 2".

Basic Stitches: Ch, sl st, sc.

Notes: For **color change** *(see Stitch Guide),* always change colors in last st made.

Use a separate ball of yarn for each section of color and fasten off each color when no longer needed.

Each square on graph equals one sc.

Graph is for center section of Afghan only; first and last sts of rows are not shown.

Afghan

Row 1: With med. green, ch 161, sc in second ch from hook, sc in each ch across, turn. *(160 sc made) Front of row 1 is right side of work.*

Rows 2–30: Ch 1, sc in each st across, turn.

Row 31: Ch 1, sc in first 62 sts changing to dk. green *(see Notes),* sc in next 12 sts changing to med. green, sc in last 86 sts, turn.

Row 32: Ch 1, sc in first 26 sts, work next 95 sts according to corresponding row of graph on page 72, sc in last 39 sts, turn.

Row 33: Ch 1, sc in first 39 sts, work next 95 sts according to corresponding row of sc in last 26 sts, turn.

Rows 34–172: Repeat rows 32 and 33 alternately, ending with row 32.

Rows 173–202: Ch 1, sc in each st across, turn. At end of last row, fasten off.

Rnd 203: Working around outer edge, join brown with sc in first st, sc in each st and in end of each row around with 3 sc in each corner, join with sl st in first sc.

Rnds 204–205: Ch 1, sc in each st around with 3 sc in each center corner st, join. At end of last rnd, fasten off.

Finishing

For **pom-pom,** wrap white around cardboard 100 times; slide loops off cardboard, tie separate 8" strand of white around center of all loops; cut loops. Trim ends to form 2" pom-pom.

Embroider cross stitch *(see Stitch Guide)* on Afghan according to graph on page 72.

Sew pom-pom to Afghan according to placement line on graph. ●

Continued on page 72

1 ST PLACE

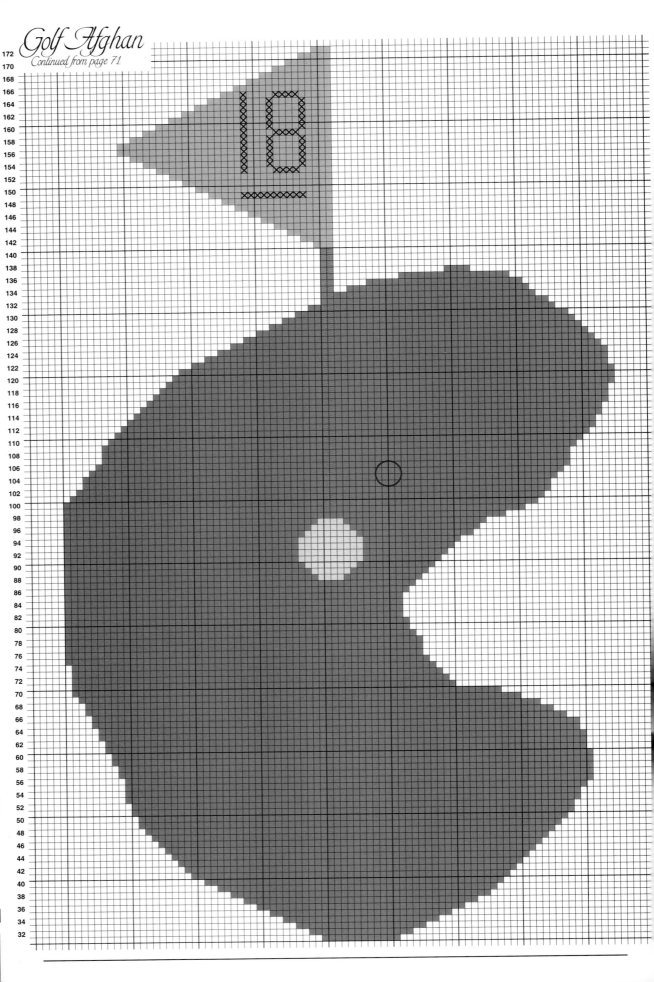

Cross Stitch:
(See instructions for working information.)
X = White

Key:

□ = Med. Green	▨ = White
▨ = Dk. Green	○ = Pom-Pom Placement
▨ = Red	
□ = Tan	

chapter 5

Fourth Fever

Create and inspire culinary fireworks with a surefire Independence Day favorite.

Red, White & Blue Berry Pie

3 pints fresh strawberries
½ pint fresh blueberries
⅔ cup strawberry jelly
1 prepared pie shell, baked

Wash and hull strawberries. Microwave jelly for 1 minute or until it becomes liquid. Toss the berries with the jelly and spoon into pie shell. Gently press the berries into the shell without mashing the berries. Refrigerate for 2 hours.

Li-bear-ty Wreath

Designed by Jocelyn Sass

Finished Size: 15" across.

Materials:
- Worsted-weight yarn:
    1 oz. each red and blue
    ½ oz. white
- 14" straw wreath
- 5" flocked and jointed bear
- 4 yds. red, white and blue 1½" craft ribbon
- Small flag on a pick
- Tacky craft glue
- Polyester fiberfill
- Tapestry needle
- F hook or hook needed to obtain gauge

Gauge: 9 sc = 2"; 5 sc rows = 1".

Basic Stitches: Ch, sl st, sc.

Plain Heart (make 1 blue, 1 red)
Front
Row 1: Ch 5, sc in second ch from hook and in each ch across, turn. *(4 sc made)*
Rows 2–3: Ch 1, 2 sc in first st, sc in each st across to last st, 2 sc in last st, turn. *(6, 8)*
Row 4: Ch 1, sc in each st across to last st, 2 sc in last st, turn. *(9)*
Row 5: Ch 1, 2 sc in first st, sc in each st across, turn. *(10)*
Row 6: Ch 1, sc first 2 sts tog, sc in each st across to last st, 2 sc in last st, turn. *(10)*
Row 7: Ch 1, 2 sc in first st, sc in next 5 sts, (sc next 2 sts tog) across, turn. *(9)*
Rows 8–9: Ch 1, sc in each st across, turn.
Row 10: Ch 1, 2 sc in each of first 2 sts, sc in next 5 sts, sc last 2 sts tog, turn. *(10)*
Row 11: Ch 1, sc first 2 sts tog, sc in next 7 sts, 2 sc in last st, turn. *(10)*
Row 12: Ch 1, sc in first 8 sts, sc last 2 sts tog, turn. *(9)*
Row 13: Ch 1, sc first 2 sts tog, sc in each st across, turn. *(8)*
Rows 14–15: Ch 1, sc first 2 sts tog, sc in each st across to last 2 sts, sc last 2 sts tog, turn. *(6, 4)*
Rnd 16: Working in ends of rows and in each st, sc around outer edge of Heart with 3 sc in point, join with sl st in first sc. Fasten off.
For **trim,** join white with sc in any **front lp** *(see Stitch Guide)* of rnd 16, ch 3, (sc in next st, ch 3) around, join. Fasten off.
With white, make eight French Knots *(see Stitch Guide)* in a 1¾" circle on Front.

Continued on page 81

Uncle Sam Windsock

Designed by Karin Strom

Finished Size: 34" long without hanger.

Materials:
- Worsted yarn:
    - 6½ oz. blue
    - 4 oz. white
    - 3½ oz. red
    - 1 oz. beige
    - 1 oz. black
- Felt:
    - 4" x 7" white piece
    - 4" square beige piece
    - 3" square pink piece
    - 1" x 3" red piece
    - 2" square blue piece
    - 1½" square rose piece
- Metal rings:
    - 7" diameter
    - 1" diameter
- 16 gold 18mm jingle bells
- Monofilament line
- Craft glue
- Tapestry needle
- H hook or hook needed to obtain gauge

Gauge: 7 sc = 2"; 7 sc rows = 2".

Basic Stitches: Ch, sl st, sc.

Windsock

Note: *When changing colors (see Stitch Guide), drop first color to wrong side of work, pick up next color. Always change to next color in last st made.*

Rnd 1: Starting at top, with blue, ch 80, sl st in first ch to form ring, ch 1, sc in each ch around, join with sl st in first sc, **turn.** *(80 sc made)*

Rnds 2–22: Ch 1, sc in each st around, join, **turn.** At end of last rnd, fasten off.

Rnd 23: Join white with sc in first st, sc in next 4 sts changing to red *(see Note)* in last st, (sc in next 5 sts changing to white in last st, sc in next 5 sts changing to red in last st) 7 times, sc in last 5 sts changing to white in last st, join, **turn.**

Rnds 24–27: Ch 1, sc in first 5 sts changing to red in last st, (sc in next 5 sts changing to white in last st, sc in next 5 sts changing to red in last st) 7 times, sc in last 5 sts changing to white in last st, join, **turn.**

Rnd 28: Working this rnd only in **back lps** *(see Stitch Guide),* ch 1, sc in first 31 sts changing to beige in last st; for **face,** sc in next 18 sts changing to white in last st; sc in last 31 sts, join, **turn.**

Rnds 29–45: Working in **both lps,** ch 1, sc in first 31 sts changing to beige in last st, sc in next 18 sts changing to white in last st, sc in next last 31 sts, join. **turn.** At end of last rnd, fasten off white and beige.

Rnd 46: For **body,** join blue with sc in first st, sc in each st around, join, **turn.**

Rnds 47–75: Ch 1, sc in each st around, join, **turn.** At end of last rnd, fasten off.

First Streamer

Row 1: Join red with sc in first st on rnd 75, sc in next 4 sts leaving remaining sts unworked, turn. *(5 sc made)*

Rows 2–44: Ch 1, sc in each st across, turn. At end of last row, fasten off.

Row 45: Join black with sc in first st, sc in last 4 sts, turn.

Rows 46–50: Ch 1, sc in each st across, turn. At end of last row, fasten off.

Second Streamer

Row 1: Join white with sc in next st on rnd 75, sc in next 4 sts, turn. *(5 sc made)*

Rows 2–44: Ch 1, sc in each st across, turn. At end of last row, fasten off.

Row 45: Join black with sc in first st, sc in last 4 sts, turn.

Rows 46–50: Ch 1, sc in each st across, turn. At end of last row, fasten off.

For **Next 14 Streamers,** repeat Second Streamer alternating red and white for a total of 16 Streamers.

Brim

Rnd 1: With rnd 75 toward you, working in remaining lps on rnd 27, join blue with sl st in first st, sl st in each st around, join with sl st in first sl st. *(80 sl sts made)*

Rnd 2: Working over the sl sts and into rnd 27 again; ch 1, sc in first 5 sts, 2 sc in next st, (sc in next 2 sts, 2 sc in next st) 23 times, sc in last 5 sts, join. *(104 sc made)*

Rnd 3: Ch 1, sc in each st around, join.

Rnd 4: Ch 1, sc in first 8 sts, 2 sc in next st, (sc in next 9 sts, 2 sc in next st) 9 times, sc in next 3 sts, 2 sc in next st, sc in last st, join. *(115)*

Rnd 5: Ch 1, sc in each st around, join. Fasten off.

For **hair strand** *(make 9),* with white, ch 9. Fasten off.

Arrange and sew nine hair strands to center bottom of face for beard.

Cut all felt pieces according to pattern pieces on page 86.

For **stripes,** cut two white pieces and one red piece each ¼" x 3" from felt.

Arrange and glue three white stars over rnds

Continued on page 86

Stars & Stripes
Pillow & Potholders

Designed by Delores Spagnuolo

Finished Sizes: Pillow is 16" square. Potholders are 9" square.

Materials:
- 3½ oz. each red, winter white and blue worsted yarn
- 16" square pillow form
- 2 plastic 1" rings
- H hook or hook needed to obtain gauge

Gauge: 3 sc = 1"; 4 sc rows = 1".

Basic Stitches: Ch, sl st, sc, hdc, dc.

Note: For amount of motifs and Stars needed, see individual Pillow and Potholder instructions.

Motif A

Row 1: For **first half,** with blue, ch 31, sc in second ch from hook, sc in each ch across, turn. *(30 sc made)*

Rows 2–14: Ch 1, sc first 2 sts tog, sc in each st across to last 2 sts, sc last 2 sts tog, turn. At end of last row *(4).*

Row 15: Ch 1, sc first 2 sts tog, sc last 2 sts tog, turn. *(2)*

Row 16: Ch 1, sc 2 sts tog, turn. Fasten off.

Row 17: For **second half,** working in starting ch on opposite side of row 1, join red with sc in first ch, sc in each ch across, turn. *(30)*

Rows 18–21: Ch 1, sc first 2 sts tog, sc in each st across to last 2 sts, sc last 2 sts tog, turn. At end of last row, fasten off. *(22)*

Row 22: Join white with sl st in first st, ch 1, sc same st as sl st and next st tog, sc in each st across to last 2 sts, sc last 2 sts tog, turn. *(20)*

Rows 23–26: Ch 1, sc first 2 sts tog, sc in each st across to last 2 sts, sc last 2 sts tog, turn. At end of last row, fasten off. *(12)*

Row 27: Join red with sl st in first st, ch 1, sc same st as sl st and next st tog, sc in each st across to last 2 sts, sc last 2 sts tog, turn. *(10)*

Rows 28–30: Ch 1, sc first 2 sts tog, sc in each st across to last 2 sts, sc last 2 sts tog, turn. At end of last row *(4).*

Row 31: Ch 1, sc first 2 sts tog, sc last 2 sts tog, turn. *(2)*

Row 32: Ch 1, sc 2 sts tog, turn. Fasten off.

Rnd 33: Working around outer edge, join white with sc in first st, 2 sc in same st as last sc *(corner made),* sc in end of each row around with 3 sc in each corner, join with sl st in first sc. Fasten off. *(72)*

Motif B

Row 1: For **first half,** with red, ch 31, sc in second ch from hook, sc in each ch across, turn. *(30 sc made)*

Rows 2–5: Ch 1, sc first 2 sts tog, sc in each st across to last 2 sts, sc last 2 sts tog, turn. At end of last row, fasten off. *(22)*

Row 6: Join white with sl st in first st, ch 1, sc same st as sl st and next st tog, sc in each st across to last 2 sts, sc last 2 sts tog, turn. *(20)*

Rows 7–10: Ch 1, sc first 2 sts tog, sc in each st across to last 2 sts, sc last 2 sts tog, turn. At end of ff. *(12)*

Row 11: Join red with sl st in first st, ch 1, sc same st as sl st and next st tog, sc in each st across to last 2 sts, sc last 2 sts tog, turn. *(10)*

Rows 12–14: Ch 1, sc first 2 sts tog, sc in each st across to last 2 sts, sc last 2 sts tog, turn. At end of last row *(4).*

Row 15: Ch 1, sc first 2 sts tog, sc last 2 sts tog, turn. *(2)*

Row 16: Ch 1, sc 2 sts tog, turn. Fasten off.

Row 17: For **second half,** working in starting ch on opposite side of row 1, join white with sc in first ch, sc in each ch across, turn. *(30)*

Rows 18–21: Ch 1, sc first 2 sts tog, sc in each st across to last 2 sts, sc last 2 sts tog, turn. At end of last row, fasten off. *(22)*

Row 22: Join red with sl st in first st, ch 1, sc same st as sl st and next st tog, sc in each st across to last 2 sts, sc last 2 sts tog, turn. *(20)*

Rows 23–26: Ch 1, sc first 2 sts tog, sc in each st across to last 2 sts, sc last 2 sts tog, turn. At end of last row, fasten off. *(12)*

Row 27: Join white with sl st in first st, ch 1, sc same st as sl st and next st tog, sc in each st across to last 2 sts, sc last 2 sts tog, turn. *(10)*

Rows 28–32: Repeat rows 28–32 of Motif A. At end of last row, **do not fasten off.**

Rnd 33: Working around outer edge, ch 1, 3 sc in first st *(corner made),* sc in end of each row around with 3 sc in each corner, join with sl st in first sc. Fasten off. *(72)*

Motif C

Row 1: For **first half,** with blue, ch 31, sc in second ch from hook, sc in each ch across, turn. *(30 sc made)*

Rows 2–14: Ch 1, sc first 2 sts tog, sc in each st across to last 2 sts, sc last 2 sts tog, turn. At end of last row *(4).*

Continued on page 80

Stars & Stripes Pillow & Potholders

Continued from page 79

Row 15: Ch 1, sc first 2 sts tog, sc last 2 sts tog, turn. *(2)*

Row 16: Ch 1, sc 2 sts tog, turn. Fasten off.

Row 17: For **second half,** working in starting ch on opposite side of row 1, join blue with sc in first ch, sc in each ch across, turn. *(30)*

Rows 18–32: Repeat rows 2–16. At end of last row, **do not fasten off.**

Rnd 33: Working around outer edge, ch 1, 3 sc in first st *(corner made),* sc in end of each row around with 3 sc in each corner, join with sl st in first sc. Fasten off. *(72)*

Small Star

Rnd 1: With white, ch 3, sl st in first ch to form ring, ch 1, 10 sc in ring, join with sl st in first sc. *(10 sc made)*

Rnd 2: Ch 2 *(counts as hdc),* hdc in same st as ch-2, 2 hdc in each st around, join with sl st in top of ch-2. *(20 hdc)*

Rnd 3: (Ch 2, dc in next st, ch 1, sc in next st, sl st in next 2 sts) 4 times, ch 2, dc in next st, ch 1, sc in next st, sl st in last st, join. Fasten off.

Large Star

Rnd 1: With white, ch 3, sl st in first ch to form ring, ch 1, 10 sc in ring, join with sl st in first sc. *(10 sc made)*

Rnd 2: Ch 2, hdc in as same st ch-2, 2 hdc in each st around, join with sl st in top of ch-2. *(20 hdc)*

Row 3: For **first point,** ch 1, sc in first 4 sts leaving remaining sts unworked, turn. *(4 sc)*

Row 4: Ch 1, sc first 2 sts tog, sc last 2 sts tog, turn. *(2)*

Row 5: Ch 1, sc 2 sts tog, **do not turn.** Fasten off.

Row 3: For **second point,** join white with sc in next unworked st on rnd 2, sc in next 3 sts leaving remaining sts unworked, turn. *(4 sc)*

Row 4: Ch 1, sc first 2 sts tog, sc last 2 sts tog, turn. *(2)*

Row 5: Ch 1, sc 2 sts tog, **do not turn.** Fasten off.

For **third–fourth points,** repeat rows 3–5 of Second Point two more times.

Rows 3–5: For **fifth point,** repeat rows 3–5 of Second Point. At end of last row, **do not fasten off.**

Rnd 6: Working around outer edge, ch 1, sc in end of each row and sc in each st at top of each Point around, join with sl st in first sc. Fasten off.

Pillow
First Side

Work four Motifs A.

Work four Small Stars.

For **Assembly,** working in **back lps** *(see Stitch Guide),* using white, sl st Motifs together *(see illustration).*

Center and sew one Small Star on first

half of each Motif A.

For **Edging,** with right side facing you, working around outer edge, join white with sc in any center corner st, 2 sc in same st, sc in each st and in each seam around with 3 sc in each center corner st, join with sl st in first sc. Fasten off.

Second Side

Work two Motifs B and two Motifs C.

Work two Small Stars and one Large Star.

For **Assembly,** working in **back lps,** using white, sl st Motifs together *(see illustration).*

Center and sew one Small Star on first half of one Motif C and one Small Star on second half of same Motif. Center and sew Large Star to other Motif C.

For **Edging,** with right side facing you, working around outer edge, join white with sc in any center corner st, 2 sc in same st, sc in each st and in each seam around with 3 sc in each center corner st, join with sl st in first sc. Fasten off.

Assembly

Hold First and Second Sides wrong sides together, working through both thickness and **back lps,** matching sts, join white with sc in any center corner st, **reverse sc** *(see Stitch Guide)* in each st around, inserting pillow form before closing, join with sl st in first sc. Fasten off.

Potholder
Sides

Work one Motif A and one Motif B.

Assembly

Rnd 1: Hold Motifs together with stripes on Motif B perpendicular, working through both thicknesses and in **back lps,** with Motif A facing you, join white with sc in center corner st of first half, 2 sc in same st, sc in each st around with 3 sc in each center corner st, join with sl st in first sc. *(80 sc made)*

Rnd 2: Ch 1, sc in first st, ch 3, (sc; for **hanger,** work 18 sc around one ring—*see Stitch Guide,* sc) in next center st at corner, ch 3, (sc in next st, ch 3) around, join. Fasten off.

Work one Small Star. Center and sew on first half of Motif A.

Repeat for second Potholder. ●

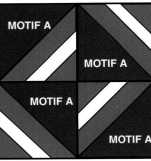

FIRST SIDE

MOTIF A   MOTIF A   MOTIF A   MOTIF A

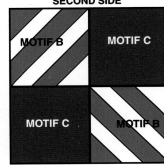

SECOND SIDE

MOTIF B   MOTIF C   MOTIF C   MOTIF B

Li-bear-ty Wreath

Continued from page 75

Back
Row 1: Ch 5, sc in second ch from hook and in each ch across, turn. *(4 sc made)*
Rows 2–15: Repeat rows 2–15 of Front.
Rnd 16: Repeat rnd 16 of Front, **do not fasten off.**
Rnd 17: Holding front and back with wrong sides together and working through both thicknesses in **back lps,** sl st in each st around, stuffing before closing, join with sl st in first sl st. Fasten off.

Flag Heart
Front
Row 1: With blue, ch 2, changing to white *(see Stitch Guide),* ch 3, sc in second ch from hook and in each ch across, changing colors according to graph, turn. *(4 sc made)*
Rows 2–15: Following color change graph, ch 1, sc in each sc across, turn.
Rnd 16: Matching colors, working in ends of rows and in each st, sc around outer edge of piece with 3 sc in point, join with sl st in first sc. Fasten off.
For **trim,** repeat trim on Plain Heart.
With white, embroider three french knots on blue part of Front.

Back
With blue, repeat Plain Heart Back.

Hat
Note: Do not join rnds unless otherwise stated.
Rnd 1: With red, ch 2, 6 sc in second ch from hook. *(6 sc made)*
Rnd 2: 2 sc in each sc around. *(12)*
Rnd 3: (Sc in next st, 2 sc in next st) around, changing to white in last st made, join with sl st in first sc. *(18)*
Rnd 4: Ch 1, working in **back lps,** sc in each st around.
Rnd 5: Sc in each st around, changing to red in last st made.
Rnd 6: Sc in each st around.
Rnd 7: Sc in each st around, changing to white in last st made.
Rnds 8–9: Repeat rnds 6–7, changing to red in last st made on rnd 9.
Rnds 10–11: Repeat rnds 6–7, changing to blue in last st made on rnd 11.
Rnd 12: With blue, working in **front lps,** 2 sc in each st around. *(36)*
Rnd 13: Sc in each st around, join. Fasten off.
Stuff Hat lightly with fiberfill. Glue Hat to bear's head.

Assembly
1: Cut 2-yd. piece of ribbon and wrap around wreath, secure in place with glue.
2: Glue Plain Hearts to right-hand side of wreath, pin in place until dry.
3: Glue bear and Flag Heart to left-hand side of wreath.
4: From remaining 2 yds. of ribbon make a loop bow and glue to top center of wreath.
5: Glue flag to bear's paw. ●

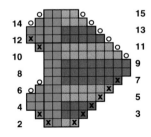

EACH SQUARE = 1 SC
■ = RED
▨ = WHITE
▦ = BLUE
X = 2 SC IN FIRST ST
○ = SC LAST 2 STS TOGETHER

Simply Patriotic Afghan

Designed by Martha Brooks Stein

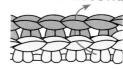

Finished Size: 46" x 62".

Materials:
- Worsted yarn:
  - 20 oz. blue
  - 16 oz. off-white
  - 12 oz. red
- Tapestry needle
- H hook or hook needed to obtain gauge

Gauge: Motif = 4" square.

Basic Stitches: Ch, sl st, sc, hdc, dc.

Motif A (make 96)

Rnd 1: With red, ch 6, sl st in first ch to form ring, ch 3 *(counts as dc)*, 2 dc in ring, ch 2, (3 dc in ring, ch 2) 3 times, join with sl st in top of ch-3. Fasten off. *(4 ch sps made)*

Rnd 2: Join off-white with sl st in any ch-2 sp; for **beginning shell (beg shell), (ch 3, 2 dc, ch 2, 3 dc) in same ch sp as sl st,** ch 1; for *shell, **(3 dc, ch 2, 3 dc)** in next ch-2 sp, ch 1; repeat from * around, join. Fasten off. *(8 ch sps)*

Rnd 3: Join blue with sl st in any ch-2 sp, beg shell, ch 1, 3 dc in next ch-1 sp, ch 1, (shell in next ch-2 sp, ch 1, 3 dc in next ch-1 sp, ch 1) 3 times, join. Fasten off.

Motif B (make 69)

Rnd 1: With red, ch 6, sl st in first ch to form ring, ch 3, 2 dc in ring, ch 2, (3 dc in ring, ch 2) 3 times, join with sl st in top of ch-3. Fasten off. *(4 ch sps made)*

Rnd 2: Join blue with sl st in any ch-2 sp, beg shell, ch 1, (shell in next ch-2 sp, ch 1) around, join. Fasten off. *(8 ch sps)*

Rnd 3: Join off-white with sl st in any ch-2 sp, beg shell, ch 1, 3 dc in next ch-1 sp, ch 1, (shell in next ch-2 sp, ch 1, 3 dc in next ch-1 sp, ch 1) 3 times, join. Fasten off.

Assembly

Using matching color yarn, sew Motifs together in **inside lps** *(see illustration)* according to assembly illustration below.

Border

Rnd 1: Working around outer edge, join blue with sc in any corner ch-2 sp, ch 2, sc in same ch sp, sc in each st, hdc in each seam and sc in each ch-1 sp around with (sc, ch 2, sc) in each corner ch-2 sp, join with sl st in first sc. Fasten off.

Rnd 2: Join red with sc in any corner ch sp, ch 2, sc in same ch sp, (ch 1, skip next st, sc in next st) across to next corner, ch 1, skip next st, *(sc, ch 2, sc) in next corner ch sp, ch 1, skip next st, (sc in next st, ch 1, skip next st) across to next corner; repeat from * around, join. Fasten off.

Rnd 3: Join off-white with sl st in any corner ch sp, ch 3, (sl st in next ch sp, ch 3) around, join with sl st in first sl st. Fasten off. ●

INSIDE LOOPS ILLUSTRATION

SIMPLY PATRIOTIC AFGHAN ASSEMBLY

Independence Angel

An Original by Annie

Finished Size: Fits 11½" fashion doll.

Materials:
- Size 10 crochet cotton thread:
    80 yds. white
    80 yds. red
    30 yds. blue
- Gold 8mm corrugated ring
- Gold 10.5mm corrugated ring
- Gold 19 x 6mm spaghetti bead
- Gold small bead cap
- 2 gold ½" sequin pins
- 2 gold star charms
- Gold eagle charm
- Gold 4mm bead
- 3 gold 3mm beads
- 12" gold metallic ¼" ribbon
- Gold mesh angel wings
- White ¾" pom-pom
- 6½" doll stand
- Orange and yellow markers
- 1" plastic ring
- Five small snaps
- Sewing thread and needle
- Craft glue
- No. 7 steel hook or hook needed to obtain gauge

Gauge: 9 sts = 1"; 10 sc rows = 1".

Basic Stitches: Ch, sl st, sc, hdc, dc, tr.

Blouse
Row 1: Starting at waist, with blue, ch 27, sc in second ch from hook, sc in each ch across, turn. *(26 sc made)*

Rows 2–4: Ch 1, sc in each st across, turn.

Row 5: Ch 1, sc in each st across with 2 sc in last st, turn. *(27)*

Row 6: Ch 1, sc in first 7 sts, (2 sc in next st, sc in next 3 sts) 3 times, 2 sc in next st, sc in last 7 sts, turn. *(31)*

Row 7: Ch 1, sc in first 8 sts, 2 sc in next st, sc in next 13 sts, 2 sc in next st, sc in last 8 sts, turn. *(33)*

Row 8: Ch 1, sc in each st across, turn.

Row 9: Ch 1, sc in first 8 sts, 2 sc in next st, sc in next 15 sts, 2 sc in next st, sc in last 8 sts, turn. *(35)*

Row 10: Ch 1, sc in each st across, turn.

Row 11: Ch 1, sc in first 8 sts, 2 sc in next st, sc in next 17 sts, 2 sc in next st, sc in last 8 sts, turn. *(37)*

Row 12: Ch 1, sc in each st across, turn.

Row 13: Ch 1, sc in first st, 2 sc in next st, sc in next 13 sts, skip next st, 10 dc in next st, skip next st, sc in next st, skip next st, 10 dc in next st, skip next st, sc in next 13 sts, 2 sc in next st, sc in last st, turn. *(53 sts)*

Row 14: Ch 1, sc in first 15 sts, skip next st, dc in next 9 sts, skip next st, sc in next st, skip next st, dc in next 9 sts, skip next st, sc in last 15 sts, turn. *(49 sts)*

Row 15: Ch 1, sc in first 14 sts, skip next st, sc in next 9 sts, skip next st, sc in next 9 sts, skip next st, sc in last 14 sts, turn. *(46 sts)*

Row 16: Ch 1, sc in first 22 sts, sc next 2 sts tog, sc in last 22 sts. Fasten off. *(45 sts)*

Sleeve (make 2)

Rnd 1: With blue, ch 17, sl st in first ch to form ring, ch 1, sc in same ch as sl st, sc in next 3 chs, hdc in next ch, 2 dc in each of next 3 chs, dc in next 2 chs, 2 dc in each of next 3 chs, hdc in next ch, sc in last 3 chs, join with sl st in first sc. *(23 sts made)*

Rnd 2: Ch 1, sc in first 7 sts, skip next st, 2 dc in each of next 8 sts, skip next st, sc in last 6 sts, join. *(29 sts)*

Rnd 3: Ch 1, sc in first 7 sts, hdc in next st, dc in next 14 sts, hdc in next st, sc in last 6 sts, join.

Rnd 4: Ch 1, sc in first st, (sc next 2 sts tog) 2 times, skip next st, dc in next st, (dc next 2 sts tog) 8 times, dc in next st, skip next st, (sc next 2 sts tog) 2 times, join. *(15 sts)*

Rnd 5: Ch 1, sc in each st around, join with sl st in first sc.

Rnd 6: Ch 3, 2 dc in same st as ch-3, 3 dc in each st around, join with sl st in top of ch-3. Fasten off.

Rnd 7: Working in remaining lps on opposite side of starting ch on rnd 1, join blue with sl st in first ch, ch 3, dc in next 4 chs, 2 tr in each of next 8 chs, dc in last 4 sts, join with sl st in top of ch-3. Leaving 12" end for sewing, fasten off.

Skip seven sts from one back edge on row 16 of Blouse, sew eight sts on rnd 7 of Sleeve to eight sts on Bodice with sc stitches on Sleeve at underarm.

Sew three snaps evenly spaced down back opening on Blouse.

Skirt

Notes: *Work all rows of Skirt in back lps (see Stitch Guide) unless otherwise stated.*

Skirt is worked from side to side.

Row 1: With red, ch 68, sc in second ch from hook, sc in each ch across, turn. Fasten off. *(67 sc made)*

Row 2: Join white with sl st in first st, sl st in next 2 sts, sc in next 6 sts, hdc in next 10 sts, dc in next 25 sts, tr in last 23 sts, turn.

Row 3: Ch 1, sc in each st across, turn. Fasten off.

Row 4: Join red with sl st in first st, sl st in next 2 sts, sc in next 6 sts, hdc in next 10 sts, dc in next 25 sts, tr in last 23 sts, turn.

Row 5: Ch 1, sc in each st across, turn. Fasten off.

Rows 6–44: Repeat rows 2–5 consecutively, ending with row 4. At end of last row, **do not turn.** Fasten off.

Skip first 14 sts on row 44 and 14 sts on opposite side of starting ch on row 1; matching sts, sew remaining sts and chs together for back seam.

For **placket,** working in remaining 14 lps on opposite side of starting ch on row 1, join red with sl st in 14th ch, ch 2, hdc in each ch across. Fasten off.

Sew two snaps evenly spaced down back opening on Skirt.

Place Blouse and Skirt on doll; place doll on stand. Tie gold metallic ribbon in bow around waist at back of doll. Glue eagle to center front of Blouse *(see photo).*

Glue wings to back of Blouse.

Halo

Rnd 1: Join white with sc around ring *(see Stitch Guide),* 48 more sc around ring, join with sl st in first sc. *(49 sc made)*

Rnds 2–4: Ch 1, sc in each st around, join.

Rnd 5: Ch 1, sc in first st; (*for **point,** ch 16, sl st in second ch from hook, sc in next 2 chs, hdc in next 3 chs, dc in next 5 chs, tr in last 4 chs *point completed;* skip next 4 sts on rnd 4*, sc in next 3 sts) 6 times; repeat between first and second *, sc in last 2 sts, join with sl st in first sc. Fasten off.

Rnd 6: Working in remaining lps on opposite side of ch-16, join red with sc in first ch of first point made, sc in next 13 chs, (sc, ch 1, sc) in last ch, sc in last 14 sts on opposite side of same point, skip next st, sc in next st, skip next st; *working in remaining lps on opposite side of ch-16 of next point, sc in first 14 chs, (sc, ch 1, sc) in last ch, sc in last 14 sts on opposite side of same point, skip next st, sc in next st, skip next st; repeat from * around, join. Fasten off.

Arrange hair as desired. Place Halo on head.

Earrings

For **Earring,** insert one sequin pin through one 3mm bead and through hole on one star, glue to secure, place in ear on doll.

Torch

1: Glue rings in following sequence to one end of spaghetti bead; 8mm corrugated ring, 10.5mm corrugated ring and small end of bead cap.

2: Trim pom-pom in flame shape. Using orange and yellow markers, color pom-pom to resemble fire. Glue flame to inside of bead cap.

3: Glue 4mm bead to opposite end of spaghetti bead, glue one 3mm bead to 4mm bead.

4: Glue Torch to one hand *(see photo).* ●

Uncle Sam Windsock

Continued from page 77

9–20 at top. Glue eyes, nose mouth and cheeks to face. Glue hand and stripes over rnds 51–66 on left side of body.

Fold rnds 1–3 of top to inside over 7" ring, sew in place.

Cut four desired lengths from monofilament line and tie to 1" ring, tie other end of lines to 7" ring. ●

CHEEK
Cut 2 from pink.

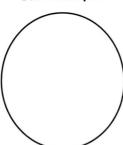

EYE
Cut 2 from blue.

HAND
Cut 1 from beige.

NOSE
Cut 1 from beige.

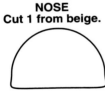

MOUTH
Cut 1 from rose.

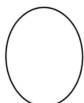

LARGE STAR
Cut 1 from white.

SMALL STAR
Cut 1 from white.

MED. STAR
Cut 1 from white.

chapter 6
Baby Bonanza

Patty cake, patty cake, baker's man. Bake me dozens of baby cakes as fast as you can!

Brownie Bites
1 Box brownie mix
Brownies cut into 1" cubes
1 Pkg. dark chocolate almond bark
1 Pkg. white chocolate almond bark

Melt dark chocolate almond bark according to package instructions. Dip brownie cubes into melted chocolate, place on wax paper until chocolate hardens. Dip brownie cubes a second time if desired. Melt small amount of white chocolate almond bark according to package instructions. Drizzle melted white chocolate over top and sides of chocolate-dipped brownie cubes.

Ribbons & Lace Booties & Bib

Ribbons & Lace Bib

Finished Sizes: Small 0-3 mos. Finished measurement: 6½" x 6¾"; Large 3-6 mos. Finished measurement: 7½" x 7¾".

Materials:
- For **Small 0-3 mos.,** 66 yds. ecru and 17 yds. pink size 20 crochet cotton thread
- For **Large 3-6 mos.,** 95 yds. ecru and 25 yds. pink size 10 crochet cotton thread
- 32" of ⅛" ribbon
- ⅜" flat button
- Sewing thread and needle
- No. 9 steel hook or hook needed to obtain gauge

Gauges: For **Small,** 11 sts = 1"; 5 dc rows = 1". For **Large,** 10 sts = 1"; 4 dc rows = 1".

Basic Stitches: Ch, sl st, sc, dc.

Bib
Row 1: Starting at **top,** with ecru, ch 52, sc in second ch from hook, sc in each ch across, turn. *(51 sc made)*

Row 2: Ch 3, dc in next 8 sts, *ch 2, skip next 2 sts; for **shell, (2 dc, ch 3, 2 dc)** in next st, ch 2, skip next 2 sts, dc in next 9 sts; repeat from * across, turn. *(36 dc, 3 shells) First ch-3 counts as first dc. Front of row 2 is right side of work.*

Rows 3–6: Ch 3, (dc in each st across to next ch sp, dc in ch sp, ch 2, shell in ch sp of next shell, ch 2, dc in next ch sp) 3 times, dc in each st across, turn. At end of last row, fasten off. *(60 dc, 3 shells)*

Row 7: For **first shoulder,** skip first 13 dc and shell, join ecru with sl st in next st, ch 3, dc in each st across to next ch sp, dc in ch sp, ch 2, shell in ch sp of next shell, ch 2, dc in next ch sp, dc in next 17 sts leaving remaining sts unworked for **second shoulder,** turn. *(36 dc, 1 shell)*

Rows 8–21: Ch 3, dc in each st across to next ch sp, dc in ch sp, ch 2, shell in ch sp of next shell, ch 2, dc in next ch sp, dc in each st across, turn. At end of last row, fasten off. *(68)*

Note: For **picot shell,** *(2 dc, ch 3, sl st in second ch from hook, dc)* in next st, ch sp or row.

Rnd 22: With right side of work facing you, working around outer edge in sts and in ends of rows, beginning on opposite side of starting ch on row 1, working in sps between sts, join pink with sc in first sp, 2 sc in same sp as first sc, sc in each sp across to last sp, 3 sc in last sp, 3 sc in each of next 4 rows, (2 sc, ch 3, picot shell—*see Note)* in next row, ch 3, picot shell in next st, ch 3, skip next 2 sts, sc in next st, ch 3, skip next 2 sts, picot shell in next st, ch 3, skip next 2 sts, sc in next st, ch 3, skip next st, picot shell in next st, ch 3, skip next ch sp, sc in next st, ch 3, skip next st, picot shell in next ch sp, ch 3, skip next st, sc in next st, ch 3, skip next ch sp, picot shell in next row, (ch 3, sc in next row, ch 3, picot shell in next row) 7 times, ch 3, picot shell in next st, ch 3, skip next 2 sts, picot shell in next st, (ch 3, skip next 2 sts, sc in next st, ch 3, skip next 2 sts, picot shell in next st) 4 times, ch 3, skip next 2 sts, sc in next st, ch 3, skip next st and next ch sp, picot shell in next st, ch 3, skip next st, sc in next ch sp, ch 3, skip next st, picot shell in next st, ch 3, skip next ch sp and next st, sc in next st, ch 3, skip next 2 sts, picot shell in next st, (ch 3, skip next 2 sts, sc in next st, ch 3, skip next 2 sts, picot shell in next st) 4 times, ch 3, skip next 2 sts, picot shell in next st, (ch 3, picot shell in next row, ch 3, sc in next row) 7 times, ch 3, picot shell in next row, ch 3, skip next ch sp, sc in next st, ch 3, skip next st, picot shell in next ch sp, ch 3, skip next st, sc in next st, ch 3, skip next ch sp, picot shell in next st, (ch 3, skip next 2 sts, sc in next st, ch 3, skip next 2 sts, picot shell in next st) 2 times, ch 3, picot shell in next row, 3 sc in each of next 4 rows, join with sl st in first sc. Fasten off.

Neck Strap
Rnd 1: With ecru, ch 50; for **buttonhole,** dc in seventh ch from hook; dc in each ch across; working in remaining lps on opposite side of starting ch, for **base,** (ch 3, sl st, ch 3, dc) in first ch; dc in next 43 chs, ch 1, skip next ch, join with sl st in next ch. Fasten off.

Rnd 2: Starting at **base,** join pink with sc in first ch, sc in next 2 chs, skip next st, sc in next 3 chs; working in sps between sts, sc in next 44 sps, 3 sc in next ch sp, 6 sc in next buttonhole sp, sc in next 44 sps, join with sl st in first sc. Fasten off.

With right sides together, hold base of Neck Strap to left shoulder at neck edge, matching sts; working through both thicknesses, sl st in each st across. Fasten off.

Sew button to rnd 1 on opposite shoulder.

Finishing
Cut two piece ribbon each 4" long and one piece ribbon 24" long.

Continued on page 95

Baby In Bassinet

Designed by Barbara Anderson

Finished Size: 5½" across.

Materials:
- Baby yarn:
  - ½ oz. yellow
  - Small amount each peach, white and green
- Blue and dk. pink six-strand embroidery floss
- 6" gift bow
- 3½" square cardboard
- Fabric stiffener
- Polyester fiberfill
- Craft glue
- Tapestry needle
- No. 4 steel hook and B hook or hooks needed to obtain gauges

Gauges: B hook, 6 sc = 1", 6 sc rows = 1"; 6 dc = 1", 2 dc rows = ¾"; 1 tr row = ½". **No. 4 hook,** 8 sts = 1".

Basic Stitches: Ch, sl st, sc, dc, tr.

Note: Use B hook unless otherwise stated.

Bassinet

Row 1: For **bottom,** with yellow, ch 13, 2 sc in second ch from hook, sc in next 10 chs, 2 sc in last ch, turn. *(14 sc made)*

Rows 2–3: Ch 1, 2 sc in first st, sc in each st across to last st, 2 sc in last st, turn. At end of last row *(18)*.

Rows 4–7: Ch 1, sc in each st across, turn.

Rows 8–10: Ch 1, sc first 2 sts tog, sc in each st across to last 2 sts, sc last 2 sts tog, turn. At end of last row, **do not turn.** *(12)*

Rnd 11: Working around outer edge, ch 1, sc in end of each row and in each st around, join with sl in first sc. *(44)*

Using crocheted piece as pattern, cut cardboard piece same size as bottom. Set aside.

Rnd 12: For **skirt,** working this rnd in **back lps** *(see Stitch Guide),* ch 3, dc in each st around, join with sl st in top of ch-3.

Rnd 13: Working this rnd in **back lps,** (ch 4, tr) in first st, 2 tr in each st around, join with sl st in top of ch-4. *(88 tr)*

Rnd 14: (Ch 5, dc) in first st, skip next st, sc in next st, skip next st, *(dc, ch 2, dc) in next st, skip next st, sc in next st, skip next st; repeat from * around, join with sl st in third ch of ch-5. *(22 ch sps, 22 sc)*

Rnd 15: (Sl st, ch 5, dc) in first ch sp, ch 1, (sc, ch 2, sc) in next sc, ch 1, *(dc, ch 2, dc) in next ch sp, ch 1, (sc, ch 2, sc) in next sc, ch 1; repeat from * around, join. *(44 ch-2 sps)*

Rnds 16–17: (Sl st, ch 5, dc) in first ch sp, ch 1, (sc, ch 2, sc) in next ch-2 sp, ch 1, *(dc, ch 2, dc) in next ch-2 sp, ch 1, (sc, ch 2, sc) in next ch-2 sp, ch 1; repeat from * around, join. At end of last rnd, fasten off.

Rnd 18: For **side,** working in **front lps** of rnd 11, join yellow with sl st in first st, ch 3, dc in each st around, join. *(44 dc)*

Rnd 19: Ch 3, dc in each st around, join.

Row 20: For **hood,** working in rows, with yellow, skip first 18 sts, join with sl st in next st, ch 3, dc in next 13 sts leaving last 12 sts unworked, turn. *(14 dc)*

Row 21: Ch 3, dc in each st across, turn.

Row 22: Ch 3, (dc next 2 sts tog) 6 times, dc in last st, turn. *(8)*

Row 23: Ch 3, (dc next 2 sts tog) 3 times, dc in last st. Fasten off. *(5)*

Row 24: For **trim,** working in ends of rows on hood, with wrong side facing you, join yellow with sc in row 20, sc in same row, 2 sc in each of next 3 rows, skip first st on row 23, sc in next 3 sts, skip last st, 2 sc in each of last 4 rows, join with sl st in next unworked st on rnd 19, turn. *(19 sc)*

Row 25: (Ch 4, skip next st, sl st in next st, ch 3, sl st in next st) across, ch 4, skip last st, sl st in next unworked st on rnd 19. Fasten off.

For **tie loops,** with wrong side of bottom facing you, working in sts of rnd 11, skip first 13 sts, (join yellow with sl st in next st, ch 5, skip next st, sl st in next st), **fasten off;** skip next 20 sts; repeat between ( ). Fasten off.

Glue cardboard to wrong side of bottom.

Lightly pat fabric stiffener on side and hood of Bassinet. Let dry.

Bow (make 2)

With green, ch 25. Fasten off. Tie each in Bow. Sew one Bow to rnd 18 on front of Bassinet and one to row 23 on center top of hood.

Ribbon

With green, ch 100. Fasten off. Starting at center of one side, weave through sts of rnd 13 on Bassinet, tie in bow.

Pillow Side (make 2)

Row 1: With yellow, ch 7, sc in second ch from hook, sc in each ch across, turn. *(6 sc made)*

Rows 2–6: Ch 1, sc in each st across, turn. At end of last row, for **first side,** fasten off; for **second side,** do not fasten off.

Hold Pillow Sides together; working through both thicknesses, stuffing lightly before closing, ch 1, sc in each st and end of each row around with 3 sc in each corner, join with sl st in first sc. Fasten off.

Baby

Note: Do not join rnds unless otherwise stated. Mark first st of each rnd.

Rnd 1: Starting at **head,** with No. 4 hook and peach, ch 2, 6 sc in second ch from hook. *(6 sc made)*

Rnd 2: 2 sc in each st around. *(12)*

Rnd 3: (2 sc in next st, sc in next 2 sts) around. *(16)*

Rnds 4–7: Sc in each st around. Stuff.

Rnd 8: Sc in next st, (sc in next st, sc next 2 sts tog) around. *(11)*

Rnd 9: (Sc next 2 sts tog) 5 times, sc in last st. *(6)*

Rnd 10: Sc in each st around. Stuff. Continue stuffing as you work.

Rnd 11: For **body,** 2 sc in each st around, join with sl st in first sc. Fasten off. *(12)*

Rnd 12: With No. 4 hook and white, join with sc in first st, sc in same st, sc in next st, (2 sc in next st, sc in next st) around, join. *(18)*

Rnd 13: Ch 3, dc in each st around, join with sl st in top of ch-3.

Rnd 14: Working this rnd in **back lps,** ch 3, dc in each st around, join.

Rnd 15: Ch 3, dc in each st around, join; for **leg openings,** skip next 9 sts, sl st in next st. Fasten off.

Rnd 16: For **first leg,** join peach with sc in first unworked st on one leg opening, sc in next 8 sts. *(9 sc)*

Rnds 17–19: Sc in each st around. At end of last rnd, fasten off. Sew opening closed.

Rnds 16–19: For **second leg,** repeat rnds 16–19 of first leg.

Rnd 20: For **skirt,** working in **front lps** of rnd 14, join white with sl st in first st, ch 3, dc in each st around, join. *(18 dc)*

Rnd 21: Ch 1, sc in first st, ch 1, (dc, ch 2, dc) in next st, *ch 1, sc in next st, ch 1, (dc, ch 2, dc) in next st; repeat from * around, ch 1, join with sl st in first sc. *(9 ch-2 sps, 9 sc)*

Rnd 22: (Ch 5, dc) in first st, ch 1, skip next ch-1 sp, sc in next ch-2 sp, ch 1, *skip next ch-1 sp, (dc, ch 2, dc) in next st, ch 1, sc in next ch-2 sp, ch 1; repeat from * around, join with sl st in third ch of ch-5.

Rnd 23: (Sl st, ch 1, sc) in first ch-2 sp, ch 1, skip next ch-1 sp, *(dc, ch 2, dc) in next sc, ch 1, skip next ch-1 sp, sc in next ch-2 sp, ch 1; repeat from * around, join with sl st in first sc.

Rnds 24–25: Repeat rnds 22–23. At end of last rnd, fasten off.

Sleeve (make 2)

Rnd 1: With No. 4 hook and white, ch 4, sl st in first ch to form ring, ch 3, 7 dc in ring, join with sl st in top of ch-3. *(8 dc made)*

Rnds 2–3: Ch 3, dc in each st around, join. At end of last rnd, fasten off.

Rnd 4: For **hand,** working this rnd in **back lps,** join peach with sc in first st, sc in next 2 sts, skip next st, sc in next 2 sts, skip next st, sc in last st, **do not join.** *(6 sc)*

Rnd 5: Sc in each st around. Leaving 6" for sewing, fasten off. Stuff lightly. Sew opening closed.

Sew rnd 1 of one Sleeve to rnds 11–12 on each side of body.

With blue, using **french knot** *(see Stitch Guide),* embroider eyes centered ¼" apart between rnds 6–7 on head.

With pink, using **straight stitch** *(see Stitch Guide),* embroider mouth between rnds 7–8 centered below eyes.

Belt

With B hook and yellow, ch 60. Fasten off. Sew center of tie to center of row 5 on bottom inside Bassinet.

Place Pillow and Baby inside Bassinet, tie Belt around waist to secure.

Tie (make 2)

With yellow, ch 80. Fasten off. Sew center of Tie to center of gift bow. Run each end through Tie loops on bottom of Bassinet, tie in bow. ●

Lullaby Lambkin

Designed by Peggy Johnston

Finished Sizes: Lambkin is 17" tall. Afghan is 11" across.

Materials:
- Worsted yarn:
  - 7 oz. off-white
  - 2 oz. lt. peach
  - 2 oz. blue variegated
  - 1½ oz. lt. blue
  - 5 yds. each of coral and dk. blue
- 20" blue ⅜" ribbon
- Blue ⅝" flat button
- Pink lipstick *(for blush)*
- Cotton swab
- Polyester fiberfill
- Blue sewing thread
- Tapestry and sewing needles
- F, G and H hooks or hooks needed to obtain gauges

Gauges: F hook, 9 sc = 2", 9 sc rnds = 2"; **G hook,** 4 sc = 1", 4 sc rnds = 1". **H hook,** 3 hdc = 1", 2 hdc rnds = 1".

Basic Stitches: Ch, sl st, sc, hdc.

Note: Work in continuous rnds, do not join or turn unless otherwise stated. Mark first st of each rnd.

Lambkin
Head
Rnd 1: Starting at center front of face, with F hook and off-white, ch 2, 6 sc in second ch from hook. *(6 sc made) Wrong side of sts is right side of work.*

Rnd 2: 2 sc in each st around. *(12)*

Rnd 3: (2 sc in next st, sc in next st) around. *(18)*

Rnd 4: Sc in each st around.

Rnd 5: (Sc in next 2 sts, 2 sc in next st) around. *(24)*

Rnd 6: (Sc in next 3 sts, 2 sc in next st) around. *(30)*

Rnd 7: (Sc in next 4 sts, 2 sc in next st) around. *(36)*

Rnds 8–9: Sc in each st around.

Rnd 10: (2 sc in next st, sc in next 3 sts) 5 times, sc in each st around. *(41) Third 2-sc group is center top of face.* Stuff.

Rnds 11–17: Sc in each st around. Stuff.

Rnd 18: (Skip next st, sc in next 3 sts) 9 times, skip next st, sc in next 4 sts. *(31)*

Rnds 19–22: Sc in each st around. Stuff, keeping bottom of Head flat.

Rnd 23: (Skip next st, sc in next st) 14 times, skip next st, sc in next 2 sts, **turn.** *(16)*

Rnd 24: Ch 1, sc in first 4 sts, (skip next st, sc in next 4 sts) 2 times, skip next st, sc in last st, join with sl st in first sc. Fasten off.

With tapestry needle and off-white, sew opening closed.

Facial Features
For **nose,** with tapestry needle and coral, embroider satin stitches *(see Stitch Guide)* over rnd 2 at top of face *(see facial features illustration).*

For **mouth,** with tapestry needle and coral, embroider straight stitches *(see Stitch Guide)* below nose *(see facial features illustration).*

For **eyelashes,** with tapestry needle and dk. blue, embroider straight stitches 1¾" apart above nose on front of face *(see facial features illustration)* indenting at center.

For **cheeks,** using cotton swab, apply small amount of lipstick to each side of face *(see photo).*

Ear (make 2)
Rnd 1: With F hook and lt. peach, ch 2, 6 sc in second ch from hook. *(6 sc made)*

Rnd 2: 2 sc in each st around. *(12)*

Rnds 3–4: Sc in each st around.

Rnd 5: (2 sc in next st, sc in next st) around. *(18)*

Rnds 6–11: Sc in each st around.

Rnd 12: (Sc next 2 sts tog) around. *(9)*

Row 13: Flatten last rnd; working through both thicknesses, ch 1, sc in each st across. Fasten off.

Sew straight edge on each Ear to each side of Head 6" apart *(see photo).*

Body
Rnd 1: Starting at bottom, with G hook and off-white, ch 25, sc in second ch from hook, sc in each ch across to last ch, 3 sc in last ch; working on opposite side of starting ch, sc in next 22 chs, 2 sc in next ch. *(50 sc made)*

Rnd 2: Sc in each st around.

Note: *For **loop st (lp st**—see Stitch Guide), insert hook in st, wrap yarn 2 times around finger, insert hook from left to right through all loops on finger, pull loops through st, drop loops from finger, yo, pull through all loops on hook. Lps are on back side of work.*

Continued on page 94

Lullaby Lambkin

Continued from page 93

Rnd 3: **Lp st** *(see Stitch Guide)* in each st around. *Back of rnd 3 is right side of work.*

Rnd 4: Sc in each st around.

Rnd 5: Lp st in each st around.

Rnds 6–15: Repeat rnds 4 and 5 alternately.

Rnd 16: (Sc in next 6 sts, sc next 2 sts tog) 6 times, sc in next 2 sts. *(44)*

Rnd 17: Lp st in each st around.

Rnd 18: (Sc in next 6 sts, sc next 2 sts tog) 5 times, sc in next 4 sts. *(39)*

Rnd 19: Lp st in each st around.

Rnd 20: (Sc in next 6 sts, sc next 2 sts tog) 4 times, sc in next 7 sts. *(35)*

Rnd 21: Lp st in each st around.

Rnd 22: Sc next 2 sts tog, (sc in next st, sc next 2 sts tog) around. *(23)*

Rnd 23: Lp st in each st around.

Rnd 24: Sc in each st around, join with sl st in first sc. Fasten off.

Turn right side out, stuff lightly.

With tapestry needle and off-white, center and sew bottom of Head to last rnd on Body.

Bottom Hoof & Leg *(make 2)*

Rnd 1: Starting at bottom of Hoof, with G hook and lt. peach, ch 2, 6 sc in second ch from hook. *(6 sc made)*

Rnd 2: 2 sc in each st around. *(12)*

Rnd 3: (Sc in next st, 2 sc in next st) around. *(18)*

Rnd 4: (Sc in next 2 sts, 2 sc in next st) around. *(24)*

Rnds 5–7: Sc in each st around. At end of last rnd, join with sl st in first sc. Fasten off.

Rnd 8: For **Leg,** join off-white with sl st in first st, lp st in same st as joining sl st, lp st in each st around. *Back of rnd 8 is right side of work.*

Rnd 9: (Sc next 2 sts tog, sc in next 4 sts) around. *(20)*

Rnd 10: Lp st in each st around.

Rnd 11: Sc in each st around.

Rnds 12–22: Repeat rnds 10 and 11 alternately, ending with rnd 10.

Rnd 23: (2 sc in next st, sc in next 4 sts) around. *(24)*

Rnds 24–32: Repeat rnds 10 and 11 alternately, ending with rnd 10. At end of last rnd, join with sl st in first sc. Turn right side out, stuff.

Row 33: Flatten last rnd, working through both thicknesses, ch 1, sc in each st across. Fasten off.

To **sculpt Hoof,** thread tapestry needle with lt. peach, (insert needle up through center bottom of Hoof and out at one side going over sts at side) 2 times, pulling yarn to form a toe indention on Hoof. Secure end and fasten off. Repeat on other Hoof.

With tapestry needle and off-white, sew flattened edge on each Bottom Leg to bottom of Body ½" apart.

Top Hoof & Leg *(make 2)*

Rnd 1: Starting at bottom of Hoof, with G hook and lt. peach, ch 2, 6 sc in second ch from hook. *(6 sc made) Back side of rnd 1 is right side of work.*

Rnd 2: 2 sc in each st around. *(12)*

Rnd 3: (Sc in next st, 2 sc in next st) around. *(18)*

Rnds 4–5: Sc in each st around. At end of last rnd, join with sl st in first sc. Fasten off.

Rnd 6: For **Leg,** join off-white with sl st in first st, lp st in same st as joining sl st, lp st in each st around.

Rnd 7: Sc in each st around.

Rnd 8: Lp st in each st around.

Rnds 9–22: Repeat rnds 7 and 8 alternately.

Rnd 23: Sc in each st around. Turn right side of sts out, stuff.

Row 24: Flatten last rnd, working through both thicknesses, ch 1, sc in each st across. Fasten off.

Sculpt Hoof same as Bottom Hoof and Leg.

With tapestry needle and off-white, sew flattened edge on each Top Leg to each side of Body 4½" apart *(see photo).*

Collar

Row 1: With G hook and lt. blue, ch 31, sc in second ch from hook, sc in each ch across, turn. *(30 sc made)*

Row 2: Ch 1, sc in each st across, turn. Fasten off.

Place Collar around neck, with tapestry needle and lt. blue, sew ends together in back.

With sewing needle and thread, sew button to center front of Collar.

Tail

Cut 12 strands of lt. peach each 12" long. Hold all strands together as one, fold in half. Tie a separate 12" strand at fold, tie fold to center st on rnd 7 at back of Body. Separate strands into three equal parts and braid strands. Tie a separate 7" strand of lt. blue yarn in bow around bottom of braid. Trim ends.

Hair *(make 22)*

For **first curl,** leaving long end, with G hook and off-white, *ch 5, 3 sc in second ch from hook, 3 sc in each of next 2 chs, (3 sc, sl st) in last ch; for **second and third curls,** repeat from * 2 more times. Leaving long end, fasten off. Tie long ends together forming a circle.

With tapestry needle and off-white, sew Hair along hairline and around back of Head.

Rosebud

With G hook and coral, ch 5, 3 sc in second ch from hook, 3 sc in each of next 2 chs, (3 sc, sl st) in last ch. Fasten off.

Tie ribbon in bow. With sewing needle and thread, sew Rosebud to center of bow. With sewing needle and thread, sew bow to top of Head.

Afghan

Rnd 1: With H hook and variegated, ch 2, 8 sc in second ch from hook. *(8 sc made)*

Rnd 2: 2 hdc in each st around. *(16 hdc)*

Rnds 3–4: (Hdc in next st, 2 hdc in next st) around. *(24, 36)*

Rnd 5: (Hdc in next 2 sts, 2 hdc in next st) around. *(48)*

Rnd 6: (Hdc in next 3 sts, 2 hdc in next st)

around. *(60)*

Rnd 7: (Hdc in next 4 sts, 2 hdc in next st) around. *(72)*

Rnd 8: (Hdc in next 5 sts, 2 hdc in next st) around. *(84)*

Rnd 9: Hdc in each st around, join with sl st in top of first hdc. Fasten off.

Ribbons & Lace
Continued from page 89

Working on one shoulder, starting on row 2 at neck edge, weave one 4" piece through ch sps on one side of shells to row 6; continue weaving through ch sps on other side of shells to row 2. Tack ends of row 1 on wrong side of Bib. Repeat on second shoulder with other 4" ribbon.

Working on center front of Bib over rows 2–21, leaving 6" ends, weave 24" ribbon through ch sps in same manner as short ribbons. Tie ends in bow at center front of Bib.

Ribbons & Lace Bib

Finished Sizes: Small 0-3 mos. Finished measurement: 3½" sole; Large 3-6 mos. Finished measurement: 4" sole.

Materials:
- For **Small 0-3 mos.,** 132 yds. pink and 55 yds. ecru size 20 crochet cotton thread
- For **Large 3-6 mos.,** 155 yds. pink and 65 yds. ecru size 10 crochet cotton thread
- 1 yd. of ⅛" ribbon
- No. 9 steel hook or hook needed to obtain gauge

Gauges: For **Small,** 11 sts = 1"; 10 sc rows = 1". For **Large,** 10 sts = 1"; 9 sc rows = 1".

Note: Work in continuous rnds; do not turn or join unless otherwise stated. Mark first st of each rnd.

Basic Stitches: Ch, sl st, sc, dc, tr.

Shoe (make 2)

Rnd 1: With pink, ch 24, sc in second ch from hook, sc in next 21 chs, 3 sc in last ch; working in remaining lps on opposite side of starting ch, sc in next 21 chs, 2 sc in last ch. *(48 sc made)*

Rnd 2: (2 sc in next st, sc in next 21 sts, 2 sc in next st, 3 sc in next st) 2 times. *(56)*

Rnd 3: (2 sc in next st, sc in next 23 sts, 2 sc in next st, sc in next st, 3 sc in next st, sc in next st) 2 times. *(64)*

Rnd 4: (2 sc in next st, sc in next 25 sts, 2 sc in next st, sc in next 2 sts, 3 sc in next st, sc in next 2 sts) 2 times. *(72)*

Rnd 5: Sc in each st around.

Rnd 6: Sc in next st, (2 sc in next st, sc in next 25 sts, 2 sc in next st, sc in next 4 sts, 3 sc in

Rnd 10: Join lt. blue with sc in first st, sc in each st around, join with sl st in first sc.

Rnd 11: Ch 1, sc in first st, ch 4, skip next st, (sc in next st, ch 4, skip next st) around, join.

Rnd 12: Ch 1, sc in first ch sp, ch 4, (sc in next ch sp, ch 4) around, join. Fasten off. •

next st), sc in next 4 sts; repeat between ( ), sc in last 3 sts. *(80)*

Rnd 7: Sc in next 2 sts, (2 sc in next st, sc in next 25 sts, 2 sc in next st, sc in next 6 sts, 3 sc in next st), sc in next 6 sts; repeat between ( ), sc in last 4 sts. *(88)*

Rnd 8: Sc in next 3 sts, (2 sc in next st, sc in next 25 sts, 2 sc in next st), sc in next 17 sts; repeat between ( ), sc in last 14 sts, join with sl st in first sc. *(92)*

Rnd 9: For **side,** ch 3, dc in each st around, join with sl st in top of ch-3. Fasten off. *(Ch-3 counts as first dc.)*

Rnd 10: Join ecru with sc in first st, sc in next 37 sts, ch 6, skip next 5 sts, sc in last 49 sts. *(87 sc, 1 ch sp)*

Rnd 11: Sc in each st around with 7 sc in ch sp. *(94)*

Rnd 12: Sc in next 35 sts, ch 5, skip next 6 sts, sc in next st, ch 5, skip next 6 sts, sc in last 46 sts. *(82 sc, 2 ch sps)*

Rnd 13: Sc in next 32 sts, ch 5, skip next 3 sts and next ch sp, sc in next st, ch 5, skip next ch sp and next 3 sts, sc in last 43 sts. *(76 sc, 2 ch sps)*

Rnd 14: Sc in next 29 sts, ch 5, skip next 3 sts and next ch sp, sc in next st, ch 5, skip next ch sp and next 3 sts, sc in last 40 sts, join with sl st in first sc. Fasten off. *(70 sc, 2 ch sps)*

Rnd 15: Join pink with sc in same st as joining sl st, sc in next 25 sts, ch 6, skip next 3 sts and next ch sp, sc in next st, ch 6, skip next ch sp and next 3 sts, sc in last 37 sts. *(64 sc, 2 ch sps)*

Rnd 16: Sc in next 23 sts, ch 6, skip next 3 sts and next ch sp, sc in next st, ch 6, skip next ch sp and next 3 sts, sc in last 34 sts. *(58 sc, 2 ch sp)*

Rnd 17: Sc in next 20 sts, ch 6, skip next 3 sts and next ch sp, sc in next st, ch 6, skip next ch sp and next 3 sts, sc in last 31 sts. *(52 sc, 2 ch sps)*

Rnd 18: Sc in next 20 sts, 6 sc in next ch sp, skip next st, 6 sc in next ch sp, sc in last 31 sts, join with sl st in first sc. Fasten off. *(63 sc)*

Row 19: For **top,** working in rows, skip first 33 sts, join pink with sl st in next st, (ch 4, tr) in same st as sl st; working in last 29 sts and first 19 skipped sts, (ch 3, skip next 2 sts, tr in next 2 sts) 12 times, turn. *(26 tr, 12 ch sps) First ch-*

Continued on page 100

Flower Package Decorations

Designed by Betty Dowler

Finished Sizes: Sizes range from 6" to 6½" including Leaves.

Materials For One:
- Small amount worsted yarn of each color used *(see individual instructions)*
- 11" of ¾" gathered lace
- Sewing thread to match lace
- Craft glue
- Tapestry and sewing needles
- K and H hooks

Basic Stitches: Ch, sl st, sc, hdc, dc, tr.

Basic Instructions

Base
Rnd 1: With K hook and desired color, ch 2, 6 sc in second ch from hook. Work in continuous rnds, **do not join.** *(6 sc made)*
Rnd 2: 2 sc in each st around. *(12)*
Rnd 3: (Sc in next st, 2 sc in next st) around. *(18)*
Rnd 4: (Sc in next 2 sts, 2 sc in next st) around. *(24)*
Rnd 5: (Sl st in next st, ch 3) around, join with sl st in first sl st. Fasten off.
Sew lace to back of rnd 4, turning under ¼" on ends.

Leaf
With green and K hook, ch 10, sl st in second ch from hook, sl st in next 2 chs, (ch 3, dc in next ch of ch-10, ch 2, sl st in top of dc just made, 2 sc around post of same dc—*see Stitch Guide,* ch 1; sl st in next 2 chs) 2 times, ch 3, dc in same ch as last sl st, ch 2, sl st in top of dc just made, 2 sc around post of same dc; working on opposite side of starting ch, sl st in next 2 chs; repeat between ( ) 2 times, sl st in last 2 chs, join with sl st in first sl st. Fasten off.

Calyx
Rnd 1: With green and K hook, ch 2, 5 sc in second ch from hook. Work in continuous rnds, **do not join.** *(5 sc made)*
Rnd 2: Sc in each st around.
Rnd 3: (Sl st in next st, ch 2) around, join with sl st in first sl st. Fasten off.

Center
With H hook and stated color, ch 4, yo, insert hook in fourth ch from hook, yo, pull long lp through ch, (yo, insert hook in same ch, yo, pull long lp through ch) 3 times, yo, pull through all lps on hook, ch 1, sl st in same ch. Fasten off.

Flowers

Peach & Orange
Rnd 1: With peach and H hook, ch 2, 6 sc in second ch from hook, **do not join.** *(6 sc made)*
Rnd 2: (Sc in next st, 2 sc in next st) around. *(9)*
Rnd 3: Sc in each st around.
Rnd 4: (Sc in next st, ch 2) around, join with sl st in first sc, **turn.**
Rnd 5: (Sl st, ch 2, dc, ch 2, sl st in second ch from hook, dc, ch 2, sl st) in each ch-2 sp around, join with sl st in first sl st. Fasten off.
Rnd 6: Working around posts of sc in rnd 4, join orange with sc around any st, sc around each st around, join.
Rnd 7: Ch 1, (sc, ch 3, sc) in each st around, join.
Rnd 8: Working in space between dc sts on rnd 5; ch 1, sc in each space around, join.
Rnd 9: Ch 1, (sc, ch 3, sc) in each st around, join. Fasten off.

Peach & Orange Assembly
1: With brown, work Basic Center. Attach to center on right side of Flower.
2: Work Basic Calyx, glue wrong side of center on Flower inside Calyx.
3: Work Base and two Leaves. Tack Leaves and Flower to Base.

Continued on page 98

Flower Package Decorations
Continued from page 97

Raspberry & Yellow
Rnd 1: With raspberry and H hook, ch 5, sl st in fifth ch from hook to form a circle, ch 1, (sc, ch 3) 5 times in circle, join with sl st in first sc.

Rnd 2: (Sl st, ch 2, 5 dc, ch 2, sl st) in each ch sp around, join with sl st in first sl st. Fasten off.

Rnd 3: Join yellow with sc in first ch-2 sp, *(sc in next st, ch 2) 5 times, sc in next ch-2 sp, ch 2, sc in next ch-2 sp; repeat from * 3 more times, (sc in next st, ch 2) 5 times, sc in next ch-2 sp, ch 2, join with sl st in first sc. Fasten off.

Rnd 4: Working around post of sc on rnd 1, join yellow with sc around any st, sc around each st around, join.

Rnd 5: Ch 3, sl st in same st, (sl st, ch 3, sl st) in each st around, join. Fasten off.

Raspberry & Yellow Assembly
1: With raspberry, work Center. Attach to center on right side of Flower.

2: Work steps 1–2 of Peach & Orange.

Red & White
Rnd 1: With white and H hook, ch 5, sl st in fifth ch from hook to form a circle, ch 1, (sc, ch 2) 5 times in circle, join with sl st

in first sc.

Rnd 2: (Sl st, ch 2, 4 hdc) in first ch-2 sp, 5 hdc in each ch-2 sp around, join with sl st in top of ch-2. Fasten off.

Rnd 3: Join red with sc in joining sl st, ch 2, sl st in second ch from hook, (sc in next st, ch 2, sl st in second ch from hook) 3 times, sc in next st, hdc in circle between sts, *(sc in next st, ch 2, sl st in second ch from hook) 4 times, sc in next st, hdc in circle between sts; repeat from * around, join. Fasten off.

Red & White Assembly
1: With bright yellow, work Center. Attach to center on right side of Flower.

2: Work steps 1–2 of Peach & Orange.

Two-Toned Yellow
Rnds 1–4: With light yellow, work rnds 1–4 of Peach & Orange. **At end of rnd 4, do not turn.**

Rnd 5: Ch 1, (sc, tr, sc, tr) in each ch-2 sp around, join, **turn.** Fasten off.

Rnd 6: With inside facing you, working around posts of sc of rnd 4, join bright yellow with sc around any st, sc around each st around, join.

Rnd 7: Ch 2, hdc in each st around, join with sl st in top of ch-2.

Rnd 8: Working in sps between hdc, (sc, ch 3) around, join. Fasten off.

Two-Toned Yellow Assembly
1: With red, work Center. Attach to center on right side of Flower.

2: Work steps 1–2 of Peach & Orange.

Pink & Yellow

Rnds 1–3: With light yellow, work rnds 1–3 of Peach & Orange.

Rnd 4: (Sc in next 2 sts, 2 sc in next st) around.

Rnd 5: Sl st in next st, ch 3, dc in each st around, join with sl st in top of ch-3. Fasten off.

Rnd 6: Join pink with sl st in last sl st, dc **front post** *(see Stitch Guide)* around ch-3, ch 3, dc **back post** around next dc, ch 3, (alternate dc back and front post sts, ch 3) around, join.

Rnd 7: Dc back post around ch-3 on rnd 5, ch 3, dc front post around next dc on rnd 5, (alternate dc back and front post sts, ch 3) around, join. Fasten off.

Pink & Yellow Assembly

1: With red, work Center. Attach to center on right side of Flower.

2: Work steps 1–2 of Peach & Orange.

White & Blue

Rnd 1: With white, work rnd 1 of Peach & Orange.

Rnd 2: (Sc, ch 2) in each st around, join with sl st in first sc, **turn.**

Rnd 3: Ch 1, (sc in next ch sp, ch 2, dc around post of sc on rnd 2, ch 2) around, join.

Rnd 4: Ch 1, (sc in next ch sp, ch 3, dc around post of sc on rnd 2, ch 3, sl st in next ch sp, ch 3) around, join. Fasten off.

Rnd 5: Working around post of sc on rnd 2, join blue with sc around any st, sc around each st around, join.

Rnd 6: Repeat rnd 3. Fasten off.

White & Blue Assembly

1: With raspberry, work Center. Attach to center on right side of Flower.

2: Work steps 1–2 of Peach & Orange.

Variegated

Rnd 1: With variegated, work rnd 1 of Peach & Orange.

Rnds 2–3: Sc in each st around.

Rnd 4: (Sc, ch 3) in each st around, join with sl st in first sc, **turn.**

Rnd 5: *(Sc, ch 2) 2 times in next ch sp, dc around post of sc on rnd 4, ch 2, (sc, ch 2) 2

times in next ch sp; repeat from * around, join. Fasten off.

Rnd 6: Working around posts of sc on rnd 4, join with sc around any st, sc around each st around, **do not join.**

Rnd 7: Working in **front lps** *(see Stitch Guide)*, (sl st, ch 3) in each st around, join.

Rnd 8: Working in **back lps** of sts on rnd 6, (sl st, ch 3) 2 times in each st around, join. Fasten off.

Variegated Assembly

1: With bright yellow, work Center. Attach to center on right side of Flower.

2: Work steps 1–2 of Peach & Orange.

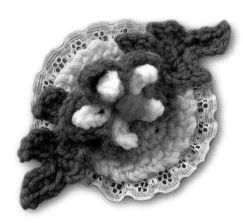

Purple & White

Rnd 1: With H hook and two strands of white yarn held together as one, ch 5, sl st in fifth ch from hook to form a circle, (sl st, ch 4, sl st in second ch from hook, ch 2) 5 times in circle, join with sl st in first sl st. Fasten off.

Rnd 2: Join purple with sl st in circle between white petals, ch 5, (dc in circle between white petals, ch 2) 4 times, join with sl st in third ch of ch-5.

Rnd 3: *(Sc, hdc, dc, ch 2, sl st in second ch from hook, dc, hdc, sc) in next ch sp, sl st around post of dc on rnd 2; repeat from * around, join. Fasten off.

Purple & White Assembly

1: With red, work Center. Attach to center on right side of Flower.

2: Work steps 1–2 of Peach & Orange. ●

Ribbons & Lace
Continued from page 95

4 counts as first tr. Rows now begin here.

Row 20: Ch 7, (2 tr in next ch sp, ch 3) across to last 2 tr, skip next tr, tr in last tr, turn. *(26 tr, 13 ch sps)*

Row 21: Ch 3, dc in first ch sp; for **picot, ch 3, sl st in third ch from hook;** (2 dc in next ch sp, picot) 11 times, dc in last ch sp, dc in last st. Fasten off.

For **trim,** with Top facing you, working in worked sts on rnd 8 of Sole and between sts on rnd 9, join pink with sc in any st, sc in each st around, join with sl st in first sc. Fasten off.

Cut 18" piece ribbon. Weave through ch sps on row 21; tie in bow •

Why God Made Little Boys

God made a world out of His dreams,
of magic mountains, oceans and streams.
Prairies and plains and wooded land,
then paused and thought "I need someone to stand
on top of the mountains, to conquer the sea,
explore the plains and climb the trees,
someone to start out small and grow
sturdy, strong like a tree" and so....
He created boys, full of spirit and fun
to explore and conquer, to romp and run
with dirty faces, banged up chins,
with courageous hearts and boyish grins.
When He had completed the task He'd begun,
He surely said, "That's a job well done."

– Author unknown

Why God Made Little Girls

God made the world with it's towering trees,
Majestic Mountains and restless seas;
Then paused and said, "It needs one more thing,
Someone to laugh and Dance and sing,
To walk in the woods and gather flowers,
To commune with nature in quiet hours."
So God made little girls
With laughing eyes and bouncing curls.
With joyous hearts and infectious smiles,
Enchanting ways and feminine wiles,
And when He'd completed the task He'd begun,
He was pleased and proud of the job He's done,
For the world, when seen through a little girls eyes
Greatly resembles paradise.

– Author unknown

chapter 7
Fright Night

A wickedly sneaky way to greet and treat each little ghost and goblin brave enough to ring the doorbell.

Dirt Cups
1 pkg. instant chocolate pudding
1 pkg. chocolate cookies
Gummy worms

Prepare instant chocolate pudding according to package instructions. Fill clear plastic cups about ⅔ full with pudding. Cover the top of the pudding with crushed chocolate cookie crumbs. Stick bottom edge of desired cookies into pudding mixture as shown in photo. Decorate with gummy worms as desired.

Halloween Set

Designed by Debra Yorston

Candy Basket

Finished Size: 9" wide x 4" high.

Materials:
- Worsted yarn:
    - 3 oz. orange
    - 2 oz. black
- Two 1½" decorative wooden cutouts
- Craft glue
- J hook or hook needed to obtain gauge

Gauge: **With two strands held together,** 5 sc = 2"; 3 sc rnds = 1".

Basic Stitches: Ch, sl st, sc.

Note: Work in continuous rnds; do not join or turn unless otherwise stated. Mark first st of each rnd.

Basket

Rnd 1: With one strand each of orange and black held together, ch 2, 6 sc in second ch from hook. *(6 sc made)*

Rnd 2: 2 sc in each st around. *(12)*

Rnd 3: (2 sc in next st, sc in next st) around. *(18)*

Rnd 4: (2 sc in next st, sc in next 2 sts) around. *(24)*

Rnd 5: (2 sc in next st, sc in next 3 sts) around. *(30)*

Rnd 6: (2 sc in next st, sc in next 4 sts) around. *(36)*

Rnd 7: (2 sc in next st, sc in next 5 sts) around. *(42)*

Rnd 8: (2 sc in next st, sc in next 6 sts) around. *(48)*

Rnd 9: (2 sc in next st, sc in next 7 sts) around. *(54)*

Rnd 10: (2 sc in next st, sc in next 8 sts) around. *(60)*

Rnd 11: (2 sc in next st, sc in next 9 sts) around. *(66)*

Rnd 12: (2 sc in next st, sc in next 10 sts) around. *(72)*

Rnds 13–20: Sc in each st around. At end of last rnd, fasten off black. Continue working with two strands of orange.

Rnd 21: Sc in first 15 sts; for **Handle,** ch 10, skip next 6 sts; sc in next 30 sts; for **Handle,** ch 10, skip next 6 sts, sc in last 15 sts, join with sl st in first sc. *(60 sc, 20 chs)*

Rnd 22: Ch 1, **reverse sc** *(see Stitch Guide)* in each st and in each ch around, join. Fasten off. Center and glue wooden cutouts to one side of Basket between Handles *(see photo).*

Continued on page 104

Halloween Set
Continued from page 103

Trick or Treat Bag

Finished Size: 10" wide x 11" high.

Materials:
- Worsted yarn:
    - 4 oz. orange
    - 4 oz. black
    - 4 oz. white
- 4" decorative wooden cutout
- Craft glue
- K hook or hook needed to obtain gauge

Gauge: With three strands held together, 7 sc = 3"; 5 sc rows = 2".

Basic Stitches: Ch, sl st, sc.

Bag

Row 1: With one strand of each color held together, ch 7, sc in second ch from hook, sc in each ch across, turn. *(6 sc made)*

Rows 2–21: Ch 1, sc in each st across, turn.

Note: *Work in continuous rnds; do not join or turn unless otherwise stated. Mark first st of each rnd.*

Rnd 22: Working around outer edge, 3 sc in first st, sc in next 4 sts, 3 sc in next st, sc in end of next 21 rows; working in remaining lps on opposite side of starting ch, 3 sc in first ch, sc in next 4 chs, 3 sc in next ch, sc in end of next 21 rows. *(62 sc made)*

Rnd 23: Working this rnd in **back lps** *(see Stitch Guide)*, sc in each st around.

Rnds 24–41: Working in **both lps,** sc in each st around.

Rnd 42: Sc in first 19 sts; for **Handle,** ch 8, skip next 8 sts; sc in next 23 sts; for **Handle,** ch 8, skip next 8 sts; sc in last 4 sts.

Rnd 43: Sc in each st and in each ch around.

Rnd 44: Sc in each st around, join with sl st in first sc. Fasten off.

Glue wooden cutout to side of Bag *(see photo).*

Hot Pad & Potholders

Finished Sizes: Hot Pad is 9" square; Potholders are 7½" square.

Materials:
- Worsted yarn:
    - 4 oz. white
    - 2 oz. orange
    - Small amount each yellow and green
- Scrap of black felt
- Craft glue
- Tapestry needle
- I and J hooks or hooks needed to obtain gauge

Gauge: **With two strands held together and J hook,** 8 sc = 3"; 4 sc rows = 1½".

Basic Stitches: Ch, sl st, sc, hdc, dc.

Potholder (make 2)

Row 1: With two strands white held together and J hook, ch 15, sc in second ch from hook, sc in each ch across, turn. *(14 sc made)*

Rows 2–14: Ch 1, sc in each st across, turn. At end of last row, **do not turn.**

Rnd 15: For **Border,** working around outer edge, sc in end of next 14 rows; working in remaining lps on opposite side of starting ch on row 1, 3 sc in first ch, sc in next 12 chs, 3 sc in last ch, sc in end of next 14 rows, 3 sc in first st, sc in next 12 sts, 3 sc in last st for corner, join with sl st in first sc. Fasten off. *(Center sc of 3-sc group is corner st.)*

Rnd 16: With two strands orange held together and J hook, join with sc in any corner st, ch 3, skip next st, (sc in next st, ch 3, skip next st) around, join. Fasten off.

Candy Corn

Row 1: With one strand of yellow and I hook, ch 9, 2 sc in second ch from hook, sc in each ch across to last ch, 2 sc in last ch, turn. *(10 sc made)*

Row 2: Ch 1, sc in each st across, turn. Fasten off.

Row 3: Join one strand of orange with sc in first st, sc in each st across, turn.

Row 4: Sc first 2 sts tog, sc in each st across to last 2 sts, sc last 2 sts tog, turn. *(8)*

Row 5: Ch 1, sc in each st across, turn.

Rows 6–9: Repeat rows 4 and 5 alternately. At end of last row, fasten off. *(6, 4)*

Row 10: Join one strand of white with sc in first st, sc in each st across, turn.

Row 11: Sc first 2 sts tog, sc last 2 sts tog, turn.

Row 12: Sc first and last sts tog. Fasten off.

With tapestry needle and matching color yarn, sew Candy Corn to center of Potholder *(see photo).*

Hot Pad

Row 1: With two strands white held together and J hook, ch 19, sc in second ch from hook, sc in each ch across, turn. *(18 sc made)*

Rows 2–18: Ch 1, sc in each st across, turn.

Rnd 19: For **Border,** working around outer edge, sc in end of next 18 rows; working in remaining lps on opposite side of starting ch on row 1, 3 sc in first ch, sc in next 16 chs, 3 sc in last ch, sc in end of next 18 rows, 3 sc in first st, sc in next 16 sts, 3 sc in last st, join with sl st in first st. Fasten off. *(Center sc of 3-sc group is corner st.)*

Rnd 20: With two strands orange held together and J hook, join with sc in any corner st, ch 3, (skip next st, sc in next st, ch 3) around, join. Fasten off.

Continued on page 114

Spider Door Knobbie

Designed by Cynthia Harris

Finished Size: Fits standard doorknob.

Materials:
- 2 oz. black worsted yarn
- Two 12mm wiggle eyes
- One thin ponytail elastic band
- Craft glue or glue gun
- Small amount fiberfill
- Tapestry needle
- H hook or size needed to obtain gauge

Gauge: Inner Circle = 4" across.

Basic Stitches: Ch, sl st, sc.

Spider
Inner Circle
Rnd 1: Ch 2, 6 sc in second ch from hook, **do not join rnds.** *(6 sc made)*
Rnd 2: 2 sc in each sc around. *(12)*
Rnd 3: (Sc in next sc, 2 sc in next sc) around. *(18)*
Rnd 4: (Sc in next 2 sts, 2 sc in next st) around. *(24)*
Rnd 5: (Sc in next 3 sts, 2 sc in next st) around. *(30)*
Rnd 6: (Sc in next 4 sts, 2 sc in next st) around,

join with sl st in first sc. Fasten off. *(36)*

Body
Rnds 1–6: Repeat rnds 1–6 Inner Circle. At end of rnd 6, **do not join, do not fasten off.**
Rnds 7–10: Sc in each st around.
Rnd 11: Holding wrong side of Inner Circle to wrong side of rnd 10 on Body, matching sts and working through both thicknesses, sc in each st around, stuffing with fiberfill before closing.
Rnds 12–17: Sc in each st around.
Rnd 18: Working over elastic band, sc in each st around.
Rnd 19: Sc in each st around, join with sl st in first sc. Fasten off.

Leg (make 8)
With black, leaving 6" length for sewing at beginning of ch, ch 12, sc in second ch from hook and in each ch across. Fasten off.

Finishing
1: With 6" lengths, sew 4 Legs evenly spaced to each side of Body at rnd 10.
2: Glue eyes close together to head as shown in photo. ●

Jack O'Lantern Pillow

Designed by Karen Robison

Finished Size: 24¾" square.

Materials:
- Worsted yarn:
  - 13 oz. green
  - 3½ oz. orange
  - 1½ oz. yellow
  - 1 oz. black
- 16" square pillow form
- Tapestry needle
- H hook or hook needed to obtain gauge

Gauge: 7 hdc = 2"; 7 hdc rows = 2½".

Basic Stitches: Ch, sl st, sc, hdc.

Special Stitch: To **join with hdc,** place slip knot on hook, yo, insert hook in st, yo, pull through st, yo, pull through all lps on hook.

Notes: When changing colors *(see Stitch Guide),* always change colors in last st made. Carry and work over dropped color.
Each square on graph equals one hdc.

Pillow
Row 1: With green, ch 145, hdc in second ch from hook, hdc in each ch across, turn. *(144 hdc made)*

Rows 2–6: Ch 1 *(ch-1 at beginning of rnds is not counted as a st),* hdc in each st across, turn.

Row 7: Ch 1, hdc in first 67 sts changing to orange *(see Notes),* hdc in next 6 sts changing to green, hdc in each st across, turn. *Front of row 7 is right side of work.*

Rows 8–42: Ch 1, hdc in first 46 sts changing colors according to corresponding rows, work according to graph across to last 46 sts, hdc in last 46 sts, turn.

Rows 43–47: Ch 1, hdc in each st across, turn. At end of last row, fasten off.

With wrong side facing you, fold right side over 12" and left side over 13" overlapping *(see illustration).* Sew top right side edges together and bottom edges together leaving overlapped edges unsewn for pillow opening. Insert pillow.

Ruffle
Rnd 1: With green, ch 240, sl st in first ch to form ring, ch 1, hdc in each ch around being careful not to twist chain, join with sl st in first hdc. *(240 hdc made)*

Rnd 2: Ch 1, hdc in first 3 sts, 2 hdc in next st, (hdc in next 3 sts, 2 hdc in next st) around, join. Fasten off. *(300 hdc)*

Rnd 3: Join yellow with hdc *(see Special Stitch)* in first st, ch 1, skip next st, (hdc in next st, ch 1, skip next st) around, join. *(150 hdc)*

Rnd 4: Ch 1, hdc in first st, ch 1, (hdc, ch 1, hdc) in next st, ch 1, *hdc in next st, ch 1, (hdc, ch 1, hdc) in next st, ch 1; repeat from * around, join. Fasten off. *(225 hdc, 225 ch sps)*

Rnd 5: Join green with hdc in first st, hdc in each st and in each ch around, join. Fasten off. *(450 hdc)*

Rnd 6: Join orange with hdc in first st, ch 1, skip next st, ch 1, (hdc in next st, ch 1, skip next st) around, join. *(225 hdc)*

Rnd 7: Ch 1, hdc in first st, ch 1, (hdc, ch 1, hdc) in next st, ch 1, *hdc in next st, ch 1, (hdc, ch 1, hdc) in next st, ch 1; repeat from * around to last st, hdc in last st, ch 1, join. Fasten off. *(337 hdc, 337 ch sps)*

Rnd 8: Join green with hdc in first st, hdc in each st and in each ch around with 2 hdc in last ch, join. *(675 sc)*

Rnd 9: Ch 1, (hdc, ch 1, hdc, ch 1, hdc) in first st, ch 1, skip next st, sc in next st, *ch 1, skip next st, (hdc, ch 1, hdc, ch 1, hdc) in next st, ch 1, skip next st, sc in next st; repeat from * around, ch 1, join. Fasten off.

Sew Ruffle to outer edge of Pillow. ●

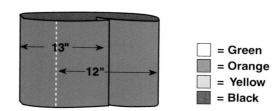

□ = Green
▨ = Orange
▧ = Yellow
■ = Black

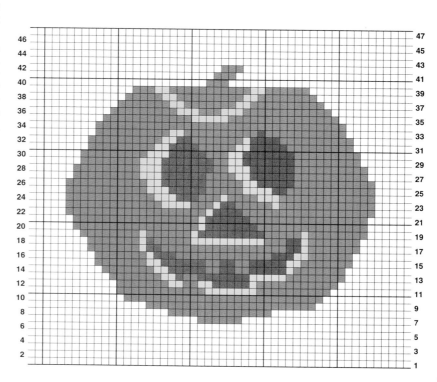

Spider Witch

Designed by Beverly Mewhorter

Finished Size: 9½" tall.

Materials:
- Worsted yarn:
  - 2½ oz. orange
  - 1 oz. black
- 18" black ³⁄₁₆" ribbon
- 12 wiggle 4mm eyes
- Small miniature plastic frog
- 6" craft witch broom
- 5½" witch air freshener doll
- Hot glue gun and glue
- Tapestry needle
- G hook or hook needed to obtain gauge

Gauge: 4 dc = 1"; 2 dc rows = 1".

Basic Stitches: Ch, sl st, sc, dc.

Dress
Bodice
Row 1: Starting at waist, with orange, ch 21, sc in second ch from hook, sc in each ch across, turn. *(20 sc made)*

Row 2: Ch 1, sc in first 4 sts; for **armhole**, ch 5, skip next 2 sts; sc in next 8 sts; for **armhole**, ch 5, skip next 2 sts; sc in last 4 sts, turn. *(16 sc, 10 chs)*

Row 3: Ch 1, sc in first 4 sts, sc in next 5 chs, sc in next 2 sts, (sc next 2 sts tog) 2 times, sc in next 2 sts, sc in next 5 chs, sc in last 4 sts, turn. *(24 sc)*

Row 4: Ch 1, sc in first 4 sts, (sc next 2 sts tog) 8 times, sc in last 4 sts. Fasten off. *(16 sc)*

Row 5: For **neck ruffle**, join black with sl st in first st, ch 3, 3 dc in same st as joining sl st, (4 sc in next st, 4 dc in next st) 7 times, sc in last st. Fasten off.

Skirt
Row 1: Working in starting ch on opposite side of row 1 on Bodice, join orange with sl st in first ch, ch 3, 3 dc in same ch as joining sl st, 4 dc in each ch across, turn. *(80 dc made)*

Rows 2–9: Ch 3, dc in each st across, turn. At end of last row, **do not turn.** Fasten off.

Row 10: For **ruffle**, join black with sl st in first st, ch 3, 3 dc in same st as joining sl st, (4 sc in next st, 4 dc in next st) 39 times, sc in last st. Fasten off.

Sew ends of rows 1–10 on Skirt together.

Sleeve (make 2)
Rnd 1: With orange, ch 7, sl st in first ch to form ring, ch 3, dc in each ch around, join with sl st in top of ch-3. *(7 dc made)*

Rnds 2–4: Ch 3, dc in each st around, join. At end of last rnd, fasten off.

Rnd 5: For **ruffle**, join black with sc in first st, 2 sc in same st as joining sc, 4 sc in each st around, join with sl st in first sc. Fasten off.

Using orange, sew one Sleeve in each armhole.

Spider (make 6)
With black, ch 2, 8 sc in second ch from hook *(body made)*, (sl st, ch 1, 2 sc, sl st) in first sc *(head made)*. Fasten off.

Hat
Rnd 1: With black, ch 2, 4 sc in second ch from hook, join with sl st in first sc. *(4 sc made)*

Rnd 2: Ch 1, 2 sc in each st around, join. *(8 sc)*

Rnds 3–4: Ch 1, sc in each st around, join.

Rnd 5: Ch 1, sc in first st, 2 sc in next st, (sc in next st, 2 sc in next st) around, join. *(12 sc)*

Rnds 6–7: Ch 1, sc in each st around, join.

Rnd 8: Ch 1, sc in first st, 2 sc in next st, (sc in next st, 2 sc in next st) around, join. *(18 sc)*

Rnd 9: Ch 1, sc in each st around, join.

Rnd 10: Ch 1, sc in first st, 2 sc in next st, (sc in next st, 2 sc in next st) around, join. *(27 sc)*

Rnd 11: Ch 1, sc in each st around, join.

Rnd 12: Ch 3, dc in next st, 2 dc in next st, (dc in next 2 sts, 2 dc in next st) around, join with sl st in top of ch-3. Fasten off.

Finishing
1: Using black, sew Spiders evenly spaced over rows 5 and 6 of Skirt.
2: For **legs,** using black, embroider four ½" long **straight stitches** *(see Stitch Guide)* on each side of Spiders body.
3: Glue two eyes to each Spider head.
4: Place Dress on doll; using orange, sew ends of rows 1–4 on Bodice together.
5: Starting at center front, weave ribbon through sts on row 4 of Bodice; tie ends in bow.
6: Glue Hat to doll's head. Glue frog to front of Hat. Glue broom handle in doll's right hand. ●

Jack O'Lantern Afghan

Designed by Martha Brooks Stein

Finished Size: 43" x 55½".

Materials:
- Worsted yarn:
  - 21 oz. orange
  - 20½ oz. black
  - ½ oz. rust
- Two 12mm wiggle eyes
- Tapestry needle
- I hook or size needed to obtain gauge

Gauge: Each Square is 2½" across.

Basic Stitches: Ch, sl st, sc, hdc, dc.

Afghan
Solid Square
(make 164 tangerine, 146 black, 2 rust)
Rnd 1: Ch 4, sl st in first ch to form ring, ch 3

(counts as dc), 2 dc in ring, (ch 2, 3 dc in ring) 3 times, join with hdc in top of ch-3 *(joining ch sp made). (12 dc, 4 ch sps made)*
Rnd 2: (Ch 3, 2 dc, ch 2, 3 dc) in joining ch sp, ch 1, (3 dc, ch 2, 3 dc, ch 1) in each ch sp around, join. Fasten off.

Half-Color Square
(make 20 tangerine/black and 4 rust/black)
Rnd 1: With first color, ch 4, sl st in first ch to form ring, (ch 3, 2 dc, ch 2, 3 dc) in ring, ch 1 changing to second color *(see illustration)*, ch 1, (3 dc, ch 2, 3 dc) in ring, join with hdc in top of ch-3 *(joining ch sp made). (12 dc, 4 ch sps made)*
Rnd 2: (Ch 3, 2 dc) in joining ch sp, ch 1, change to first color, 3 dc in same ch sp as last dc made, ch 1, (3 dc, ch 2, 3 dc) in next

Continued on page 114

Assembly Illustration

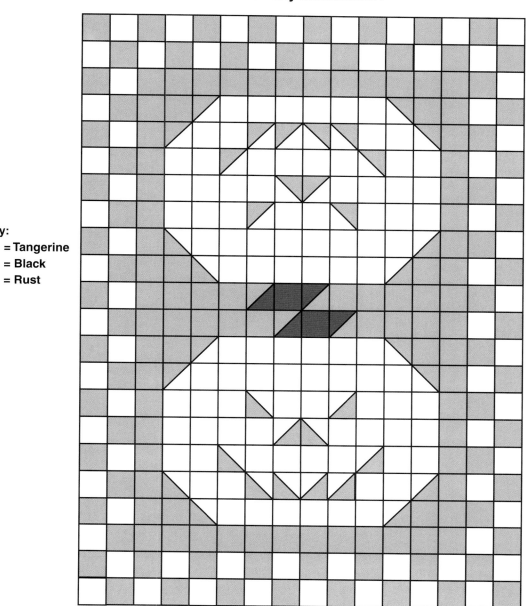

Key:
☐ = Tangerine
▨ = Black
▣ = Rust

Plant Pokes

Designed by Cynthia Harris

General Information

Finished Sizes: About 3½" to 5" tall.

Materials For Each:
- 12" of ⅛" wooden dowel
- Craft glue
- Polyester fiberfill
- Tapestry and sewing needles
- G hook or hook needed to obtain gauge
- Additional materials are listed with each individual pattern

Gauge: 4 sc = 1"; 4 sc rnds = 1".

Basic Stitches: Ch, sl st, sc, hdc, dc.

Note: Work in continuous rnds; do not join or turn unless otherwise stated. Mark first st of each rnd.

Basic Head & Body
Rnd 1: Ch 3, sl st in first ch to form ring, ch 1, 2 sc in each ch around. *(6 sc made)*
Rnd 2: 2 sc in each st around. *(12)*
Rnds 3–5: Sc in each st around.
Rnd 6: (Sc next 2 sts tog) around. *(6)*
Rnd 7: 2 sc in each st around. *(12)*
Rnds 8–12: Sc in each st around.
Rnd 13: (Sc next 2 sts tog) around. Stuff firmly. *(6)*
Rnd 14: Skip first st, sl st in next st, (skip next st, sl st in next st) 2 times. Fasten off.

Basic Arm (make 2)
Rnd 1: Ch 2, 4 sc in second ch from hook. *(4 sc made)*
Rnds 2–5: Sc in each st around. At end of last rnd, leaving long end for sewing, fasten off. Stuff firmly. Flatten rnd 5 and sew closed. Sew one Arm to each side of Body.

Witch

Additional Materials:
- Small amount each of black, green, gold, purple and med. brown worsted yarn
- Scrap piece of black felt
- 2 gold 5mm sequins
- Two 7mm wiggle eyes
- Black permanent marker

Head & Body
Rnds 1–6: With green, work rnds 1–6 of Basic Head and Body. At end of last rnd, fasten off.
Rnds 7–9: Join black with sl st in first st, work rnds 7–9 of Basic Head and Body.
Rnd 10: Working in **back lps** (see Stitch Guide), sl st in next st, ch 1, sc in each st around.

Rnds 11–14: Work rnds 11–14 of Basic Head and Body.

Arm (make 2)
Rnd 1: With green, work rnd 1 of Basic Arm. Fasten off.
Rnds 2–5: Join black with sl st in first st, work rnds 2–5 of Basic Arm.

Skirt
Rnd 1: With top of Head facing you, working in remaining **front lps** of rnd 9, join black with sl st in st at center back of Body, (ch 3, dc) in first st, 2 dc in each st around, join with sl st in top of ch-3. *(24 dc made)*
Rnds 2–3: Ch 3, dc in each st around, join. Fasten off.

Hair
Cut 16 strands of purple each 7" long; gather together and tie another strand around center of all strands. Using tie, attach Hair to top of Head.

Hat
Rnd 1: With black, ch 2, 4 sc in second ch from hook. *(4 sc made)*
Rnd 2: Sc in each st around.

Rnd 3: Sc in first st, 2 sc in next st, sc in next st, 2 sc in next st. *(6)*

Rnd 4: Sc in each st around.

Rnd 5: 2 sc in first st, sc in next 2 sts, 2 sc in next st, sc in next 2 sts. *(8)*

Rnd 6: 2 sc in first st, sc in next 3 sts, 2 sc in next st, sc in next 3 sts. *(10)*

Rnd 7: 2 sc in first st, sc in next 4 sts, 2 sc in next st, sc in next 4 sts. *(12)*

Rnd 8: 2 sc in first st, sc in next 5 sts, 2 sc in next st, sc in next 5 sts. *(14)*

Rnd 9: Working in **front lps,** (sl st, ch 2, hdc) in first st, 2 hdc in each st around, join with sl st in top of ch-2. Fasten off.

Stuff Hat lightly. Working in remaining **back lps** of rnd 8, sew Hat to top of Head spreading Hair evenly around as you work.

Broom

1: For **handle,** with two strands med. brown held together as one, ch 10; working in **back bar** *(see Stitch Guide)* of ch, sl st in second ch from hook, sl st in each ch across. Fasten off.

2: For **bristles,** cut thirty strands of gold each 2" long and separate into two equal groups. Gather one group of bristles together with ends even, lay 1" of handle on top of bristles, gather remaining group of bristles and lay on top of handle. Tie another strand of gold around bristles, enclosing end of handle, knot tightly.

3: Place glue on handle inside bristles and press bristles against handle.

4: Glue handle to Witch's left Arm.

Finishing

1: For **nose,** with green, ch 3, sl st in second ch from hook, sc in next ch. Leaving long end for sewing, fasten off. Sew to center of face.

2: Glue eyes above nose.

3: For **eyebrows,** cut two thin strips of black felt ³⁄₈" long, glue above eyes.

4: For **mouth,** cut one thin strip of black felt ½" long, glue below nose.

5: Glue sequins to front of Body above Skirt.

6: Color dowel with black marker, let dry. Cover end of dowel with glue; insert glued end into bottom of Body through center of rnd 14.

Scarecrow

Additional Materials:

- Small amount each of off-white, dk. green, blue, lt. yellow, med. brown and black worsted yarn
- Scrap pieces of gold, red, black and tan felt
- Two 7mm wiggle eyes
- 2 small wooden beads or buttons
- Orange permanent marker

Head & Body

Rnds 1–6: With off-white, work rnds 1–6 of Basic Head and Body on page 112. At end of last rnd, fasten off.

Rnd 7: Working in **back lps** *(see Stitch Guide),* join dk. green with sl st in first st, 2 sc in each st around.

Rnds 8–10: Work rnds 8–10 of Basic Head and Body. At end of last rnd, fasten off.

Rnds 11–14: Join blue with sl st in first st, work rnds 11–14 of Basic Head and Body.

Arm (make 2)

Rnd 1: With off-white, work rnd 1 of Basic Arm. Fasten off.

Rnds 2–5: Join dk. green with sl st in first st, work rnds 2–5 of Basic Arm.

Hat

Rnd 1: With med. brown, ch 3, join with sl st in first ch to form ring, 2 sc in each ch around. *(6 sc made)*

Rnd 2: Sc in first st, 2 sc in next st, (sc in next st, 2 sc in next st) 2 times. *(9)*

Rnd 3: Sc in first 2 sts, 2 sc in next st, (sc in next 2 sts, 2 sc in next st) 2 times, sc in last st. *(12)*

Rnd 4: 2 sc in first st, sc in next 3 sts, (2 sc in next st, sc in next 3 sts) 2 times. *(15)*

Rnd 5: 2 sc in first st, sc in next 4 sts, (2 sc in next st, sc in next 4 sts) 2 times. *(18)*

Rnd 6: Working in **front lps,** sl st in next st, ch 1, 2 sc in first st, sc in next 2 sts, (2 sc in next st, sc in next 2 sts) around, join with sl st in first sc. Fasten off.

Stuff Hat firmly. Working in remaining **back lps** of rnd 7, sew Hat to top of Head.

Crow

Rnd 1: With black, ch 2, 4 sc in second ch from hook. *(4 sc made)*

Rnd 2: Sc in each st around.

Continued on page 114

Plant Pokes
Continued from page 113

Rnd 3: Skip first st, sc in next st, skip next st, sc in next st. *(2)*
Rnds 4–5: Sc in each st around.
Rnd 6: Sc 2 sts tog. Fasten off.

Wings
With black, leaving long end for sewing, ch 4, sl st in second ch from hook, sc in next 2 chs. Fasten off.
Sew wings to sides of Crow between rnds 2 and 3.

Finishing
1: For neck straw, cut 24 strands of lt. yellow each 3" long. Holding two strands together, fold in half, pull fold through one remaining **front lp** on rnd 6 of Head and Body, pull loose ends through fold. Trim ends to ¼" and separate strands. Repeat in each remaining front lp on rnd 6.

2: For **strap (make 2),** leaving long end for sewing, with blue, ch 15. Leaving long end, fasten off. Sew first ch of each strap to rnd 8 on front of Body *(see photo),* drape straps over shoulders, cross straps in back, sew last ch to rnd 8 on back of Body.
3: Glue wiggle eyes to rnd 1 of Crow.
4: For beak, cut diamond shape from gold felt, fold in half and glue below eyes.
5: Sew Crow to right Arm.
6: For **eyes,** cut two ¼" X's from black felt and glue over rnd 4 at center front of Head.
7: For **nose,** cut small triangle from gold felt and glue between eyes.
8: For **mouth,** cut small crescent from red felt and glue below nose.
9: Glue two small beads or buttons to front of Body as shown in photo.
10: For **patches,** cut three small squares of tan felt and glue randomly around Hat.
11: Color dowel with orange marker, let dry. Cover end of dowel with glue; insert glued end into bottom of Body through center of rnd 14. ●

Jack O' Lantern Afghan

Continued from page 111

ch sp, ch 1, 3 dc in next ch sp, ch 1 change to second color, 3 dc in same ch sp as last dc made, ch 1, (3 dc, ch 2, 3 dc) in last ch sp, ch 1, join with sl st in top of ch-3. Fasten off.

Assembly
Arrange Squares according to assembly illustration; using black to sew Squares together in **back lps** *(see Stitch Guide).*

Border
Rnd 1: Working this rnd in **back lps,** join black with sc in first ch at top of right corner ch sp, ch 2, sc in next ch of same corner ch sp (corner made), *evenly space 145 sc across to next corner ch sp, sc in next ch at corner, ch 2, sc in next ch sp at corner, evenly space 196 sc across to next corner*, sc in next ch at corner, ch 2, sc in next ch; repeat between first and second *, join with sl st in first sc.
Rnd 2: Ch 1, **reverse sc** *(see Stitch Guide),* ch 2, skip next st or next ch sp, (reverse sc in next st or ch sp, ch 2, skip next st or next ch sp) around, join. Fasten off. ●

Halloween Set
Continued from page 104

Pumpkin
Note: Starting ch of each rnd is not worked into or counted as a stitch.
Rnd 1: With one strand of orange and I hook, ch 3, 12 dc in third ch from hook, join with sl st in first dc. *(12 dc made)*
Rnd 2: Ch 2, 2 dc in each st around, join. *(24)*
Rnd 3: Ch 1, sl st in first 2 sts, 2 sc in next st, hdc in next st, (2 dc in next st, dc in next st) 3 times, 2 hdc in next st, sl st in next st, 2 hdc in next st, (dc in next st, 2 dc in next st) 4 times, dc in next st, 2 hdc in next st, sc in last st, join with sl st in first sl st. Fasten off.
For **Stem,** with one strand of green and I hook, join with sl st in first st of last rnd, ch 5, sl st in second ch from hook, sl st in next 3 chs, sl st in same st as joining sl st. Fasten off.

With tapestry needle and orange, sew Pumpkin to center of Hot Pad leaving Stem unsewn *(see photo.)*
Trace and cut eyes and mouth from black felt according to pattern pieces. Glue to Pumpkin as shown in photo. ●

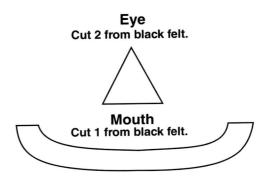

Eye
Cut 2 from black felt.

Mouth
Cut 1 from black felt.

chapter 8

Giving Thanks

Serve up the heavenly scent of freshly baked bread in a unique serving.

Pumpkin Bread in Pots

16 oz. can pumpkin
1½ cup sugar
⅔ cup vegetable oil
2 tsp. vanilla
4 eggs
3 cups self-rising flour
3 tsp. pumpkin pie spice
½ cup chopped nuts

Mix pumpkin, sugar, oil, vanilla and eggs in large bowl. Stir in remaining ingredients. Pour into well-greased 3" clay pots. Bake in 350 degree oven for 30 minutes or until toothpick comes out clean.

Turkey & Tracks Ripple Afghan

Designed by Sandra Smith

Finished Size: 60" x 70".

Materials:
- Worsted yarn:
  - 40 oz. brown
  - 12 oz. yellow
  - 12 oz. orange
- H hook or hook needed to obtain gauge

Gauge: 8 dc = 3"; 2 dc rows = 1¼".

Basic Stitches: Ch, sl st, dc.

Special Stitches: For **picot,** ch 9, sl st in front lp and left bar of last st made *(see Stitch Guide).*

For **decrease,** yo, insert hook in next st, yo, pull through st, yo, pull through 2 lps on hook, keeping last 2 lps on hook, skip next st, yo, insert hook in next st, yo, pull through st, yo, pull through 2 lps on hook, yo, pull through all 3 lps on hook.

For **spike stitch (spike st),** skipping sts behind worked sts; yo, insert hook in second st before decrease two rows below, yo, pull long lp up through st, yo, pull through 2 lps on hook, leaving last 2 lps on hook, yo, insert hook in decrease two rows below, yo, pull long lp up, yo, pull through 2 lps on hook, yo, insert hook in second st past decrease st 2 rows below, yo, pull long lp up through st, yo, pull through 2 lps on hook, yo, pull through all 4 lps on hook.

To **set picot on right side,** dc in one lp of center ch on next picot 2 rows below *(this is the contrasting color row)* and in **both lps** of next dc on this row at same time.

To **set picot on wrong side,** dc in **both lps** of next dc on this row and in one lp of center ch on next picot 2 rows below *(this is the contrasting color row)* at same time.

Note: The photographed item may contain inconsistencies in the crocheting. We have endeavored to make the instructions consistent. Please keep this in mind when comparing the instructions with the photograph.

Afghan

Row 1: With brown, ch 198, dc in fourth ch from hook, dc in next 7 chs, *(dc, **picot**—*see Special Stitches,* dc) in next ch, dc in next 9 chs, work **decrease** *(see Special Stitches)* over 3 chs, dc in next 9 chs; repeat from * 7 more times, (dc, picot, dc) in next ch, dc in next 8 chs, skip next ch, dc in last ch, turn. *(188 dc made) Front of row 1 is right side of work.*

Notes: *Hold picots worked on last row to right side of work throughout.*

To make **Braid,** *starting with the first picots on the first row, slip the picot on the 2nd row through the first picot on the first row; slip the third picot through the second; slip the fourth through the third; continue slipping picots as you work each row using the center picots on rows where 3-picot groups are worked.*

Rows 2–3: Ch 3, dc in next 8 sts, skip next st, *(dc, picot, dc) in sp at bottom of next picot, dc in next 9 sts, work decrease over 3 sts, dc in next 9 sts; repeat from * 7 more times, (dc, picot, dc) in sp at bottom of next picot, dc in next 8 sts, skip next st, dc in last st, turn. Fasten off.

Row 4: To **join with dc,** with orange, **place slip knot on hook, yo, insert hook in first st, yo, pull lp through st, (yo, pull through 2 lps on hook) 2 times;** skip next st, dc in next 8 sts, *(dc, picot 3 times, dc) in sp at bottom of next picot, dc in next 9 sts, work **spike st** *(see Special Stitches),* dc in next 9 sts; repeat from * 7 more times, (dc, picot 3 times, dc) in sp at bottom of next picot, dc in next 8 sts, skip next st, dc in last st, turn. Fasten off.

Row 5: Join brown with dc in first st, skip next st, dc in next 8 sts, *(dc, picot, dc) in next sp at bottom of center picot, dc in next 9 sts, decrease, dc in next 9 sts; repeat from * 7 more times, (dc, picot, dc) in next sp at bottom of center picot, dc in next 8 dc, skip next st, dc in last st, turn.

Row 6: Ch 3, skip next st, dc in next 8 sts, *(dc, picot, dc) in next sp at bottom of picot, dc in next 9 sts, decrease, dc in next 9 sts; repeat from * 7 more times, (dc, picot, dc) in last sp at bottom of picot, dc in next 8 sts, skip next st, dc in last st, turn. Fasten off.

Row 7: Join yellow with dc in first st, skip next st, dc in next 4 sts, **set picot on right side** *(see Special Stitches)* of first picot, dc in next 3 sts, *(dc, picot 3 times, dc) in next sp at bottom of picot, dc in next 3 sts, set picot on right side of third picot of same picot group, dc in next 5 sts, work spike st, dc in next 5

Continued on page 121

Turkey Towel Holder

Designed by Maggie Weldon

Finished Size: 6½" across.

Materials:
- Small amount each tan, red, gold, dk. brown and med. brown worsted yarn
- Plastic canvas:
    6" circle
    6 x 36-hole piece of 7-mesh
- Oval 15mm eye
- 8" of ⅜" satin ribbon
- Hot glue gun and glue
- Stitch marker
- Tapestry needle
- H hook of hook needed to obtain gauge

Gauge: Rnds 1 and 2 = 2½" across.

Basic Stitches: Ch, sl st, sc, dc, tr.

Tail Feathers

Rnd 1: With tan, ch 4, 11 dc in fourth ch from hook, join with sl st in top of ch-4. *(12 dc made)*

Rnd 2: (Ch 3, dc) in first st, 2 dc in each st around, join with sl st in top of ch-3. *(24 dc)*

Row 3: Working this row in **front lps** *(see Stitch Guide)*, ch 1, sc in first st, (ch 4, skip next st, sc in next st) 10 times, sl st in next st leaving last 2 sts unworked. Fasten off. *(10 ch sps)*

Rnd 4: Working this rnd in **back lps** of rnd 2, join gold with sl st in first st, ch 3, 2 dc in next st, (dc in next st, 2 dc in next st) around, join. *(36 dc)*

Row 5: Working this row in **front lps**, ch 1, sc in first st, (ch 4, skip next st, sc in next st) 15 times, sl st in next st leaving last 4 sts unworked. Fasten off. *(15 ch sps)*

Rnd 6: Working this rnd in **back lps** of rnd 4, join red with sl st in first st, ch 3, dc in next st, 2 dc in next st, (dc in next 2 sts, 2 dc in next st) around, join. *(48 dc)*

Row 7: Working this row in **front lps,** ch 1, sc in first st, (ch 4, skip next st, sc in next st) 21 times, sl st in next st leaving last 4 sts unworked. Fasten off. *(21 ch sps)*

Rnd 8: Working this rnd in **back lps** of rnd 6, join med. brown with sl st in first st, ch 3, dc in next 2 sts, 2 dc in next st, (dc in next 3 sts, 2 dc in next st) around, join. *(60 dc)*

Row 9: Ch 1, sc in first st, (ch 4, skip next st, sc in next st) 26 times, sl st in next st, leaving last 6 sts unworked. Leaving 18" end for sewing, fasten off. *(26 ch sps)*

For **first tie,** join med. brown with sl st in 14th sc at center top of row 9, ch 60. Fasten off.

For **second tie,** repeat first tie, joining in same st.

Head & Neck

Rnd 1: Starting at Head, with dk. brown, ch 4, 11 dc in fourth ch from hook, join with sl st in top of ch-4. *(12 dc made) Front of rnd 1 is right side of work.*

Row 2: For **Neck,** ch 1, 2 sc in first st, sc in next st, 2 sc in next st; place marker in next st, leaving remaining sts unworked, turn. *(5 sc)*

Row 3: Ch 1, sc in each st across, turn.

Row 4: Ch 1, 2 sc in first st, sc in next 3 sts, 2 sc in last st, turn. *(7 sc)*

Rows 5–8: Ch 1, sc in each st across, turn.

Row 9: Ch 1, sc first 2 sts tog, sc in next 3 sts, sc last 2 sts tog, turn. Fasten off. *(5 sc)*

Wattle

With right side of Head facing you, join red with sl st in marked st on rnd 1, remove marker and place in next st, (ch 3, tr, ch 3, sl st) in same st as first sl st. Fasten off.

Beak

With right side of Head facing you, join gold with sc in marked st on rnd 1, remove marker, (insert hook in next st, yo, pull through st, yo, pull through one lp on hook) 2 times, yo, pull through all lps on hook. Fasten off.

Finishing

1: Sew row 9 of Head and Neck centered on unworked sts of front on Tail Feathers.

2: Trim plastic canvas circle to fit on back of rnd 8 on Tail Feathers; for **towel hanger,** trim edges on plastic canvas strip at an angle to fit 1¼" from bottom of circle *(see illustration).*

3: Place wrong side of Tail Feathers on one side of plastic canvas circle, place plastic canvas strip on opposite side of circle; working through all thicknesses, with 18" end, sew outer edge of rnd 8 to outer edge of circle and plastic canvas strip at same time.

4: Tie ribbon in bow; glue between rows 4 and 5 on Neck. Glue eye on Head close to Beak. ●

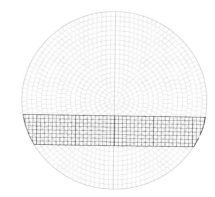

Pumpkin Basket

Designed by Rosemarie Walter

Finished Size: 8½" x 14".

Materials:
- Worsted yarn:
    9 oz. orange-brown
    5½ oz. gold
- 300 yds. dk. yellow size 10 crochet cotton thread
- 10" yellow D-ring
- Craft glue
- Polyester fiberfill
- Tapestry needle
- F and H hooks or hooks needed to obtain gauges

Gauges: **F hook,** 9 sc = 2"; 9 sc rows = 2". **H hook,** 7 sc = 2"; 7 sc rows = 2".

Basic Stitches: Ch, sl st, sc.

Note: Do not join rnds unless otherwise stated. Mark first st of each rnd.

Outside Layer

Rnd 1: Starting at bottom, with H hook and 1 strand each orange and crochet cotton, ch 2, 6 sc in second ch from hook. *(6 sc made)*

Rnd 2: 2 sc in each st around. *(12)*

Rnd 3: (Sc in next st, 2 sc in next st) around. *(18)*

Rnd 4: (Sc in next 2 sts, 2 sc in next st) around. *(24)*

Rnd 5: (Sc in next 3 sts, 2 sc in next st) around. *(30)*

Rnd 6: (Sc in next 4 sts, 2 sc in next st) around. *(36)*

Rnd 7: (Sc in next 5 sts, 2 sc in next st) around. *(42)*

Rnd 8: (Sc in next 6 sts, 2 sc in next st) around. *(48)*

Rnd 9: (Sc in next 7 sts, 2 sc in next st) around. *(54)*

Rnd 10: (Sc in next 8 sts, 2 sc in next st) around. *(60)*

Rnd 11: (Sc in next 9 sts, 2 sc in next st)

around. *(66)*

Rnd 12: (Sc in next 10 sts, 2 sc in next st) around. *(72)*

Rnd 13: (Sc in next 11 sts, 2 sc in next st) around. *(78)*

Rnd 14: (Sc in next 12 sts, 2 sc in next st) around. *(84)*

Rnd 15: (Sc in next 13 sts, 2 sc in next st) around. *(90)*

Rnd 16: (Sc in next 14 sts, 2 sc in next st) around. *(96)*

Rnd 17: Sc in each st around, join with sl st in first sc.

Row 18: For **first side panel,** working in rows, ch 1, sc in first 12 sts leaving remaining sts unworked, turn. *(12 sc)*

Row 19: Ch 1, sc in each st across, turn.

Row 20: Ch 1, 2 sc in first st, sc in each st across to last st, 2 sc in last st, turn. *(14)*

Rows 21–29: Repeat rows 19 and 20 alternately, ending with row 19 and *(22 sts)*.

Row 30: Ch 1, sc first 2 sts tog, sc in each st across to last 2 sts, sc last 2 sts tog, turn. *(20)*

Row 31: Ch 1, sc in each st across, turn.

Rows 32–39: Repeat rows 30 and 31 alternately. At end of last row, fasten off. *(12)*

Row 18: For **second side panel,** join with sc in next unworked st on row 17, sc in next 11 sts leaving remaining sts unworked, turn. *(12 sc)*

Rows 19–39: Repeat rows 19–39 of first panel.

For **remaining panels,** repeat second panel 6 more times.

Rnd 40: Working around outer edge, join with sc in any st, sc in each st and in end of each row around, join with sl st in first sc. Fasten off.

Inside Layer
With F hook and gold yarn, work same as Outside Layer.

Assembly
1: Working in **front lps** *(see Stitch Guide),* sew 4 panels on each side of Inside Layer together leaving sts between 4-panel sections and 12 sts at top of panels unsewn.

2: For basket, hold Inside and Outside Layers wrong sides together, matching sts; lightly stuff bottom between layers; working on 4 panels on each side of layers through both thicknesses, sew **both lps** of Outside Layer and **back lps** of Inside Layer together leaving sts between 4-panel sections and 12 sts at top of panels unsewn.

3: Place basket inside handle with flat edge of handle centered at bottom. Pull layers to outside of handle on each side. Sew **front lps** of unsewn inside panels together leaving 12 sts at top of each panel unsewn. Matching sts, sew **back lps** of outside panels to **front lps** of inside panels.

4: Working through **back lps,** sew sts at top of panels together, stuffing each panel lightly before closing.

5: Glue basket to bottom of handle.

6: Sew top of basket to handle on each side. •

Turkey & Tracks Ripple Afghan
Continued from page 119

sts, set picot on right side of first picot of next picot group, dc in next 3 sts; repeat from * 7 more times, (dc, picot 3 times, dc) in last sp at bottom of picot, dc in next 3 sts, set picot on right side of third picot of same picot group, dc in next 4 sts, skip next st, dc in last st, turn. Fasten off.

Rows 8–9: Repeat rows 5 and 6.

Row 10: Join orange with dc in first st, skip next st, dc in next 4 sts, **set picot on wrong side** *(see Special Stitches)* of first picot, dc in next 3 sts, *(dc, picot 3 times, dc) in next sp at bottom of picot, dc in next 3 sts, set picot on wrong side of third picot of same picot group, dc in next 5 sts, work spike st, dc in next 5 sts, set picot on wrong side of first picot of next picot group, dc in next 3 sts; repeat from * 7 more times, (dc, picot 3 times, dc) in last sp at bottom of picot, dc in next 3 sts, set picot on wrong side of third picot of same picot group, dc in next 4 sts, skip next st, dc in last st, turn. Fasten off.

Rows 11–13: Repeat rows 5–7.

Rows 14–97: Repeat rows 8–13 consecutively.

Row 98: Repeat row 5.

Row 99: Ch 3, skip next st, dc in next 8 sts, *(dc, ch 2, dc) in next sp at bottom of picot, dc in next 9 sts, decrease, dc in next 9 sts; repeat from * 7 more times, (dc, ch 2, dc) in last sp at bottom of picot, dc in next 8 sts, skip next st, dc in last st, turn.

Row 100: Ch 3, skip next st, dc in next 4 sts, working on yellow row, set picot on wrong side of first picot, dc in next 3 sts, *(dc, ch 2, dc) in next ch-2 sp and in center lp of picot on brown row below at same time, dc in next 3 sts, working on yellow row, set picot on wrong side of third picot of same picot group, dc in next 5 sts, decrease, dc in next 5 sts, working on yellow row, set picot on wrong side of first picot of next picot group, dc in next 3 sts; repeat from * 7 more times, (dc, ch 2, dc) in last ch-2 sp and in center lp of picot on brown row below at same time, dc in next 3 sts, working in yellow row, set picot on wrong side of third picot of same picot group, dc in next 4 sts, skip next st, dc in last st, turn. Fasten off. •

Autumn Harvest Angel

An Original by Annie

Finished Size: Fits 11½" fashion doll.

Materials:
- No. 8 pearl cotton or size 20 crochet cotton thread:
  - 100 yds. med. gold
  - Small amount each dk. lavender, dk. brown, med. yellow-green, lt. yellow and dk. red
- No. 5 pearl cotton or size 10 crochet cotton thread:
  - 40 yds. med. gold
  - 16 yds. lt. gold
  - 18 yds. med. yellow
  - 19 yds. tangerine
  - 35 yds. burnt orange
  - 22 yds. red
  - 23 yds. burgundy
  - 23 yds. dk. violet
  - 23 yds. royal blue
  - 23 yds. dk. baby blue
- 7 each red and gold 20 x 14mm oak leaves
- 13 gold 15 x 10mm dogwood leaves
- Brass oval blank
- Three 36" lengths and one 42" length of ⅛" ribbon desired colors
- 6" gold braid
- Wooden angel wings
- Hot glue gun and glue sticks
- Small amount polyester fiberfill
- Straight pins
- Brass jump ring
- 3 small snaps
- Fabric stiffener
- Tapestry needle
- Sewing needle and gold sewing thread
- Nos. 7 and 12 steel hooks or hook needed to obtain gauge

Gauge: No. 7 hook and size 10 thread, 7 dc = 1"; 4 dc rows = 1".

Basic Stitches: Ch, sl st, sc, hdc, dc.

Notes: Use No. 7 steel hook with No. 5 thread and No. 12 steel hook with No. 8 thread throughout.
Work in rnds, do not join or turn unless otherwise stated. Mark first st or ch sp of each rnd.

Dress
Bodice
Row 1: With No. 5 med. gold, ch 40, sc in second ch from hook, sc in each ch across, turn. *(39 sc made)*

Rows 2–3: Ch 1, sc in each st across, turn.

Row 4: Ch 1, sc in first 16 sts, skip next st, 10 dc in next st, skip next st, sc in next st, skip next st, 10 dc in next st, skip next st, sc in last 16 sts, turn. *(33 sc, 20 dc)*

Row 5: Ch 1, sc in first 15 sts, (skip next st, dc in next 9 sts, skip next st), sc in next st; repeat between ( ), sc in last 15 sts, turn. *(31 sc, 18 dc)*

Row 6: Ch 1, sc in first 15 sts, (skip next st, sc in next 7 sts, skip next st), sc in next st; repeat between ( ), sc in last 15 sts, turn. *(45 sc)*

Rows 7–8: Ch 1, sc in first 22 sts, sl st in next st, sc in last 22 sts, turn. *(44 sc, 1 sl st)*

Row 9: Ch 1, sc in first 9 sts; for **armhole**, ch 14, skip next 2 sts; sc in next 11 sts, sl st in next st, sc in next 11 sts; for **armhole**, ch 14, skip next 2 sts; sc in last 9 sts, turn. *(40 sc, 28 chs, 1 sl st)*

Row 10: Ch 1, sc in first 7 sts, (sc next 2 sts tog, skip next ch, sc in next 12 chs, skip next ch, sc next 2 sts tog), sc in next 9 sts, sl st in next st, sc in next 9 sts; repeat between ( ), sc in last 7 sts, turn. *(60 sc, 1 sl st)*

Row 11: For **First Front**, ch 1, sc in first 6 sts, sc next 2 sts tog, skip next st, sc in next 11 sts, sl st in next 2 sts leaving remaining sts unworked, turn. *(18 sc, 2 sl sts)*

Row 12: Skip first 2 sl sts, sc in next 9 sts, sc next 3 sts tog, sc in last 6 sts. Fasten off.

Row 11: For **Second Front,** join No. 5 med. gold with sc in first st on opposite end of row 10, sc in next 5 sts, sc next 2 sts tog, skip next st, sc in next 11 sts, sl st in next 2 sts leaving remaining sts unworked, turn. *(18 sc, 2 sl sts)*

Row 12: Repeat row 12 of First Front.

Row 13: Working in remaining lps on opposite side of starting ch on row 1 of Bodice, join No. 5 med. gold with sc in first ch, sc in each ch across. Fasten off. *(39 sc made)*

For **edging,** working in sts and in ends of rows around neck opening, with right side facing you, join No. 5 med. gold with sc in first st on left side at back opening, **reverse sc** *(see Stitch Guide)* in each st across to right side of back opening. Fasten off.

Sleeve (work in each armhole)
Row 1: Skip first 4 chs of ch-14 on armhole, join No. 5 med. gold with sc in next ch, 2 sc in each of next 4 chs, sc in next ch, turn. *(10 sc made)*

Row 2: Skip first st, sc in next 8 sts, sl st in last st, turn. *(8 sc, 1 sl st)*

Row 3: Skip first sl st, sc in next 7 sts, sl st in last st, turn.

Row 4: Skip first sl st, sc in next 7 sts, sc in end of row 3, sc ends of rows 2 and 1 tog, sc in

Continued on page 124

Autumn Harvest Angel

Continued from page 123

next 3 chs, sc next ch and next st tog, turn. *(13 sc)*

Rnd 5: Working in rnds, ch 1, sc in first 4 sts, sc next 2 sts tog, sc in next 7 sts, sc in ends of rows 4, 3 and 2, sc end of row 1 and next ch tog, sc in next 2 chs, sc next ch and next st tog, join with sl st in first sc, **turn.** *(19)*

Rnd 6: Ch 1, sc first 2 sts tog, sc in next 11 sts, sc next 2 sts tog, sc in next 2 sts, sc last 2 sts tog, join, **turn.** *(16)*

Rnds 7–9: Ch 1, sc in each st around, join, **turn.**

Rnds 10–11: Ch 1, skip first st, sc in each st around, join, **turn.** *(15, 14)*

Rnds 12–14: Ch 1, sc in each st around, join, **turn.** At end of last rnd, fasten off.

Rnd 15: Join No. 8 med. gold with sc in first st, (ch 3, sc in next st) around, ch 2, join with hdc in first sc. *(14 ch sps)*

Rnd 16: Ch 1, sc in first ch sp, (ch 4, sc in next ch sp) around, ch 2, join with hdc in first sc.

Rnds 17–24: Ch 1, sc in first ch sp, (ch 5, sc in next ch sp) around, ch 3, join with dc in first sc. At end of last rnd, fasten off.

Skirt

Row 1: Working in **back lps** *(see Stitch Guide)* of row 13 on Bodice, join No. 5 lt. gold with sl st in first st, ch 3, dc in same st, (dc in next 3 sts, 2 dc in next st) 9 times, dc in last 2 sts, turn. *(49 dc made)*

Row 2: (Ch 3, dc) in first st, (dc in next 5 sts, 2 dc in next st) across, turn. *(58)*

Rows 3–4: Ch 3, dc in each st across, turn. At end of last row, fasten off.

Row 5: Join med. yellow with sl st in first st, ch 3, dc in same st; for **long dc (ldc), yo, insert hook in st on row below last, working over last row, yo, pull long lp through st, (yo, pull through 2 lps on hook) 2 times;** (dc in next 2 sts, ldc in next st) across to last 2 sts, dc in next st, 2 dc in last st, turn. *(41 dc, 19 ldc)*

Row 6: Ch 3, dc in next 8 sts, 2 dc in next st, (dc in next 9 sts, 2 dc in next st) across, turn. *(66 dc)*

Rows 7–8: Ch 3, dc in each st across, turn. At end of last row, fasten off.

Row 9: Join tangerine with sl st in first st, ch 3, ldc in next st, (dc in next 2 sts, ldc in next st) 21 times, dc in last st, turn. *(44 dc, 22 ldc)*

Row 10: Ch 3, dc in next 9 sts, 2 dc in next st, (dc in next 14 sts, 2 dc in next st) 3 times, dc in last 10 sts, turn. *(70 dc)*

Rows 11–12: Ch 3, dc in each st across, turn. At end of last row, fasten off.

Row 13: Join burnt orange with sl st in first st, ch 3, dc in next st, ldc in next st, (dc in next 2 sts, ldc in next st) across to last st, dc in last st, turn. *(46 dc, 24 ldc)*

Rnd 14: Working in rnds, (ch 3, dc) in first st, (dc in next 11 sts, 2 dc in next st) 5 times, dc in last 9 sts, join with sl st in top of ch-3, **turn.** *(76 dc)*

Rnds 15–16: Ch 3, dc in each st around, join, **turn.** At end of last rnd, fasten off.

Rnd 17: Join No. 5 red with sl st in first st, ch 3, (ldc in next st, dc in next 2 sts) around, join, **turn.** *(51 dc, 25 ldc)*

Rnd 18: (Ch 3, dc) in first st, (dc in next 12 sts, 2 dc in next st) 5 times, dc in last 10 sts, join, **turn.** *(82 dc)*

Rnds 19–20: Ch 3, dc in each st around, join, **turn.** At end of last rnd, fasten off.

Rnd 21: Join No. 5 burgundy with sl st in first st, ch 3, (ldc in next st, dc in next 2 sts) around, join, **turn.** *(55 dc, 27 ldc)*

Rnds 22–24: Ch 3, dc in each st around, join, **turn.** At end of last rnd, fasten off. *(82 dc)*

Rnd 25: Join No. 5 dk. violet with sl st in first st, ch 3, (ldc in next st, dc in next 2 sts) around, join, **turn.** *(55 dc, 27 ldc)*

Rnds 26–28: Ch 3, dc in each st around, join, **turn.** At end of last rnd, fasten off. *(82 dc)*

Rnd 29: Join royal blue with sl st in first st, ch 3, (ldc in next st, dc in next 2 sts) around, join, **turn.** *(55 dc, 27 ldc)*

Rnds 30–32: Ch 3, dc in each st around, join, **turn.** At end of last rnd, fasten off. *(82 dc)*

Rnd 33: Join dk. baby blue with sl st in first st, ch 3, (ldc in next st, dc in next 2 sts) around, join, **turn.** *(55 dc, 27 ldc)*

Rnds 34–36: Ch 3, dc in each st around, join, **turn.** At end of last rnd, fasten off. *(82 dc)*

Overskirt

Row 1: Working in remaining **front lps** of row 13 on Bodice, join No. 8 med. gold with sl st in first st, (ch 5, sc) in same st, (ch 5, sc in next st) across to last st, (ch 5, sc, ch 2, dc) in last st, turn. *(40 ch sps made)*

Rows 2–9: Ch 1, sc in first ch sp, (ch 5, sc in next ch sp) across to last ch sp, ch 2, dc in last ch sp, turn. *(32 ch sps at end of row 9)*

Rnd 10: Working in rnds, ch 1, sc in first ch sp, (ch 5, sc in next ch sp) around to last ch sp, ch 2, dc in last ch sp, join with sl st in third ch of first ch-5. *(31 ch sps)*

Rnds 11–41: Ch 1, sc in first ch sp, (ch 5, sc in next ch sp) around. At end of last rnd, fasten off.

Pumpkin

Rnd 1: With burnt orange, ch 2, 6 sc in second ch from hook, **do not join.** *(6 sc made)*

Rnd 2: 2 sc in each st around. *(12 sc)*

Rnd 3: (Sc in next st, 2 sc in next st) around. *(18)*

Rnd 4: (Sc in next 2 sts, 2 sc in next st) around. *(24)*

Rnd 5: (Sc in next 3 sts, 2 sc in next st) around. *(30)*

Rnd 6: (Sc in next 4 sts, 2 sc in next st) around. *(36)*

Rnds 7–14: Sc in each st around.

Rnd 15: (Sc in next 4 sts, sc next 2 sts tog) around. *(30)*

Rnd 16: (Sc in next 3 sts, sc next 2 sts tog) around. *(24)*

Rnd 17: (Sc in next 2 sts, sc next 2 sts tog)

around. *(18)*

Rnd 18: (Sc in next st, sc next 2 sts tog) around. Stuff. *(12)*

Rnd 19: (Sc next 2 sts tog) around, join with sl st in first sc. Leaving a 24" end of thread, fasten off. *(6)*

To **shape Pumpkin,** thread tapestry needle with 24" end and weave through sts of last rnd; pull to close opening. Insert needle through center of Pumpkin and out of center on opposite side; bring thread out over side of Pumpkin and down through center again, pulling thread tightly enough to make a crease in side of Pumpkin; repeat five more times evenly spacing the creases. Secure thread and cut off remaining end of thread.

For **Pumpkin Stem,** with dk. brown, ch 6, sl st in second ch from hook, sl st in each ch across; working on opposite side of ch, sl st in each ch across. Leaving a long end of thread, fasten off.

Using end of thread, sew Stem to center top of Pumpkin.

For **Pumpkin Leaf,** with yellow-green, ch 5, (sc, hdc, dc) in second ch from hook, (hdc, sc) in next ch, (sc, hdc, dc) in next ch, (hdc, sc, ch 3, sc, hdc) in next ch; working in remaining lps on opposite side of ch, (dc, hdc, sc) in next ch, (sc, hdc) in next ch, (dc, hdc, sc) in next ch. Leaving a long end of thread, fasten off.

Using end of thread, sew Leaf to center top of Pumpkin beside Stem.

Apple (make 2)

Rnd 1: Starting at top, with No. 8 dk. red, ch 2, 6 sc in second ch from hook. *(6 sc made)*

Rnd 2: 2 sc in each st around. *(12)*

Rnd 3: (2 sc in next st, sc in next st) around. *(18)*

Rnds 4–5: Sc in each st around.

Rnd 6: (Sc next 2 sts tog, sc in next st) around. Stuff. *(12)*

Rnd 7: (Sc next 2 sts tog) around. *(6)*

Leaving a long end of thread, fasten off.

Thread tapestry needle with end of thread and weave through sts of last rnd; pull to close opening. Insert needle through center of Apple and out at center top. Bring thread back out at bottom. Pull thread to indent top of Apple slightly. Secure end of thread.

For **Stem,** with dk. brown, ch 6, sl st in second ch from hook, sl st in each ch across. Leaving a long end of thread, fasten off.

Using end of thread, sew Stem to center top of Apple.

For **Leaf,** with yellow-green, ch 6, sl st in second ch from hook, sc in next 3 chs, sl st in last ch. Leaving a long end of thread, fasten off.

Using end of thread, sew Leaf to center top of Apple beside Stem.

PEAR (make 2)

Rnd 1: Starting at bottom, with No. 8 lt. yellow, ch 2, 6 sc in second ch from hook. *(6 sc made)*

Rnd 2: (2 sc in next st, sc in each of next 2 sts) 2 times. *(8)*

Rnds 3–4: Sc in each st around.

Rnd 5: (2 sc in next st, sc in next st) around. *(12)*

Rnd 6: (2 sc in next st, sc in next 2 sts) around. *(16)*

Rnds 7–8: Sc in each st around.

Rnd 9: (Sc next 2 sts tog, sc in next 2 sts) around. Stuff. *(12)*

Rnd 10: (Sc next 2 sts tog) around. *(6)* Leaving a long end of thread, fasten off.

Thread tapestry needle with end of thread and weave through sts of last rnd; pull to close opening. Secure end.

For **Stem,** with dk. brown, ch 5, sl st in second ch from hook, sl st in each ch across. Leaving a long end of thread, fasten off.

Using end of thread, sew Stem to center top of Pear.

For **Leaf,** with yellow-green, ch 6, sl st in second ch from hook, sc in next 3 chs, sl st in last ch. Leaving a long end of thread, fasten off.

Using end of thread, sew Leaf to center top of Pear beside Stem.

Grape Cluster (make 2)

Rnd 1: Starting at bottom, leaving a long end of thread, with No. 8 dk. lavender, ch 3, sl st in first ch to form ring *(Center made)*.

Row 2: Ch 3, sl st in third ch from hook, (ch 2, sl st in same ch) 5 times.

Row 3: Sl st in Center, ch 3, sl st in third ch from hook, (ch 2, sl st in same ch) 7 times.

Rows 4–6: Sl st in Center, ch 3, sl st in third ch from hook, (ch 2, sl st in same ch) 9 times. At end of last row, leaving a long end of thread, fasten off.

Continued on page 132

Thanksgiving Favors

Designed by Cindy Harris

Pilgrim Boy

Finished Size: 7" tall.

Materials:
- Worsted yarn:
  1 oz. each lt. apricot and black
  Small amount each brown, white and yellow
- 75 yds. tan raffia straw
- Small piece red felt
- Polyester fiberfill
- Two 10mm wiggly eyes
- 6" piece ¼" elastic for (optional) Doorknob Cover
- Craft glue
- Tapestry needle
- D, F and G hooks or hooks needed to obtain gauges

Gauges: D hook, 4 hdc = 1", 3 hdc rows = 1"; 2 post sts and 2 hdc = 1", 4 post st and hdc rows = 1". **F hook,** 9 sts = 2"; 9 sc rows = 2"; 7 hdc rows = 2". **G hook,** 4 sc = 1", 4 sc rows = 1".

Basic Stitches: Ch, sl st, sc, hdc, dc.

Boy
Inner Head
Rnd 1: With G hook and lt. apricot, ch 3, sl st in first ch to form ring, ch 1, 2 sc in each ch around, **do not join rnds.** *(6 sc made)*
Rnd 2: 2 sc in each st around. *(12)*
Rnd 3: (2 sc in next st, sc in next st) around. *(18)*
Rnd 4: (2 sc in next st, sc in next 2 sts) around. *(24)*
Rnd 5: (2 sc in next st, sc in next 3 sts) around. *(30)*
Rnd 6: (2 sc in next st, sc in next 4 sts) around. Fasten off. *(36)*

Outer Head
Rnds 1–6: Starting at front, work same as rnds 1–6 of Inner Head, **do not fasten off.**
Rnds 7–8: Sc in each st around.
Rnd 9: Matching sts, hold wrong sides of Inner and Outer Head pieces together; working through both thicknesses, sc in each st around stuffing before closing.
Rnd 10: (Sc in next 4 sts, sc next 2 sts tog) around. *(30)*
Rnds 11–17: Sc in each st around. At end of last rnd, join with sl st in first sc. Leaving 8" strand for weaving, fasten off.
For **Basket Head,** stuff. Weave 8" strand through sts; pull tight to gather. Secure ends.
For **Doorknob Cover,** weave elastic through sts in last rnd. Sew ends together to secure.

Nose
With G hook and lt. apricot, ch 3, sl st in first ch to form ring, ch 1, sc in each ch around, join with sl st in first sc. Leaving 6" strand for sewing, fasten off.
Sew Nose centered on front of Head.

Ear (make 2)
With G hook and lt. apricot, ch 2, (2 sc, sl st) in second ch from hook. Leaving 6" strand for sewing, fasten off.
Sew Ears on each side of Head.

Shirt
Rnd 1: With G hook and black, ch 3, sl st in first ch to form ring, ch 1, 2 sc in each ch around. *(6 sc made)*
Rnd 2: 2 sc in each st around. *(12)*
Rnds 3–12: Sc in each st around.
Rnd 13: (Sc next 2 sts tog) around. *(6)*
Rnd 14: (Sl st in next st, skip next st) around. Fasten off.
Flatten Shirt.
Sew Shirt centered on bottom of Head leaving 1" extending on each side for **Shoulders.**

Collar
Row 1: With G hook and white, ch 21, sc in second ch from hook, sc in each ch across, turn. *(20 sc made)*
Rnd 2: Working in rnds, ch 1, 2 sc in first st, sc in next 18 sts, 2 sc in last st; working in remaining lps on opposite side of starting ch on row 1, 2 sc in first ch, sc in next 18 ch, 2 sc in last ch, join with sl st in first sc. Fasten off.
Place Collar around neck and tack ends of row 1 together at center front.
For **Tie,** cut a separate 8" strand of black and tie in bow; tack to center front of Collar; tack Collar to front of Shirt at same place.

Hair
Cut 18 strands of brown each 4" long; tie a separate 6" strand around center of all strands held together.
Tack center of Hair to center top of Head evenly spacing strands around front and sides of Head.

Hat
Rnd 1: With G hook and black, ch 3, sl st in first ch to form ring, ch 1, 2 sc in each ch around. *(6 sc made)*
Rnd 2: 2 sc in each st around. *(12)*
Rnd 3: (2 sc in next st, sc in next st) around. *(18)*
Rnd 4: Working in **back lps** *(see Stitch Guide)*, sc in each st around.
Rnds 5–8: Sc in each st around.
Rnd 9: (Sc in next 5 sts, 2 sc in next st) around. *(21)*
Rnds 10–12: Sc in each st around.
Rnd 13: (Sc in next 6 sts, 2 sc in next st) around. *(24)*
Rnd 14: For **Brim,** (sl st, ch 2, hdc) in next st, (hdc in next st, 2 hdc in next st) around, join with sl st in top of ch-2. Fasten off. *(35 hdc)*
Stuff Hat; sew centered on top of Head.
With two strands of yellow, using **straight**

Continued on page 128

Thanksgiving Favors
Continued from page 127

Continued from page 127

stitch *(see Stitch Guide)*, embroider buckle over two rows on center front of Hat above Brim *(see photo)*.

Finishing
1: Trim Hair to desired length.
2: Glue eyes to front of Head centered above Nose 1" apart.
3: Cut Mouth from felt according to pattern piece; glue on front of Head centered below Nose.

**MOUTH
Cut 1.**

Note: For Doorknob Cover, omit Sleeve, Hand, Shoe and Basket.

Sleeve (make 2)
Rnd 1: With F hook and black, starting at wrist, ch 9, join with sl st in first ch to form ring, ch 1, sc in each ch around, join with sl st in first sc. *(9 sc made)*
Rnd 2: Ch 2, (hdc in next st, 2 hdc in next st) around, join with sl st in first ch-2. *(13 hdc)*
Rnds 3–7: Ch 2, hdc in each st around, join. At end of last rnd, fasten off.
Flatten Sleeve.
Sew rnd 7 of Sleeves to Shoulders on Shirt.

Hand (make 2)
Rnd 1: With G hook and lt. apricot, starting at wrist, ch 2, 6 sc in second ch from hook. *(6 sc made)*
Rnd 2: 2 sc in each st around. *(12)*
Rnd 3: (Sc in next st, 2 sc in next st) around, join with sl st in first sc. *(18)*
Rnd 4: Ch 1, sc in first 2 sts; for **Thumb**, 5 dc in next st, drop lp from hook, insert hook in top of first dc of group, pull dropped lp through st; sc in last 15 sts. *(17 sc, 1 Thumb)*
Rnd 5: Sc in first 2 sts, skip Thumb, sc in each st around.
Rnd 6: Sc in first st, (sc next 2 sts tog) 2 times, sc in next 4 sts, sc next 2 sts tog, sc in last 6 sts. *(14)*
Rnd 7: Sc in first 6 sts, (sc next 2 sts tog) 2 times, sc in last 4 sts. Stuff. *(12)*
Rnd 8: (Sc next 2 sts tog) around, join with sl st in first sc. Leaving 6" strand for sewing, fasten off. *(6)* Sew opening closed.
For **Fingers**, working from bottom to top, over rnds 5–8, sculpture fingers as shown *(see illustration)*.
Sew Hands to rnd 1 of Sleeves.

Shoe (make 2)
Rnd 1: With F hook and black, starting at bottom, ch 10, sc in second ch from hook, sc in next 6 chs, 2 hdc in next ch, 3 hdc in last ch; working in remaining lps on opposite side of ch, 2 hdc in next ch, sc in next 6 chs, 2 sc in last ch. *(22 sts made)*
Rnd 2: 2 sc in first st, sc in next 8 sts, 2 sc in next 3 sts, sc in next 8 sts, 2 sc in last 2 sts. *(28 sc)*
Rnd 3: Sc in each st around, join with sl st in first sc.
Rnd 4: Working in **back lps** *(see Stitch Guide)*, ch 1, sc first 2 sts tog, sc next 2 sts tog, sc in next 5 sts, (sc next 2 sts tog) 4 times, sc in next 7 sts, (sc next 2 sts tog) 2 times. *(20)*
Rnd 5: Sc first 2 sts tog, sc in next 6 sts, (sc next 2 sts tog) 2 times, sc in next 6 sts, sc last 2 sts tog. *(16)*
Rnd 6: Sc first 2 sts tog, sc in next 4 sts, (sc next 2 sts tog) 2 times, sc in next 4 sts, sc last 2 sts tog, join with sl st in first sc. Fasten off. *(12 sc)*
Matching sts, sew last row together.

Basket
Rnd 1: With D hook and raffia, starting at bottom, ch 3, sl st in first ch to form ring, ch 2, 9 hdc in ring, join with sl st in top of ch-2. *(10 hdc made)*
Rnd 2: Ch 2, hdc in same st, 2 hdc in each st around, join. *(20)*
Rnd 3: Ch 2, 2 hdc in next st, (hdc in next st, 2 hdc in next st) around, join. *(30)*
Rnd 4: Ch 2, hdc in next st, 2 hdc in next st, (hdc in next 2 sts, 2 hdc in next st) around, join. *(40)*

Rnd 5: Ch 2, hdc in next 2 sts, 2 hdc in next st, (hdc in next 3 sts, 2 hdc in next st) around, join. *(50)*

Rnd 6: Working in **back lps,** ch 2, hdc in each st around, join.

Rnd 7: Ch 2; for **dc front post (fp**—*see Stitch Guide),* yo, insert hook from right to left around post of hdc on previous row, complete as dc; (hdc in next hdc, fp around next hdc) around, join with sl st in top of ch-2.

Rnd 8: Ch 2, (hdc in next dc, fp around next hdc) around to last st, hdc in last dc, join with sl st in top of ch-2.

Rnds 9–13: Repeat rnds 7 and 8 alternately, ending with rnd 7.

Rnd 14: Working in **back lps,** ch 1, sc in first 2 sts, (sc next 2 sts tog, sc in next 2 sts) around, join with sl st in first sc. *(38 sc)*

Rnd 15: Working this rnd in **front lps of rnd 13,** ch 1, **reverse sc** *(see Stitch Guide)* in each st around, join with sl st in first sc. Fasten off.

Assembly
Arrange Boy around Basket and sew in place. Sew Shoes to front of Basket.

Pilgrim Girl
Finished Size: 5" tall.

Materials:
- Worsted yarn:
  1 oz. lt. apricot,
  Small amount each black, white and yellow
- 75 yds. tan raffia straw
- Small piece red felt
- Polyester fiberfill
- Two 10mm wiggly eyes
- 6" piece ¼" elastic for (optional) Doorknob Cover
- Craft glue
- Tapestry needle
- D, F and G hooks or hooks needed to obtain gauges

Gauges: D hook, 4 hdc = 1", 3 hdc rows = 1"; 2 post sts and 2 hdc = 1", 4 post st and hdc rows

= 1". **F hook,** 9 sts = 2"; 9 sc rows = 2"; 7 hdc rows = 2". **G hook,** 4 sc = 1", 4 sc rows = 1".

Basic Stitches: Ch, sl st, sc, hdc, dc.

Girl
Inner Head, Outer Head, Nose, Shirt, Collar, Sleeve, Hand & Shoe
Work same as Pilgrim Boy Inner Head, Outer Head, Nose, Shirt, Collar, Sleeve, Hand and Shoe.
Note: *For Doorknob Cover, omit Sleeve, Hand, Shoe and Basket.*

Hair
Cut 18 strands of yellow each 5" long; tie a separate 7" strand around center of all strands held together.
Tack center of Hair to center top of Head evenly spacing strands around front and sides of Head.

Hat
Row 1: With G hook and white, ch 17, sc in second ch from hook, sc in each ch across, turn. *(16 sc made)*

Rows 2–7: Ch 1, sc in each st across, turn.

Rnd 8: Working around outer edge in sts and in ends of rows, ch 1, sc first 2 sts tog, (sc next 2 sts tog) 7 times, (sc next 2 rows tog) 3 times, skip last row; for **Brim,** working in remaining lps on opposite side of staarting ch of row 1, 3 hdc in first ch, hdc in each ch across with 3 hdc in last ch; skip next row, (sc next 2 rows tog) 3 times, join with sl st in first sc. Leaving long strand for sewing, fasten off.
Sew Hat centered on top of Head.

Finishing
Work same as Pilgrim Boy Finishing on page 128.

Basket
Work same as Pilgrim Boy Basket on page 128.

Indian
Finished Size: 7" tall including feather.

Materials:
- Worsted yarn:
  1 oz. each tan and brown
  Small amount each black, green, yellow, red, purple, blue and orange
- 75 yds. tan raffia straw
- Small piece red felt
- Polyester fiberfill
- Two 10mm wiggly eyes
- 6" piece ¼" elastic for (optional) Doorknob Cover;
- Craft glue
- Tapestry needle
- D, F and G hooks or hooks needed to obtain gauges

Continued on page 130

Thanksgiving Favors

Continued from page 129

Gauges: D hook, 4 hdc = 1", 3 hdc rows = 1"; 2 post sts and 2 hdc = 1", 4 post st and hdc rows = 1". **F hook**, 9 sts = 2"; 9 sc rows = 2"; 7 hdc rows = 2". **G hook**, 4 sc = 1", 4 sc rows = 1".

Basic Stitches: Ch, sl st, sc, hdc, dc.

Indian
Inner Head, Outer Head & Nose
Work Pilgrim Boy Inner Head, Outer Head and Nose with tan.

Shirt
Work Pilgrim Boy Shirt with brown.

Yoke
Row 1: With F hook and brown, ch 2, 2 sc in second ch from hook, turn. *(2 sc made)*

Row 2: Ch 1, 2 sc in first st, sc in last st, turn. *(3)*

Row 3: Ch 1, sc in each st across with 2 sc in last st, turn. *(4)*

Row 4: Ch 1, 2 sc in first st, sc in each st across, turn. *(5)*

Rows 5–10: Ch 1, sc in each st across, turn.

Row 11: Ch 1, sc in first 3 sts, sc last 2 sts tog, turn. *(4)*

Row 12: Ch 1, sc first 2 sts tog, sc in last 2 sts, turn. *(3)*

Row 13: Ch 1, sc in first st, sc last 2 sts tog. Fasten off. *(2)*

Sew rows 2–12 on straight edge of Yoke to top edge of Shirt.

For each **Fringe,** cut one strand brown 3" long; fold in half, insert hook in st or end of row, pull fold through st or end of row, pull ends through fold, tighten.

Fringe two times in each st and in unsewn row at each end on straight edge of Yoke.

Hair
Cut 21 strands of black each 15" long; tack center of each strand to center top of Head evenly spaced over 1¼" from front to back.

Cut two 4" strands of black; tie Hair 2" below center on each side of Head and tack to Head.

For **Ties,** cut four strands of red each 8" long.

For each **Braid,** wrap one tie several times around Hair at same place black strand was tied and secure ends. Separate Hair into three equal sections, braid tightly; tie separate 4" strand of black ½" from end and trim ends evenly. Wrap one tie several times around braid ½" from end covering black tie. Secure ends.

Headband
Row 1: With G hook and yellow, ch 2, sc in second ch from hook, turn. *(1 sc made)*

Rows 2–35: Ch 1, sc in sc, turn. At end of last row, leaving 6" strand for sewing, fasten off.

Sew row 1 and row 35 together.

With purple, using straight stitch *(see Stitch Guide)*, embroider zig-zag design around Headband *(see photo)*.

Tack Headband in place on Head.

Feather
With G hook and green, ch 10, 2 sc in second ch from hook, sc in each ch across, ch 3 for **Tip;** working in remaining lps on opposite side of starting ch, sc in each ch across with 2 sc in last ch, join with sl st in first sc. Leaving 6" strand for sewing, fasten off.

With tip pointing up, sew opposite end of Feather to center back of Headband.

Finishing
1: Glue eyes to front of Head centered above Nose 1" apart.

2: Cut Mouth from felt according to pattern piece on page 128 on Boy Pilgrim; glue on front of Head centered below Nose.

3: With two strands of blue, embroider war paint on each side of face *(see photo)*. Repeat with two strands of orange below blue.

Note: *For Doorknob Cover, omit Sleeve, Shoe, Hand and Basket.*

Sleeve & Shoe
Work Pilgrim Boy Sleeve and Shoe with brown.

Hand
Work Pilgrim Boy Hand with tan on page 128.

Basket
Work same as Pilgrim Boy Basket on page 128.

Turkey

Finished Size: 4½" tall.

Materials:
- Worsted yarn:
  1 oz. brown
  Small amount each yellow, red and orange
- Polyester fiberfill
- Two 10mm wiggly eyes
- 6" piece ¼" elastic for *(optional)* Doorknob Cover;
- Craft glue
- Tapestry needle
- F and G hooks or hooks needed to obtain gauges

Gauge: F hook, 9 sts = 2"; 9 sc rows = 2".
G hook, 4 sc = 1", 4 sc rows = 1".

Basic Stitches: Ch, sl st, sc, hdc.

Turkey
Body
Work Pilgrim Boy Inner and Outer Head on page 127 with brown.

Head
Rnds 1–3: With brown, repeat rnds 1–3 of Pilgrim Boy Inner Head on page 127.
Rnds 4–5: Sc in each st around.
Rnd 6: (Sc next 2 sts tog) 6 times, sc in next 6 sts. *(12)*
Rnds 7–9: (Sc in next 6 sts, hdc in next 6 sts) around.
Rnd 10: Sc in each st around. Leaving a 6" strand for sewing, fasten off. Stuff.
Sew centered on front of Body.

Feathers (make 3 yellow, 2 orange, 2 red)
Rnd 1: With G hook, ch 3, sl st in first ch to form ring, ch 1, 2 sc in each ch around. *(6 sc made)*
Rnds 2–8: Sc in each st around. Leaving 6" strand for sewing, fasten off. Stuff.
Sew one yellow Feather centered on top of Body and one orange Feather on each side of yellow Feather *(see photo)*; sew one red Feather on each side of orange Feathers and one yellow feather on each side of red Feathers.

Beak
With F hook and orange, ch 3, sl st in second ch from hook, sc in next ch. Leaving 6" strand for sewing, fasten off.
Sew Beak centered on front of Head.

Comb
With F hook and red, ch 5, hdc in third ch from hook, sl st in next ch, 2 hdc in next ch, sl st in last ch. Leaving 6" strand for sewing, fasten off.
Sew Comb centered on top of Head from front to back.

Wattle
With F hook and red, ch 5, hdc in third ch from hook, sc in next ch, sl st in last ch. Leaving 6" strand for sewing, fasten off.
Sew Wattle centered on front of Head below Beak.

Foot (make 2)
With F hook and orange, ch 9, sl st in second ch from hook, sl st in next 2 ch, (ch 4, sl st in second ch from hook, sl st in next 2 chs) 2 times, sl st in last 5 chs. Leaving 6" strand for sewing, fasten off.
Sew Feet to bottom of Body 1½" apart.

Finishing
Glue eyes to front of Head centered above Beak 1" apart. ●

Thread tapestry needle with starting end of thread. Insert needle through center ch of ch-3 on each row. Insert tapestry needle threaded with remaining end of thread through center of each row and down through center again. Tie ends together and trim. Shape Grape Cluster.

For **Grape Leaf,** with yellow-green, ch 5, sc in second ch from hook, hdc in next ch, (hdc, ch 2, sl st in top of last hdc made, hdc) in next ch, (sc, ch 2, sl st, sc) in last ch; working in remaining lps on opposite side of ch, (hdc, ch 2, sl st in top of last hdc made, hdc) in next ch, hdc in next ch, (sc, sl st) in next ch. Leaving a long end of thread, fasten off.

Using end of thread, sew Leaf to top of Grape Cluster.

For **Tendril,** cut a 6" piece from No. 8 yellow-green. Leaving a long end of thread unstiffened, saturate 2" at one end of 6" piece with fabric stiffener; wrap around a straight pin and allow to dry. Remove pin carefully.

Using unstiffened end of thread, sew Tendril to top of Grape Cluster beside Leaf.

Corn (make 2)

Rnd 1: With No. 8 lt. yellow, ch 2, 3 sc in second ch from hook. *(3 sc made)*

Rnd 2: 2 sc in each st around. *(6)*

Rnds 3–8: Sc in each st around. At end of last rnd, join with sl st in first st. Leaving a long end, fasten off.

Thread tapestry needle with long end of thread and weave through sts of last rnd; pull to close opening.

For **Shuck,** with No. 8 yellow-green, ch 6, sl st in second ch from hook, sc in each ch across, ch 5, sl st in second ch from hook, sc in each ch across, ch 6, sl st in second ch from hook, sc in each ch across. Leaving a long end of thread, fasten off.

Place Shuck over end of Corn; using end of thread, tack in place.

Finishing

1: For **Halo,** arrange eight decorative leaves in a 1¾" circle as desired; cover leaves with a thick circle of hot glue. Place eight more leaves in a circle over glue. Cut two 3" pieces from 42" length of ribbon. Braid doll's hair and glue one 3" piece of ribbon 1" from end of braid. Glue Halo in place. Cut an 18" piece from each color of ribbon. Tie all pieces of ribbon together in a bow. Glue bow to back of doll's head below Halo.

2: For **Necklace,** place one leaf on a brass jump ring; place jump ring on remaining 3" piece of ribbon. Glue ribbon around doll's neck.

3: For **Earring** *(make 2),* place one dogwood leaf on each straight pin. Apply glue to post of pins. Push one pin into each of doll's earlobes.

4: For **Tray,** glue gold braid around edge of oval blank. Arrange fruit, vegetables and remaining leaves on Tray as desired and glue in place. Tie a knot in center of remaining ribbon and glue knot to bottom of Tray.

5: Sew three snaps evenly spaced down back opening of Dress. Place Dress on doll. Tack or glue Wings to back of Bodice. ●

chapter 9

Santa Surprises

*A yuletide delicacy
to tease and prompt
a joyful ho ho ho
from family, friends
and Santa.*

Reindeer Feed

½ cup butter or margarine
1 pouch instant onion soup mix
10 cups assorted snack
    crackers, cereal and pretzels

Place butter in 2-cup glass measure.
Cover with waxed paper; microwave
for 45 seconds or until melted. Stir in
soup mix. Place cracker mix in 4-quart
microwave-safe bowl. Pour butter mixture
over cracker mix, toss to mix well.
Microwave uncovered for 5 minutes or
until hot, stirring twice during heating.
Cool. Store mixture in airtight container.

Santa Moon Pillow

Designed by Wilma Bonner

Finished Size: 10" × 10½" without lace.

Materials:
- 300 yds. ecru size 20 crochet cotton thread
- 2 pieces cotton fabric each 10½" × 11"
- 1¾ yds. of 2" flat lace
- 1½ yds. of ¼" decorative cord
- Fiberfill
- Sewing thread to match fabric
- Sewing needle
- Fabric glue
- No. 10 steel hook or hook needed to obtain gauge

Gauge: 4 mesh = 1"; 9 dc rows = 2".

Basic Stitches: Ch, sl st, dc.

Special Stitches: For **beginning block (beg block)**, ch 3, dc in next 3 sts, **or,** ch 3, 2 dc in first ch sp, dc in next st.
For **beginning mesh (beg mesh)**, ch 5, skip next 2 sts or chs, dc in next st.
For **block,** dc in next 3 sts, **or,** 2 dc in next ch sp, dc in next st.

For **mesh,** ch 2, skip next 2 sts or chs, dc in next st.

Pillow Cover
Row 1: Ch 123, dc in fourth ch from hook, dc in each ch across, turn. *(121 dc made) Front of row 1 is right side of work.*
Note: *See Special Stitches above for working pattern instructions.*
Row 2: Beg block, 38 mesh, block, turn.
Rows 3–47: Work according to corresponding numbered rows on graph across, turn. At end of last row, fasten off.

Finishing
1: Holding fabric pieces right sides together, allowing ¼" for seam, sew three sides together. Clip corners. Turn right side out. Stuff. Fold raw edges ¼" to the inside; sew together. Center and glue crocheted Pillow Cover on fabric. Let dry.
2: Glue lace around outer edge of fabric pillow *(see photo)*.
3: Glue cord around outer edge of crocheted Pillow Cover. ●

Pillow Cover

Santa & Mrs. Claus

Designed by Donna Collinsworth

Santa

Finished Size: Fits 12" male fashion doll.

Materials:
- Worsted yarn:
  - 4 oz. red
  - 1½ oz. white
  - 1 oz. black
- Small amount white baby yarn
- 4 small snaps
- ¾" × 1" piece of gold felt
- Double-sided tape
- Sewing needle and thread
- Tapestry needle
- E and G hooks or hook needed to obtain gauge

Gauge: G hook and worsted yarn, 4 sc = 1"; 4 sc rows = 1".

Basic Stitches: Ch, sl st, sc, hdc, dc.

Note: Use G hook and worsted yarn throughout unless otherwise stated.

Pants
Row 1: With red, ch 27, sc in second ch from hook, sc in each ch across, turn. *(26 sc made)*

Row 2: Ch 1, sc in first 5 sts, 2 sc in next st, sc in next 14 sts, 2 sc in next st, sc in last 5 sts, turn. *(28)*

Row 3: Ch 1, sc in first 5 sts, 2 sc in next st, sc in next 16 sts, 2 sc in next st, sc in last 5 sts, turn. *(30)*

Row 4: Ch 1, sc in first 5 sts, 2 sc in next st, sc in next 18 sts, 2 sc in next st, sc in last 5 sts, turn. *(32)*

Row 5: Ch 1, sc in first 5 sts, 2 sc in next st, sc in next 20 sts, 2 sc in next st, sc in last 5 sts, turn. *(34)*

Rnd 6: Working in rnds, ch 1, sc in each st across to last 2 sts, overlap last 2 sts over first 2 sts, working through both thicknesses, sl st in last 2 sts, **turn.** *(32)*

Rnds 7–8: Ch 1, sc in each st around, join with sl st in first sc, **turn.**

Rnd 9: Ch 1, sc in each st around, ch 6, skip first 16 sts, sl st in next st. Fasten off.

Rnd 10: For **first leg,** join red with sc in third ch of ch-6, sc in next 2 chs, sc in next 16 sts, sc in last 3 chs, join with sl st in first sc, **turn.**

Rnds 11–14: Ch 1, sc in each st around, join, **turn.**

Rnd 15: Ch 1, sc in first 5 sts, sc next 2 sts tog, sc in next 8 sts, sc next 2 sts tog, sc in last 5 sts, join, **turn.** *(20)*

Rnds 16–19: Ch 1, sc in each st around, join, **turn.**

Rnd 20: Ch 1, sc in first 5 sts, sc next 2 sts tog, sc in next 6 sts, sc next 2 sts tog, sc in last 5 sts, join, **turn.** *(18)*

Rnds 21–28: Ch 1, sc in each st around, join, **turn.** At end of last rnd, fasten off.

Rnd 10: For **second leg,** working on opposite side of ch-6 on rnd 9, join red with sc in third ch, sc in next 2 chs, sc in next 16 sts, sc in last 3 chs, join with sl st in first sc, **turn.**

Rnds 11–28: Repeat rnds 11–28 of first leg. Sew snap to top of back opening.

Trim (make 2)
With white, make ch to fit around rnd 28 of legs *(ch will stretch as it is worked into)*, sc in second ch from hook, (ch 1, sc, ch 1) in same ch as first sc, (sc, ch 1, sc, ch 1) in each ch across; working on opposite side of ch, (sc, ch 1, sc, ch 1) in each ch across, join with sl st in first sc. Fasten off.

Sew Trim to bottom of each leg as shown in photo.

Coat
Row 1: Starting at bottom, with red, ch 37, sc in second ch from hook, sc in each ch across, turn. *(36 sc made)*

Rows 2–5: Ch 1, sc in each st across, turn.

Row 6: Ch 1, sc in first 5 sts, sc next 2 sts tog, sc in next 22 sts, sc next 2 sts tog, sc in last 5 sts, turn. *(34)*

Rows 7–8: Ch 1, sc in each st across, turn.

Row 9: Ch 1, sc in first 5 sts, sc next 2 sts tog, sc in next 20 sts, sc next 2 sts tog, sc in last 5 sts, turn. *(32)*

Row 10: Ch 1, sc in each st across, turn.

Row 11: Ch 1, sc in first 5 sts, sc next 2 sts tog, sc in next 18 sts, sc next 2 sts tog, sc in last 5 sts, turn. *(30)*

Rows 12–15: Ch 1, sc in each st across, turn.

Row 16: For **first front,** ch 1, sc in first 5 sts, sc next 2 sts tog leaving remaining sts unworked, turn. *(6)*

Rows 17–20: Ch 1, sc in each st across, turn.

Row 21: Ch 1, sc in each st across to last 2 sts, sc last 2 sts tog, turn. *(5)*

Row 22: Ch 1, sc first 2 sts tog, sc in each st across, turn. *(4)*

Row 23: Ch 1, sc in each st across to last 2 sts, sc last 2 sts tog, turn. Fasten off. *(3)*

Row 16: For **back,** skip next 3 sts on row 15, join red with sc in next st, sc in next 9 sts leaving remaining sts unworked, turn. *(10)*

Rows 17–22: Ch 1, sc in each st across, turn. At end of last row, fasten off.

Row 16: For **second front,** join red with sc in last st on row 15, sc in next 4 sts, sc next 2 sts tog leaving remaining sts unworked, turn. *(6)*

Rows 17–23: Repeat rows 17–23 of first front.

Matching sts, sew shoulders together.

Sew one snap to row 16 and one to row 20 on front side of Coat.

Collar
Row 1: Join red with sc in end of row 21 on first front, evenly space 13 more sc around neck opening ending in end of row 21 on second front, turn. *(14 sc made)*

Row 2: Ch 1, sc first 2 sts tog, sc in next 10 sts, sc last 2 sts tog. Fasten off.

Sleeve
Rnd 1: Join red with sc in center st on one arm-

Continued on page 138

Santa & Mrs. Claus

Continued from page 137

hole, sc in next st, evenly space 16 hdc in ends of rows around to last st, sc in last st, join with sl st in first sc, **turn**. *(19 sts made)*

Rnd 2: Ch 1, sc in each sc and hdc in each hdc around, join, **turn**.

Rnd 3: Ch 1, sc in first st, hdc in next 4 sts, (hdc next 2 sts tog, hdc in next st) 3 times, hdc in next 3 sts, sc in last 2 sts, join, **turn**. *(16 sts)*

Rnds 4–7: Ch 1, sc in each st around, join, **turn**.

Rnd 8: Ch 1, sc in first 4 sts, (sc next 2 sts tog, sc in next st) 3 times, sc in last 3 sts, join, **turn**. *(13)*

Rnds 9–11: Ch 1, sc in each st around, join, **turn**.

Rnd 12: Ch 1, sc in first 4 sts, (sc next 2 sts tog, sc in next st) 2 times, sc in last 3 sts, join, **turn**. *(11)*

Rnds 13–15: Ch 1, sc in each st around, join, **turn**. At end of last rnd, fasten off.

Repeat on other armhole.

For **Coat Trim**, work same as Pants Trim, making ch to fit across edge of Coat, starting at top of left front going across to bottom edge on right front. Sew to outer edge of Coat as shown in photo.

For **Sleeve Trim**, work same as Pants Trim, making ch to fit around bottom of Sleeve. Sew to last rnd on Sleeve. Repeat on other Sleeve.

Belt

Row 1: With black, ch 3, sc in second ch from hook, dc in last ch, turn. *(2 sts made)*

Row 2: Ch 1, sc in first st, dc in last st, turn.

Rows 3–26: Repeat row 2 or to fit around waist of Coat. At end of last row, fasten off.

Sew one snap to one end of Belt.

For **buckle**, cut out ½" square in center of felt piece.

Center and sew buckle to center front of Belt.

Hat

Rnd 1: Starting at bottom, with red, ch 24, sl st in first ch to form ring, ch 1, sc in each ch around, join with sl st in first sc, **turn**. *(24 sc made)*

Rnd 2: Ch 1, sc in first 4 sts, sc next 2 sts tog, sc in next 12 sts, sc next 2 sts tog, sc in last 4 sts, join, **turn**. *(22)*

Rnd 3: Ch 1, sc in first 4 sts, sc next 2 sts tog, sc in next 10 sts, sc next 2 sts tog, sc in last 4 sts, join, **turn**. *(20)*

Rnd 4: Ch 1, sc in first 4 sts, sc next 2 sts tog, sc in next 8 sts, sc next 2 sts tog, sc in last 4 sts, join, **turn**. *(18)*

Rnd 5: Ch 1, sc in first 4 sts, sc next 2 sts tog, sc in next 6 sts, ssc next 2 sts tog, sc in last 4 sts, join, **turn**. *(16)*

Rnd 6: Ch 1, sc in first 4 sts, sc next 2 sts tog, sc in next 4 sts, sc next 2 sts tog, sc in last 4 sts, join, **turn**. *(14)*

Rnd 7: Ch 1, sc in first 3 sts, sc next 2 sts tog, sc in next 4 sts, sc next 2 sts tog, sc in last 3 sts, join, **turn**. *(12)*

Rnds 8–9: Ch 1, sc in each st around, join, **turn**.

Rnd 10: Ch 1, sc in first 2 sts, sc next 2 sts tog, sc in next 4 sts, sc next 2 sts tog, sc in last 2 sts, join, **turn**. *(10)*

Rnd 11–12: Ch 1, sc in each st around, join, **turn**.

Rnd 13: Ch 1, sc in first 2 sts, sc next 2 sts tog, sc in next 2 sts, sc next 2 sts tog, sc in last 2 sts, join, **turn**. *(8)*

Rnds 14–17: Ch 1, sc in each st around, join, **turn**. At end of last rnd, fasten off.

Sew opening at top closed.

For **bottom Trim**, work same as Pants Trim, making ch to fit around bottom edge of Hat. Sew to rnd 1 of Hat as shown in photo.

For **top Trim**, work same as Pants Trim, making ch to fit around top of Hat. Sew to last rnd at top of Hat. Tack top of Hat to bottom Trim for back of Hat.

Boot (make 2)

Rnd 1: With black, ch 6, sc in second ch from hook, sc in next 3 chs, 3 dc in next ch; working on opposite side of ch, sc in next 4 chs, join with sl st in first sc, **turn**. *(12 sts made)*

Rnd 2: Ch 1, sc in each st around, join, **turn**.

Rnd 3: Ch 1, sc in first 4 sts, (dc next 2 sts tog) 2 times, sc in last 4 sts, join, **turn**. *(10)*

Rnd 4: Ch 1, sc in first 4 sts, sc next 2 sts tog, sc in last 4 sts, join, **turn**. *(9)*

Rnd 5: Ch 1, sc in each st around, join, **turn**.

Rnd 6: Ch 1, sc in first 2 sts, 2 sc in next st, sc in next 3 sts, 2 sc in next st, sc in last 2 sts, join, **turn**. *(11)*

Rnds 7–8: Ch 1, sc in each st around, join, **turn**. At end of last rnd, fasten off.

Beard

Row 1: With baby yarn and E hook, ch 11, sc in second ch from hook, sc in each ch across, turn *(should fit under lower lip from ear to ear)*. *(10 sc made)*

Rows 2–5: Ch 1, sc first 2 sts tog, sc in each st across to last 2 sts, sc last 2 sts tog, turn. At end of last row *(2 sts)*. Fasten off.

Row 6: For **first sideburn**, join baby yarn with sc in last st of row 5, turn.

Row 7: Ch 1, sc in st. Fasten off.

Row 6: For **second sideburn**, join baby yarn with sc in first st of row 5, turn.

Row 7: Ch 1, sc in st. Fasten off.

With tapestry needle and baby yarn, making loops of various lengths, embroider across rows and stitches of Beard and sideburns. Cut loops and trim.

For **moustache**, with baby yarn and E hook, ch 4. Fasten off. Embroider loops across ch. Cut loops and trim.

Using tape, attach Beard and Moustache to face.

Mrs. Claus

Finished Size: Fits 11½" fashion doll.

Materials:
- Worsted yarn:

4 oz. red
2 oz. white
- 3 small snaps
- Sewing needle and thread
- Tapestry needle
- G hook or hook needed to obtain gauge

Gauge: 4 sc = 1"; 4 sc rnds = 1"; 2 dc rnds = 1".

Basic Stitches: Ch, sl st, sc, hdc.

Dress
Bodice
Row 1: Starting at waist, with red, ch 18, sc in second ch from hook, sc in each ch across, turn. *(17 sc made)*

Row 2: Ch 1, sc in first 5 sts, 2 sc in next st, sc in next 5 sts, 2 sc in next st, sc in last 5 sts, turn. *(19)*

Row 3: Ch 1, sc in each st across, turn.

Row 4: Ch 1, sc in first 5 sts, 2 sc in next st, sc in next 7 sts, 2 sc in next st, sc in last 5 sts, turn. *(21)*

Row 5: Ch 1, sc in each st across, turn.

Row 6: Ch 1, sc in first 8 sts, 2 sc in each of next 2 sts, sc in next 2 sts, 2 sc in each of next 2 sts, sc in last 7 sts, turn. *(25)*

Row 7: Ch 1, sc in each st across, turn.

Row 8: Ch 1, sc in first 11 sts, sc next 2 sts tog, sc in last 12 sts, turn. *(24)*

Row 9: Ch 1, sc in each st across, turn.

Row 10: Ch 1, sc in first 11 sts, sc next 2 sts tog, sc in last 11 sts, turn. *(23)*

Row 11: For **first back side,** ch 1, sc in first 4 sts leaving remaining sts unworked, turn. *(4)*

Row 12: Ch 1, sc first 2 sts tog, sc in last 2 sts, turn. *(3)*

Row 13: Ch 1, sc in each st across, turn.

Row 14: Ch 1, sc in first st, sc last 2 sts tog, turn. *(2)*

Row 15: Ch 1, sc in each st across, turn. Fasten off.

Row 11: For **front,** skip next 3 sts on row 10, join red with sc in next st, sc in next 2 sts, sc next 2 sts tog, sc in next 4 sts leaving remaining sts unworked, turn. *(8)*

Row 12: Ch 1, sc in each st across, turn.

Row 13: Ch 1, sc in first 3 sts, sc next 2 sts tog, sc in last 3 sts, turn. *(7)*

Row 14: Ch 1, sc in first 2 sts, sl st in next 3 sts, sc in last 2 sts, turn.

Row 15: Ch 1, sc in each sc, sl st in each sl st across, turn. Fasten off.

Row 11: For **second back side,** join red with sc in last st on row 10, sc in next 3 sts leaving remaining sts unworked, turn. *(4)*

Rows 12–15: Repeat rows 12–15 of first back side. Matching sts, sew shoulders together.

Collar
Row 1: Join white with sc in end of last row on back, sc in end of next row, sc in next seam, sc in end of next 2 rows on front, sc in next st, 2 sc in next st, sc in next st, sc in end of next 2 rows, sc in next seam, sc in end of last 2 rows on back, turn. *(14 sc made)*

Row 2: Ch 1, sc in each st across, turn.

Row 3: Ch 1, sc in first st, (ch 3, sc) in each st across, turn.

Row 4: Ch 1, sc in first ch sp, *(sc, ch 2, sc, ch 4, sc, ch 2, sc) in next ch sp, sc in next ch sp; repeat from * across. Fasten off.

Skirt
Row 1: Working in starting ch on opposite side of row 1 on Bodice, join red with sl st in first ch, ch 2 *(counts as hdc),* (2 hdc in next ch, hdc in next ch) across, turn. *(25 hdc made)*

Row 2: Ch 2, (hdc in next 2 sts, 2 hdc in next st) across, turn. *(33)*

Row 3: Ch 2, (hdc in next 3 sts, 2 hdc in next st) across, turn. *(41)*

Row 4: Ch 2, (hdc in next 4 sts, 2 hdc in next st) across, turn. *(49)*

Rnd 5: Working in rnds, ch 2, hdc in each st across to last 2 sts, overlap last 2 sts over first 2 sts; working through both thicknesses, sl st in last 2 sts, **turn.**

Rnds 6–22: Ch 2, hdc in each st around, join with sl st in top of ch-2, **turn.** At end of last rnd, fasten off.

Sew three snaps evenly spaced down back opening of Bodice.

Sleeve
Rnd 1: Join red with sc in center st on one armhole, sc in next st, evenly space 16 hdc in ends of rows around to last st, sc in last st, join with sl st in first sc, **turn.** *(19 sts made)*

Rnd 2: Ch 1, sc in first st, (hdc in next 2 sts, 2 hdc in next st) 5 times, hdc in next st, sc in last 2 sts, join, **turn.** *(24 sts)*

Rnd 3: Ch 1, sc in first 6 sts, sc next 2 sts tog, (sc in next 6 sts, sc next 2 sts tog) around, join, **turn.** *(21 sts)*

Rnd 4: Ch 1, sc in first 5 sts, sc next 2 sts tog, (sc in next 5 sts, sc next 2 sts tog) around, join, **turn.** *(18)*

Rnd 5: Ch 1, sc in first 4 sts, sc next 2 sts tog, (sc in next 4 sts, sc next 2 sts tog) around, join, **turn.** *(15)*

Rnd 6: Ch 1, sc in first 3 sts, (sc next 2 sts tog, sc in next st) 3 times, sc in last 3 sts, join, **turn.** *(12)*

Rnd 7: Ch 1, sc in first 3 sts, (sc next 2 sts tog, sc in next st) 2 times, sc in last 3 sts, join, **turn.** Fasten off. *(10)*

Rnd 8: Join white with sc in first st, sc in each st around, join, **turn.**

Rnd 9: Ch 1, sc in first st, ch 3, (sc in next st, ch 3) around, join, **turn.**

Rnd 10: Ch 1, sc in first ch sp, (sc, ch 2, sc, ch 4, sc, ch 2, sc) in next ch sp, *sc in next ch sp, (sc, ch 2, sc, ch 4, sc, ch 2, sc) in next ch sp; repeat from * around, join. Fasten off.

Repeat on other armhole.

Apron
Row 1: With white, ch 76. Fasten off. *(76 chs made)*

Row 2: Skip first 33 chs for **tie,** join white with

Continued on page 148

Granny's Christmas Afghan

Designed by Jannie Lute

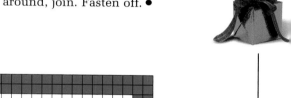

Finished Size: 72" square.

Materials:
- Worsted yarn:
  - 36 oz. off-white
  - 24 oz. green
  - 20 oz. burgundy
- Tapestry needle
- J hook or hook needed to obtain gauge

Gauge: Block is 3½" square.

Basic Stitches: Ch, sl st, sc, dc.

Off-White Block (make 108)
Rnd 1: Ch 3, sl st in first ch to form ring, ch 3 *(counts as dc)*, 2 dc in ring, ch 2, (3 dc in ring, ch 2) 3 times, join with sl st in top of ch-3.
Rnd 2: Sl st in next 2 sts, (sl st, ch 3, 2 dc, ch 2, 3 dc) in first ch sp, (3 dc, ch 2, 3 dc) in each ch sp around, join.
Rnd 3: Ch 1, sc in each st around with 3 sc in each ch-2 sp, join with sl st in first sc. Fasten off.

Burgundy/Off-White Block (make 100)
Rnd 1: With burgundy, ch 3, sl st in first ch to form ring, ch 3 *(counts as dc)*, 2 dc in ring, ch 2, (3 dc in ring, ch 2) 3 times, join with sl st in top of ch-3.
Rnd 2: Sl st in next 2 sts, (sl st, ch 3, 2 dc, ch 2, 3 dc) in first ch sp, (3 dc, ch 2, 3 dc) in each ch sp around, join. Fasten off.
Rnd 3: Join off-white with sc in first st, sc in each st around with 3 sc in each ch-2 sp, join with sl st in first sc. Fasten off.

Green/Off-White Block (make 192)
Rnd 1: With green, ch 3, sl st in first ch to form ring, ch 3, 2 dc in ring, ch 2, (3 dc in ring, ch 2) 3 times, join with sl st in top of ch-3.
Rnd 2: Sl st in next 2 sts, (sl st, ch 3, 2 dc, ch 2, 3 dc) in first ch sp, (3 dc, ch 2, 3 dc) in each ch sp around, join. Fasten off.

Rnd 3: Join off-white with sc in first st, sc in each st around with 3 sc in each ch-2 sp, join with sl st in first sc. Fasten off.

Assembly
Arrange Blocks according to assembly illustration; using tapestry needle and off-white, sew Blocks together in **back lps** *(see Stitch Guide)*.

Edging
Rnd 1: Join off-white with sc in any corner ch sp, 2 sc in same ch sp as joining sc, evenly space 198 sc across to next corner ch sp, (3 sc in next corner ch sp, evenly space 198 sc across to next corner ch sp) around, join with sl st in first sc. Fasten off. *(Center sc of each 3-sc group is corner st.)*
Rnd 2: Join burgundy with sc in any corner st, 2 sc in same st as joining sc, sc in each st around with 3 sc in each corner st, join.
Rnd 3: (Ch 1, sc, ch 2, 2 dc) in first st, skip next st, *(sc, ch 2, 2 dc) in next st, skip next 2 sts; repeat from * around, join. Fasten off. ●

Christmas Stocking

Designed by Colleen Sullivan

Finished Size: 6" wide x 18" long.

Materials:
- Worsted yarn:
  - 3 oz. green
  - 2½ oz. each of red and white
- Tapestry needle
- H hook or hook needed to obtain gauge

Gauge: 7 sc = 2"; 7 sc rows = 2".

Basic Stitches: Ch, sl st, sc, hdc, dc.

Note: When **changing colors** *(see Stitch Guide),* drop first color to wrong side of work, pick up next color, work over dropped color. Always change colors in last st made.

Stocking

Rnd 1: Starting at top, with white, ch 40, sl st in first ch to form ring, ch 1, sc in first 4 chs changing to red in last st made *(see Note),* sc in next 4 sts changing to white, (sc in next 4 sts changing to red, sc in next 4 sts changing to white) around, join with sl st in first sc. *(40 sc made)*

Rnd 2: Ch 1, sc in first 4 sts changing to red, sc in next 4 sts changing to white, (sc in next 4 sts changing to red, sc in next 4 sts changing to white) around, join.

Rnd 3: Ch 1, sc in first 4 sts changing to red, (sc in next 4 sts changing to white, sc in next 4 sts changing to red) around to last 4 sts, sc in last 4 sts, join.

Rnds 4–5: Ch 1, sc in first 4 sts changing to white, sc in next 4 sts changing to red, (sc in next 4 sts changing to white, sc in next 4 sts changing to red) around, join.

Rnd 6: Ch 1, sc in first 4 sts changing to white, (sc in next 4 sts changing to red, sc in next 4 sts changing to white) around to last 4 sts, sc in last 4 sts, join.

Rnds 7–8: Ch 1, sc in first 4 sts changing to red, sc in next 4 sts changing to white, (sc in next 4 sts changing to red, sc in next 4 sts changing to white) around, join.

Rnd 9: Ch 1, sc in first 4 sts changing to red, (sc in next 4 sts changing to white, sc in next 4 sts changing to red) around to last 4 sts, sc in last 4 sts, join.

Rnds 10–27: Repeat rnds 4–9 consecutively. At end of last rnd, fasten off both colors.

Row 28: Working in rows, for bottom half of **heel,** skip first 30 sts, join green with sc in next st, sc in next 19 sts leaving remaining sts unworked, turn. *(20 sc)*

Rows 29–36: Ch 1, sc first 2 sts tog, sc in each st across to last 2 sts, sc last 2 sts tog, turn. At end of last row *(4).*

Row 37: Ch 1, sc first 2 sts tog, sc last 2 sts tog, turn. *(2)*

Row 38: For top half of **heel,** ch 1, sc in each st across, turn.

Row 39: Ch 1, 2 sc in each st across, turn. *(4)*

Rows 40–47: Ch 1, 2 sc in first st, sc in each st across with 2 sc in last st, turn. At end of last row, fasten off. *(20)*

Using green, sew ends of rows on sides of top and bottom heel together.

Rnd 48: Working in rnds, for **foot,** working in unworked sts on rnd 27 and in sts on row 47, join red with sc in next unworked st on rnd 27, sc in next st changing to white, (sc in next 4 sts changing to red, sc in next 4 sts changing to white) 4 times, sc in next 4 sts changing to red, sc in last 2 sts, join with sl st in first sc. *(40)*

Rnd 49: Ch 1, sc in first 2 sts changing to white, (sc in next 4 sts changing to red, sc in next 4 sts changing to white) 4 times, sc in next 4 sts changing to red, sc in last 2 sts, join.

Rnd 50: Ch 1, sc in first 2 sts changing to white, (sc in next 4 sts changing to red, sc in next 4 sts changing to white) 4 times, sc in next 4 sts changing to red, sc in last 2 sts changing to white, join.

Rnds 51–52: Ch 1, sc in first 2 sts changing to red, (sc in next 4 sts changing to white, sc in next 4 sts changing to red) 4 times, sc in next 4 sts changing to white, sc in last 2 sts, join.

Rnd 53: Ch 1, sc in first 2 sts changing to red, (sc in next 4 sts changing to white, sc in next 4 sts changing to red) 4 times, sc in next 4 sts changing to white, sc in last 2 sts changing to red, join.

Rnds 54–55: Ch 1, sc in first 2 sts changing to white, (sc in next 4 sts changing to red, sc in next 4 sts changing to white) 4 times, sc in next 4 sts changing to red, sc in last 2 sts, join.

Rnd 56: Ch 1, sc in first 2 sts changing to white, (sc in next 4 sts changing to red, sc in next 4 sts changing to white) 4 times, sc in next 4 sts changing to red, sc in last 2 sts changing to white, join.

Rnds 57–59: Ch 1, sc in first 2 sts changing to red, (sc in next 4 sts changing to white, sc in next 4 sts changing to red) 4 times, sc in next 4 sts changing to white, sc in last 2 sts, join. At end of last rnd, fasten off both colors.

Rnd 60: For **toe,** join green with sc in first st, sc in each st around, join.

Rnd 61: Ch 1, sc in first 6 sts, sc next 2 sts tog,

Continued on page 153

Holly Lion

Designed by Karin Strom

Finished Size: 15" tall.

Materials:
- Worsted yarn:
  - 8 oz. burgundy
  - 4 oz. cream
  - 3½ oz. tan
  - 1 oz. green
  - 5 yds. black
  - 2 yds. pink
- 2½ yds. ecru braid
- 39" of ⅞" cream ribbon
- 24" of ¼" cream picot ribbon
- 16" of ⅜" burgundy ribbon
- 2 oz. doll hair
- 2 yds. cream marbou boa
- 2 black ⅜" shank buttons
- ⅞" decorative shank button
- Cardboard pieces:
  - 2" square
  - 1½" square
- Polyester fiberfill
- Craft glue
- 4" x 15" Styrofoam® cone
- Tapestry needle
- G hook or hook needed to obtain gauge

Gauge: 4 sc = 1"; 4 sc rows = 1".

Basic Stitches: Ch, sl st, sc, hdc, dc.

Lion
Cone Cover Top
Notes: *Work in continuous rnds; do not join or turn unless otherwise stated. Mark first st of each rnd.*

Cut 4" off top of cone.

Rnd 1: With tan, ch 6, sl st in first ch to form ring, ch 1, 12 sc in ring. *(12 sc made)*
Rnd 2: 2 sc in each st around. *(24)*
Rnds 3–18: Sc in each st around.
Rnd 19: 2 sc in next st, sc in each st around. *(25)*
Rnd 20: Sc in each st around.
Rnds 21–30: Repeat rnds 19 and 20 alternately. At end of last rnd *(30)*.
Rnd 31: 2 sc in next st, sc in next 14 sts, 2 sc in next st, sc in each st around. *(32)*
Rnd 32: Sc in each st around.
Rnd 33: 2 sc in next st, sc in next 15 sts, 2 sc in next st, sc in each st around. *(34)*
Rnd 34: Sc in each st around.
Rnd 35: 2 sc in next st, sc in next 16 sts, 2 sc in next st, sc in each st around. *(36)*
Rnd 36: Sc in each st around.
Rnd 37: 2 sc in next st, sc in next 17 sts, 2 sc in next st, sc in each st around. *(38)*
Rnd 38: Sc in each st around.

Rnd 39: 2 sc in next st, sc in next 18 sts, 2 sc in next st, sc in each st around. *(40)*
Rnd 40: Sc in each st around.
Rnd 41: 2 sc in next st, sc in next 19 sts, 2 sc in next st, sc in each st around. *(42)*
Rnd 42: Sc in each st around.
Rnd 43: 2 sc in next st, sc in next 20 sts, 2 sc in next st, sc in each st around. *(44)*
Rnd 44: Sc in each st around.
Rnd 45: 2 sc in next st, sc in next 21 sts, 2 sc in next st, sc in each st around. *(46)*
Rnd 46: Sc in each st around.
Rnd 47: 2 sc in next st, sc in next 22 sts, 2 sc in next st, sc in each st around, join with sl st in first sc. Fasten off. *(48)*

Cone Cover Bottom
Rnd 1: With tan, ch 2, 6 sc in second ch from hook. *(6 sc made)*
Rnds 2–3: 2 sc in each st around. *(12, 24)*
Rnd 4: (2 sc in next st, sc in next 3 sts) around. *(30)*
Rnd 5: (2 sc in next st, sc in next 4 sts) around. *(36)*
Rnd 6: (2 sc in next st, sc in next 5 sts) around. *(42)*
Rnd 7: (2 sc in next st, sc in next 6 sts) around, join with sl st in first sc. Fasten off. *(48)*
Place Top over cone. Sew last rnd of Bottom to last rnd of Top.

Dress
Rnd 1: Starting at top of Bodice, with cream, ch 18, sl st in first ch to form ring, ch 1, 24 sc in ring. *(24 sc made)*
Rnds 2–11: Sc in each st around.
Rnd 12: 2 sc in next st, sc in each st around. *(25)*
Rnd 13: Sc in each st around, join with sl st in first sc.
Row 14: For **Skirt,** working this row in **back lps** *(see Stitch Guide)*, ch 1, 3 sc in first st, 2 sc in next st, (3 sc in next st, 2 sc in next st) 9 times leaving last 5 sts unworked for **center front,** turn. *(50)*
Rows 15–42: Ch 1, sc in each st across, turn. At end of last row, fasten off.

Edging
Row 1: Join cream with sc in end of row 14 on Skirt at top right-hand side, sc in end of each row and in each st across ending at opposite side of row 14, turn. *(108 sc made)*
Row 2: Ch 2, hdc in next 2 sts, (sl st in next 2 sts, ch 2, hdc in next 2 sts) 26 times, sl st in last st. Fasten off.

Continued on page 146

Holly Lion
Continued from page 145

Inset
Row 1: Working in **back lps** of unworked sts on Bodice, join cream with sc in first unworked st, sc in same st as joining sc, 2 sc in each of last 4 unworked sts, turn. *(10 sc made)*

Row 2: Ch 1, 2 sc in first st, sc in each st across with 2 sc in last st, turn. *(12)*

Row 3: Ch 1, sc in each st across, turn.

Row 4: Ch 1, 2 sc in first st, sc in each st across with 2 sc in last st, turn. *(14)*

Rows 5–29: Ch 1, sc in each st across, turn. At end of last row, fasten off.

Place Dress on cone. Tack Edging to Inset.

Waistband
Rnd 1: With cream, ch 30, sl st in first ch to form ring, ch 1, sc in each ch around, join with sl st in first sc. *(30 sc made)*

Rnds 2–4: Ch 1, sc in each st around, join.

Rnd 5: (Ch 3, 4 dc) in first st, (sl st in next 2 sts, ch 3, 4 dc in next st) 9 times, sl st in last 2 sts, join with sl st in first ch of first ch-3. Fasten off.

Rnd 6: Working in remaining lps on opposite side of starting ch on rnd 1, join cream with sl st in first ch, (ch 3, 4 dc) in same ch as joining sl st, (sl st in next 2 chs, ch 3, 4 dc in next ch) 9 times, sl st in last 2 chs, join with sl st in first ch of first ch-3. Fasten off.

Cut 16" piece and 8" piece from picot ribbon. Tie 16" piece in bow at bottom of shank on decorative button, tie 8" piece in bow at top of shank on button. Sew button between rnds 2 and 3 of Waistband at center front.

Tack Waistband over rnds 11–13 of Dress, with center front at top of Inset.

Arm (make 2)
Rnd 1: Starting at bottom of hand, with tan, ch 2, 6 sc in second ch from hook. *(6 sc made)*

Rnd 2: 2 sc in each st around. *(12)*

Rnd 3: (2 sc in next st, sc in next st) around. *(18)*

Rnds 4–8: Sc in each st around.

Rnd 9: Sc next 2 sts tog, (sc in next 6 sts, sc next 2 sts tog) around. Stuff. Continue stuffing as you work. *(15)*

Rnd 10: Sc next 2 sts tog, sc in next 4 sts, sc next 2 sts tog, sc in next 5 sts, sc next 2 sts tog. *(12)*

Rnd 11: Sc in each st around.

Rnd 12: (2 sc in next st, sc in next st) around. *(18)*

Rnds 13–27: Sc in each st around.

Rnd 28: (Sc next 2 sts tog) around. *(9)*

Rnd 29: Sc in next st, (sc next 2 sts tog) around. *(5)*

Rnd 30: Sc in next st, (sc next 2 sts tog) around. *(3)*

Rnd 31: Sc next 3 sts tog. Fasten off.

Sew last 3 rnds of Arms over rnds 3–6 on sides of Dress 4" apart.

Head
Rnd 1: With tan, ch 2, 6 sc in second ch from hook. *(6 sc made)*

Rnds 2–3: 2 sc in each st around. *(12, 24)*

Rnds 4–9: Sc in each st around.

Rnd 10: Sc in next 10 sts; for **top of face,** 2 sc in each st around. *(38)*

Rnd 11: (2 sc in next st, sc in next 18 sts) around. *(40)*

Rnd 12: (2 sc in next st, sc in next 9 sts) around. *(44)*

Rnd 13: (2 sc in next st, sc in next 10 sts) around. *(48)*

Rnds 14–18: Sc in each st around.

Rnd 19: (Sc next 2 sts tog, sc in next 6 sts) around. *(42)*

Rnd 20: Sc in each st around.

Rnd 21: (Sc next 2 sts tog, sc in next 5 sts) around. *(36)*

Rnd 22: Sc in each st around.

Rnd 23: (Sc next 2 sts tog, sc in next 4 sts) around. *(30)*

Rnd 24: (Sc next 2 sts tog, sc in next 3 sts) around. Stuff. *(24)*

Rnds 25–27: (Sc next 2 sts tog) around. At end of last rnd, join with sl st in first sc. Fasten off.

Facial Features
For **nose,** using black, embroider **satin stitches** *(see Stitch Guide)* over rnds 2 and 3 at top of face *(see illustration)*.

For **mouth,** using black, embroider **straight stitches** *(see Stitch Guide)* directly below nose *(see illustration)*.

Glue two black buttons between rnds 7 and 8 of face 1" apart for eyes *(see illustration)*.

For **large pom-pom (make 4),** wrap strand of loopie hair around 2" cardboard 50 times; slide loops off, tie separate strand around center of all loops; cut loops. Trim ends to 2" across.

For **small pom-pom,** wrap strand of loopie hair around 1½" cardboard 25 times; slide loops off, tie separated strand around center of all loops; cut loops. Trim ends to 1½" across.

Glue one large pom-pom to each side of face for **cheeks** *(see photo)*.

Glue small pom-pom to face directly below mouth for **chin** *(see photo)*.

Cut and glue several 1" or smaller strands of loopie hair to face between mouth and cheeks for **whiskers.**

For **fur,** cut one end of remaining loopie hair strands, fold strands in half. Glue folded edge across top of Head over rnds 9–12 (see photo).

Center and glue Head to top of cone and Dress (see photo).

Ear (make 2)
Row 1: With pink, ch 2, 3 sc in second ch from hook, turn. (3 sc made)

Row 2: Ch 1, 2 sc in each st across, turn. (6)

Row 3: Ch 1, 2 sc in each of first 2 sts, sc in next 2 sts, 2 sc in each of last 2 sts, turn. Fasten off.

Glue one large pom-pom to center of each Ear (pom-pom is back of Ear).

Coat
Row 1: With burgundy, ch 71, sc in second ch from hook, sc in each ch across, turn. (70 sc made)

Rows 2–33: Ch 1, sc in each st across, turn.

Row 34: Ch 1, sc first 2 sts tog, (sc next 2 sts tog) across, turn. (35)

Row 35: Ch 1, sc first 2 sts tog, sc in next st, (sc next 2 sts tog, sc in next st) 10 times, sc in last 2 sts, turn. (24)

Rows 36–38: Ch 1, sc in each st across, turn.

Row 39: For **first front side,** ch 1, sc in first 4 sts leaving last 20 sts unworked, turn. (4)

Rows 40–42: Ch 1, sc in each st across, turn.

Row 43: Sl st in first 2 sts, sc in last 2 sts, turn.

Row 44: Ch 1, sc in first 2 sts leaving remaining sts unworked, turn. Fasten off.

Row 39: For **armhole,** skip next 4 unworked sts on row 38; for **back side,** join burgundy with sc in next st, sc in next 7 sts leaving last 8 sts unworked, turn. (8)

Rows 40–42: Ch 1, sc in each st across, turn.

Row 43: Ch 1, sc in first 2 sts leaving last 6 sts unworked, turn. (2)

Row 44: Ch 1, sc in first 2 sts, turn. Fasten off.

Row 43: Skip next 4 sts on back side, join burgundy with sc in next st, sc in last st, turn.

Row 44: Ch 1, sc in first 2 sts, turn. Fasten off.

Row 39: For **second front side,** for **armhole,** skip next 4 sts on row 38, join burgundy with sc in next st, sc in last 3 sts, turn. (4)

Rows 40–42: Ch 1, sc in each st across, turn.

Row 43: Ch 1, sc in first 2 sts leaving remaining sts unworked, turn.

Row 44: Ch 1, sc in each st across, turn. Fasten off.

Matching sts, sew shoulders together.

For **Coat edging,** working around outer edge on Coat, join burgundy with sc in end of first row on one side, sc in end of each row and in each st and in each seam around, join with sl st in first sc. Fasten off.

For **armhole edging,** working in ends of rows and in unworked sts on one armhole, join burgundy with sc in center unworked st, evenly space 26 more sc around armhole, join with sl st in first sc. Fasten off. Repeat on other armhole.

Sleeve (make 2)
Rnd 1: With burgundy, ch 15, sl st in first ch to form ring, ch 1, sc in each ch around. (15 sc made)

Rnds 2–3: Sc in each st around.

Rnd 4: 2 sc in each st around. (30)

Rnds 5–17: Sc in each st around.

Rnd 18: Sc in next 6 sts, (sc next 2 sts tog, sc in next 6 sts) around. (27)

Rnds 19–20: Sc in each st around.

Rnd 21: For **top,** sc in next 15 sts leaving remaining sts unworked for bottom edge. Fasten off.

Sew last rnd of Sleeves to armholes edging.

Hood
Row 1: Starting at front, with burgundy, ch 51, sc in second ch from hook, sc in each ch across, turn. (50 sc made)

Rows 2–16: Ch 1, sc in each st across, turn. At end of last row, fasten off.

Row 17: Skip first 17 sts; for **gusset,** join burgundy with sc in next st, sc in next 15 sts leaving last 17 sts unworked, turn. (16)

Rows 18–33: Ch 1, sc in each st across, turn. At end of last row, fasten off.

For **seams,** working through both thicknesses, matching 17 unworked sts on row 16 to ends of rows on gusset, join with sc in first st, sc across. Fasten off. Repeat on other side.

Bottom Edge
Row 1: Working in ends of rows and sts, join burgundy with sl st in end of row 1, ch 1, sc same row as joining sl st and next row tog, (sc next 2 rows or next 2 sts tog) across to opposite end of row 1, turn. (24 sc made)

Row 2: Ch 1, sc first 2 sts tog, (sc next 2 sts tog) across; **do not turn.**

Row 3: Ch 1, sc in each st across row 1 of Hood, sl st in next st. Fasten off.

Sew row 2 of Bottom Edge to center 24 sts on neck of Coat.

With front of Ears facing you, glue to top of Hood 4" apart.

Glue marbou boa to outer edge of Coat.

Cut braid to fit over rnds 2 and 3 of Sleeves; glue in place. Glue remaining braid around outer edge of Hood and Coat behind marbou boa.

Place Coat on Lion. Tie 7/8" ribbon in bow around neck.

Holly
Leaves
Rnd 1: For **first leaves,** with green, ch 9, (sc, hdc) in second ch from hook, (hdc, dc, hdc) in next ch, sc in next ch, sl st in next ch, (hdc, dc) in next ch, hdc in next 2 chs, (hdc, 2 dc, hdc) in last ch, working on opposite side of starting ch, hdc in next 2 chs, (dc, hdc) in next ch, sl st in next ch, sc in next ch, (hdc, dc, hdc) in next ch, (hdc, sc) in next ch, join with sl st in first sc.

Rnd 2: Ch 1, sc in first 6 sts, sl st in next sl st,

Continued on page 148

Holly Lion
Continued from page 147

sc in next 5 sts, ch 1, sc next 2 sts tog, ch 1, sc in next 5 sts, sl st in next sl st, sc in each st around, join. Fasten off.

Rnd 3: For **last leaf,** working through both thicknesses, join green with sl st in center two sl sts on first leaves, ch 9, sl st in second ch from hook, (sc, hdc) in next ch, ch 1, dc in next ch, ch 1, (hdc, sc) in next ch, sl st in next ch, (sc, hdc) in next ch, ch 1, dc in next ch, ch 1, (hdc, sc, sl st, sc, hdc) in last ch; working on opposite side of starting ch, ch 1, dc in next ch, (hdc, sc) in next ch, sl st in next ch, (sc, hdc) in next ch, ch 1, dc in next ch, (sc, hdc) in next ch, join with sl st in first sl st. Fasten off.

Berry (make 3)
Rnd 1: With burgundy, ch 2, 6 sc in second ch from hook, join with sl st in first sc.

Rnd 2: Ch 1, sc first 2 sts tog, (sc next 2 sts tog) around, join. Fasten off.

Sew Berries to center bottom of last leaf. Sew Holly to Hood beside right Ear.

Wreath
Front Side
Rnd 1: With green, ch 18, sl st in first ch to form ring, ch 1, 24 sc in ring. *(24 sc made)*

Rnd 2: Working in **back lps,** (sc in next st, 2 sc in next st) around. *(36)*

Rnd 3: Working in **back lps,** (sc in next 2 sts, 2 sc in next st) around. *(48)*

Rnd 4: Working in **back lps,** sc in each st around, join with sl st in first sc.

Rnd 5: Ch 3, skip next st, (sl st in next st, ch 3, skip next st) around.

Rnds 6–8: Working in **remaining lps** of rnds 3–1, working in a continuous spiral, sl st in next st, (ch 3, skip next st, sl st in next st) around to last st, ch 3, sl st in last st. Fasten off.

Using burgundy, embroider three **french knots** *(see Stitch Guide)* in a cluster, embroider a total of five clusters evenly spaced around Front Side.

Back Side
Rnd 1: With green, ch 18, sl st in first ch to form ring, ch 1, 24 sc in ring. *(24 sc made)*

Rnd 2: (Sc in next st, 2 sc in next st) around. *(36)*

Rnd 3: (Sc in next 2 sts, 2 sc in next st) around. *(48)*

Rnd 4: Sc in each st around, join with sl st in first sc. Fasten off.

Sew wrong sides of Front and Back Sides together.

Tie burgundy ribbon in bow, glue to rnd 3 on Front Side. Glue Wreath to right hand of Lion *(see photo).* ●

Santa & Mrs. Claus
Continued from page 139

Row 2: Skip first 33 chs for **tie,** join white with sl st in next ch, ch 2, hdc in same ch as sl st, hdc in next 9 chs leaving remaining chs unworked for **tie,** turn. *(11 hdc)*

Rows 3–12: Ch 2, hdc in each st across, turn. At end of last row, fasten off.

Row 13: For **trim,** join white with sc in end of row 2, evenly space 18 more sc across first side, (sc, ch 2, sc) in space between first 2 sts, skip next st, sc in next 8 sts, (sc, ch 2, sc) in next space between last 2 sts; working in ends of rows on second side, evenly space 19 sc across, turn. *(50 sc)*

Row 14: Ch 1, sc in first st, (ch 3, skip next st, sc in next st) 9 times, ch 3, skip next st, sc in next ch sp, (ch 3, skip next st, sc in next st) 5 times, ch 3, sc in next ch sp, (ch 3, skip next st, sc in next st) 10 times, turn. *(26 ch sps)*

Row 15: Ch 1, sl st in first st, *sc in next ch sp, (sc, ch 2, sc, ch 4, sc, ch 2, sc) in next ch sp; repeat from * across, sl st in last sc. Fasten off. ●

Holiday Coasters

Designed by Connie Folse

Mitten Coasters

Finished Size: Each Coaster is 4¾" x 5".

Materials:
- 3½ oz. each red, green and white worsted yarn
- G hook or hook needed to obtain gauge

Gauge: 4 sc = 1"; 4 sc rows = 1".

Basic Stitches: Ch, sl st, sc, dc.

Mitten (make 2 green and 2 red)

Row 1: Ch 7, sc in second ch from hook, sc in each ch across, turn. *(6 sc made)*

Rows 2–3: Ch 1, sc in each st across, turn.

Rows 4–6: Ch 1, 2 sc in first st, sc in each st across with 2 sc in last st, turn. *(8, 10, 12)*

Row 7: Ch 1, sc in each st across, turn.

Row 8: For **thumb**, (ch 3, 2 dc) in first st, 2 dc in next st leaving remaining sts unworked, turn. *(5 dc)*

Row 9: Ch 2, dc in next 2 sts, dc last 2 sts tog, **do not turn.** Fasten off.

Row 8: Join with sc in first st at beginning of row 7, sc in last 9 sts, turn. *(10 sc)*

Rows 9–11: Ch 1, sc in each st across, turn.

Rows 12–13: Ch 1, sc first 2 sts tog, sc in each st across to last 2 sts, sc last 2 sts tog, turn. *(8, 6)*

Row 14: Ch 1, sc in each st across, turn.

Row 15: Ch 1, sc first 2 sts tog, sc in next 2 sts, sc last 2 sts tog, turn. Fasten off. *(4)*

Rnd 16: Working around outer edge, for **trim,** join white with sc in first st, sc in next 3 sts, sc in end of next 15 rows; working on opposite side of starting ch on row 1, sc in next 6 chs, sc in end of next 7 rows, 2 sc in each end of next 2 rows on thumb, sc in next 3 sts on row 9 of thumb; working down opposite side of thumb, 2 sc in each end of next 2 rows, sc in end of last 8 rows, join with sl st in first sc. Fasten off.

Ornament Coasters

Finished Size: Each Coaster is 5" across.

Materials:
- 3½ oz. each red, green and white worsted yarn
- G hook or hook needed to obtain gauge

Gauge: 4 sc = 1"; 4 sc rows = 1".

Basic Stitches: Ch, sl st, sc, dc, tr.

Side (make 2 green and 2 red)

Rnd 1: Ch 2, 6 sc in second ch from hook, join with sl st in first sc. *(6 sc made)*

Rnd 2: Ch 1, 2 sc in each st around, join. *(12)*

Rnd 3: Ch 1, sc in first st, 2 sc in next st, (sc in

Continued on page 153

Angel Dining Decor

Designed by Becky Wooten

Angel & Pineapple Doily

Finished Sizes: Doily is 15" across. Each Angel is 3¼" tall, 3" across wings.

Materials:
- 150 yds. white/gold metallic size 10 crochet cotton thread
- Embroidery needle
- No. 7 steel hook or hook needed to obtain gauge

Gauge: Rnds 1–3 = 2". 7 dc = 1"; 3 dc rows = 1".

Basic Stitches: Ch, sl st, sc, hdc, dc.

Special Stitches: For **beginning shell (beg shell),** (ch 3, dc, ch 2, 2 dc) in ch sp.
For **shell,** (2 dc, ch 2, 2 dc) in next ch sp.

Angel (make 10)
Rnd 1: For **head,** ch 4, sl st in first ch to form ring, ch 3 *(counts as dc),* 11 dc in ring, join with sl st in top of ch-3. *(12 dc made) Front of rnd 1 is right side of work.*

Row 2: Working in rows, ch 3, skip next 3 sts, sl st in next st leaving remaining sts unworked, turn.

Row 3: For **wings and body,** ch 6 *(counts as dc and ch-3),* (5 dc, ch 3, dc) in ch-3 sp, turn. *(5-dc, 2 ch sps) (The ch sps are the wings and dc group is the body.)*

Row 4: Ch 5 *(counts as dc and ch-2),* (dc, ch 2) 3 times in next ch sp, 2 dc in each of next 5 sts, ch 2, (dc, ch 2) 3 times in last ch sp, dc in last st, turn. *(10-dc group, 8 ch sps)*

Row 5: Ch 4 *(counts as dc and ch-1),* (dc, ch 1, dc) in each of next 4 ch sps, ch 2, 2 dc in next st, dc in next 8 sts, 2 dc in next st, ch 2, (dc, ch 1, dc) in each of last 4 ch sps, ch 1, dc in last st, turn. *(12 dc-group, 12 ch sps)*

Row 6: Ch 6, sl st in third ch from hook *(picot made),* (dc; for **picot, ch 3, sl st in third ch from hook;** dc) in next ch sp, (picot, dc, picot, dc) in each of next 4 ch sps, picot, skip next ch sp, 2 dc in each of next 2 sts, dc in next 8 sts, 2 dc in each of next 2 sts, picot, (dc, picot, dc, picot) in each of last 5 ch sps, dc in last st, turn *(Wings and body complete).* Fasten off. *(16-dc group, 20 picots)*

Row 7: For **skirt,** join with sl st in first st of 16-dc group on body, ch 3, dc in same st as joining sl st, 2 dc in next st, dc in next 12 sts, 2 dc in each of next 2 sts leaving remaining ch sps unworked, turn. *(20 dc)*

Row 8: Ch 4, dc in next st, (ch 1, dc in next st) across, turn.

Row 9: Ch 5, dc in next st, (ch 2, dc in next st) across, turn.

Row 10: Ch 1, sc in first st, (ch 3, sc in next st) across. Fasten off.

Doily
Rnd 1: Ch 6, sl st in first ch to form ring, ch 3,

Continued on page 152

Angel Dining Decor
Continued from page 151

dc in ring, ch 2, (2 dc in ring, ch 2) 5 times, join with sl st in top of ch-3. *(6 ch sps made)*

Rnd 2: Sl st in next st, (sl st, ch 2, 3 dc, hdc) in first ch sp, (ch 3, hdc, 3 dc, hdc) in each ch sp around, ch 1, join with hdc in top of ch-2 *(joining ch sp made). (30 sts, 6 ch sps)*

Rnd 3: (Ch 3, 4 dc) in joining ch sp, ch 3, sc in center st of next 3-dc group, ch 3, (5 dc in next ch sp, ch 3, sc in center st of next 3-dc group, ch 3) around, join with sl st in top of first ch-3. *(six 5-dc groups, 6 sc)*

Rnd 4: Ch 4, dc in next st, (ch 1, dc in next st) 3 times, *ch 6, skip next 2 ch sps and next sc, dc in first st of next 5-dc group, (ch 1, dc in next st) 4 times; repeat from * 4 more times, ch 3, skip last 2 ch sps and next sc, join with dc in third ch of ch-4. *(24 ch-1 sps, 6 ch-6 sps)*

Rnd 5: Beg shell *(see Special Stitches)* in joining ch sp, (ch 3, sc in next ch-1 sp) 4 times, ch 3, *shell *(see Special Stitches)* in next ch-6 sp, (ch 3, sc in next ch-1 sp) 4 times, ch 3; repeat from * around, join with sl st in top of ch-3.

Rnd 6: Sl st in next st, (sl st, beg shell, ch 2, 2 dc) in ch sp of first shell, ch 3, skip next ch-3 sp, (sc in next ch-3 sp, ch 3) 3 times, skip next ch-3 sp, *(shell, ch 2, 2 dc) in ch sp of next shell, ch 3, skip next ch-3 sp, (sc in next ch-3 sp, ch 3) 3 times, skip next ch-3 sp; repeat from * around, join.

Rnd 7: Sl st in next st, (sl st, beg shell) in first shell, ch 3, shell in next ch-2 sp, ch 3, skip next ch-3 sp, (sc in next ch-3 sp, ch 3) 2 times, skip next ch-3 sp, *shell in next shell, ch 3, shell in next ch-2 sp, ch 3, skip next ch-3 sp, (sc in next ch-3 sp, ch 3) 2 times, skip next ch-3 sp; repeat from * around, join.

Rnd 8: Sl st in next st, (sl st, beg shell) in first shell, ch 3, sc in next ch-3 sp, ch 3, shell in next shell, ch 3, skip next ch-3 sp, sc in next ch-3 sp, ch 3, skip next ch-3 sp, (shell in next shell, ch 3, sc in next ch-3 sp, ch 3, shell in next shell, ch 3, skip next ch-3 sp, sc in next ch-3 sp, ch 3, skip next ch-3 sp) around, join.

Rnd 9: Sl st in next st, (sl st, beg shell, ch 2, 2 dc) in first shell, (ch 3, sc in next ch-3 sp) 2 times, ch 3, (shell, ch 2, 2 dc) in next shell, ch 3, skip next ch-3 sp, sc in next sc, ch 3, skip next ch-3 sp, *(shell, ch 2, 2 dc) in next shell, (ch 3, sc in next ch-3 sp) 2 times, ch 3, (shell, ch 2, 2 dc) in next shell, ch 3, skip next ch-3 sp, sc in next sc, ch 3, skip next ch-3 sp; repeat from * around, join.

Rnd 10: Sl st in next st, (sl st, beg shell) in first shell, ch 2, shell in next ch-2 sp, ch 3, skip next ch-3 sp, sc in next ch-3 sp, ch 3, skip next ch-3 sp, shell in next shell, ch 2, shell in next ch-2 sp, skip next 2 ch-3 sps and next sc, (shell in next shell, ch 2, shell in next ch-2 sp, ch 3, skip next ch-3 sp, sc in next ch-3 sp, ch 3, skip next ch-3 sp, shell in next shell, ch 2, shell in next ch-2 sp, skip next 2 ch-3 sps and next sc) around, join.

Rnd 11: Sl st in next st, ch 1, sc in first ch-2 sp, (ch 3, sc in next ch-2 sp) 2 times, (ch 3, 2 dc in next ch-3 sp) 2 times, *(ch 3, sc in next ch-2 sp) 6 times, (ch 3, 2 dc in next ch-2 sp) 2 times; repeat from * 4 more times, (ch 3, sc in next ch-2 sp) 3 times, ch 1, join with hdc in first sc *(joining ch sp made).*

Rnd 12: Ch 6, sc in next ch sp, (ch 3, sc in next ch sp) 6 times, *ch 3, dc in next ch sp, (ch 3, sc in next ch sp) 7 times; repeat from * around, ch 1, join with hdc in third ch of ch-6.

Rnd 13: Ch 1, sc in joining ch sp, (ch 3, sc in next ch sp) around, ch 1, join with hdc in first sc. Fasten off.

With right side of Angels and Doily facing you, tack heads and wings evenly spaced to last rnd of Doily. Tack third picot at end of each side on row 6 of wings together. Tack ends of rows 9 and 10 on each skirt together.

For **edging,** join with sc in any ch sp on any Angel, sc in same ch sp as joining sc, 2 sc in each ch sp around, join with sl st in first sc. Fasten off.

Angel Napkin Rings

Finished Size: Each Angel is 3" tall and 3" across wings.

Materials:
- 70 yds. white/gold metallic size 10 crochet cotton thread
- No. 7 steel hook or hook needed to obtain gauge

Gauge: 7 dc = 1"; 3 dc rows = 1".

Basic Stitches: Ch, sl st, sc, dc.

Angel (make 4)

Rnd 1: For **head,** ch 4, sl st in first ch to form ring, ch 3 *(counts as dc),* 11 dc in ring, join with sl st in top of ch-3. *(12 dc made) Front of rnd 1 is right side of work.*

Row 2: Working in rows, ch 3, skip next 3 sts, sl st in next st leaving remaining sts unworked, turn.

Row 3: For **wings and body,** ch 6 *(counts as dc and ch-3),* (5 dc, ch 3, dc) in ch-3 sp, turn. *(5-dc, 2 ch sps) (The ch sps are the wings and dc group is the body.)*

Row 4: Ch 5 *(counts as dc and ch-2),* (dc, ch 2) 3 times in next ch sp, 2 dc in each of next 5 sts, ch 2, (dc, ch 2) 3 times in last ch sp, dc in last st, turn. *(10-dc group, 8 ch sps)*

Row 5: Ch 4 *(counts as dc and ch-1),* (dc, ch 1, dc) in each of next 4 ch sps, ch 2, 2 dc in next st, dc in next 8 sts, 2 dc in next st, ch 2, (dc, ch 1, dc) in each of last 4 ch sps, ch 1, dc in last st, turn. *(12 dc-group, 12 ch sps)*

Row 6: Ch 6, sl st in third ch from hook *(picot made),* (dc; for **picot, ch 3, sl st in third ch from hook;** dc) in next ch sp, (picot, dc, picot, dc) in each of next 4 ch sps, picot, skip next ch sp, 2 dc in each of next 2 sts, dc in next 8 sts, 2 dc in each of next 2 sts, picot, skip next ch sp, (dc, picot, dc, picot) in each of last 5 ch sps, dc in last st, turn *(Wings and body complete).* Fasten off. *(16-dc group, 20 picots)*

Rnd 7: For **skirt**, working in rnds, join with sl st in first st of 16-dc group on body; for **ring**, ch 16; sl st in last st of 16-dc group, ch 3, dc in same st as ch-3, 2 dc in next st, dc in next 12 sts, 2 dc in next 2 sts, dc in each ch across ch-

16, join with sl st in top of ch-3, **do not turn.**

Row 8: Working in rows, ch 4, dc in next st, (ch 1, dc in next st) 18 times leaving remaining sts unworked, turn.

Row 9: Ch 5, dc in next st, (ch 2, dc in next st) across, turn.

Row 10: Ch 1, sc in first st, (ch 3, sc in next st) across. Fasten off. ●

Christmas Stocking
Continued from page 143

(sc in next 6 sts, sc next 2 sts tog) around, join. *(35)*

Rnd 62: Ch 1, sc in first 5 sts, sc next 2 sts tog, (sc in next 5 sts, sc next 2 sts tog) around, join. *(30)*

Rnd 63: Ch 1, sc in first 4 sts, sc next 2 sts tog, (sc in next 4 sts, sc next 2 sts tog) around, join. *(25)*

Rnd 64: Ch 1, sc in first 3 sts, sc next 2 sts tog, (sc in next 3 sts, sc next 2 sts tog) around, join. *(20)*

Rnd 65: Ch 1, sc in first 2 sts, sc next 2 sts tog, (sc in next 2 sts, sc next 2 sts tog) around, join. *(15)*

Rnd 66: Ch 1, sc in first st, sc next 2 sts tog, (sc in next st, sc next 2 sts tog) around, join. *(10)*

Rnd 67: Ch 1, sc first 2 sts tog, (sc next 2 sts tog) around, join. Fasten off.

Sew opening closed.

Cuff
Rnd 1: Working on opposite side of starting ch on rnd 1 of Stocking, join green with sc in

first ch, sc in each ch around, join with sl st in first sc. *(40 sc made)*

Rnd 2: Working in **back lps** *(see Stitch Guide),* ch 1, sc in each st around, join.

Rnd 3: Ch 1, sc in **back lp** of first st, sc in **front lp** of next st, (sc in **back lp** of next st, sc in **front lp** of next st) around, join.

Rnd 4: Ch 1, sc in **front lp** of first st, sc in **back lp** of next st, (sc in **front lp** of next st, sc in **back lp** of next st) around, join.

Rnds 5–8: Repeat rnds 3 and 4 alternately.

For **hanger,** ch 12, sl st in same st as joining sl st on rnd 8. Fasten off.

Cuff Trim
Rnd 1: With last rnd of Cuff toward you, working in **remaining lps** on rnd 1 of Cuff, join green with sc in first st, sc in each st around, join with sl st in first sc. *(40 sc made)*

Rnd 2: (Ch 4, hdc) in first st, skip next st, *(hdc, ch 2, hdc) in next st, skip next st; repeat from * around, join with sl st in second ch of ch-4. *(20 ch-2 sps)*

Rnd 3: (Sl st, ch 3, 4 dc) in first ch sp, sc in next ch sp, (5 dc in next ch sp, sc in next ch sp) around, join with sl st in top of ch-3. Fasten off. ●

Holiday Coasters
Continued from page 149

next st, 2 sc in next st) around, join. *(18)*

Rnd 4: Ch 1, sc in first 2 sts, 2 sc in next st, (sc in next 2 sts, 2 sc in next st) around, join. *(24)*

Rnd 5: Ch 1, sc in first st, 2 sc in next st, (sc in next st, 2 sc in next st) around, join. *(36)*

Rnd 6: Ch 1, sc in first 5 sts, 2 sc in next st, (sc

in next 5 sts, 2 sc in next st) around, join. Fasten off. *(42)*

Rnd 7: Working through both thicknesses with wrong side of matching Side pieces held tog, join white with sl st in first st, (ch 3, dc) in same st as joining sl st, 2 dc in next st, (dc, ch 3, sl st) in next st, sc in next 18 sts, 2 sc in next st, (dc, tr, ch 3, sl st in top of tr, dc) in next st, 2 sc in next st, sc in last 18 sts, join with sl st in first sl st. Fasten off. ●

Santa Apron

Designed by Sandra Miller Maxfield

Finsished Size: 22" long.

Materials:
- Worsted yarn:
  3 oz. red
  ¾ oz. white
  Small amount pink
- 2 wiggly 20mm eyes
- 1 Velcro® 2 piece spot
- Fabric glue
- 6" square cardboard
- H hook or hook needed to obtain gauge

Gauge: 7 sts = 2"; 3 dc rows = 2".

Basic Stitches: Ch, sl st, sc, hdc, dc.

Notes: For **color change** *(see Stitch Guide),* drop first color to wrong side of work, pick up next color. Always change colors in last st made.
Carry white yarn across wrong side of work.

Apron
Bib
Row 1: Starting at waist, with white, ch 28, dc in fourth ch from hook, dc in each ch across, turn. *(First 3 chs count as first dc—26 dc made.)*

Rows 2–6: Ch 3, dc in each st across, turn.

Rows 7–10: Ch 3, dc in next 5 sts changing to pink in last st made *(see Note),* dc in next 14 sts changing to white, dc in each st across, turn. At end of last row, fasten off pink. *Front of row 7 is right side of work.*

Row 11: Ch 3, dc in each st across changing to red in last st made, turn. Fasten off white.

Rows 12–13: Ch 3, dc in each st across, turn.

Row 14: For **strap,** ch 3, dc in next 6 sts, dc next 2 sts tog leaving last 17 sts unworked, turn. *(8)*

Row 15: Ch 3, dc in each st across, turn.

Row 16: Ch 3, dc in next 4 sts, dc next 2 sts tog, skip last st, turn. *(6)*

Rows 17–35: Ch 3, dc in each st across, turn.

Row 36: Ch 3, (dc next 2 sts tog) 2 times, dc in last st, turn. *(4)*

Row 37: Skip first st, sl st next 2 sts tog, sl st in last st. Fasten off.

Skirt
Row 1: For **tie**, with red, ch 60; working in remaining lps of row 1 on Bib on opposite side of starting ch, sc in first ch, sc in each ch across; for **tie**, ch 62, turn. *(26 sc, 122 chs made)*

Row 2: Hdc in third ch from hook, hdc in next 54 chs, (2 hdc in next ch, hdc in next ch) 2 times, 2 hdc in next ch; working in **front lps** *(see Stitch Guide),* (hdc in next st, 2 hdc in next st) 13 times, (hdc in next ch, 2 hdc in next ch) 2 times, hdc in last 56 chs, turn. Fasten off. *(165 hdc)*

Row 3: Skip first 56 sts, join red with sl st in next st, ch 4, dc in same st as joining sl st, *skip next st, dc in next st, skip next st, (dc, ch 1, dc) in next st; repeat from * 12 more times leaving last 56 sts unworked, turn.

Row 4: Ch 3, (dc, ch 1, dc) in first ch sp, *skip next st, **dc back post** *(bp, see Stitch Guide)* around next st, skip next st, (dc, ch 1, dc) in next ch sp; repeat from * across, turn.

Row 5: Ch 3, (dc, ch 1, dc) in first ch sp, *skip next st, **dc front post** *(fp, see Stitch Guide)* around next st, skip next st, (dc, ch 1, dc) in next ch sp; repeat from * across, turn.

Row 6: Ch 3, (dc, ch 1, dc) in first ch sp,*skip next st, dc bp around next st, skip next st, (dc, ch 1, dc) in next st; repeat from * across, turn.

Row 7: Ch 3, (dc, ch 1, dc) in first ch sp, [skip next st, dc fp around next st, skip next st, (dc, ch 1, 3 dc, ch 1, dc) in next ch sp, *skip next st, dc fp around next st, skip next st, (dc, ch 1, dc) in next ch sp*; repeat between first and second * 2 more times, skip next st, dc fp around next st, skip next st, (dc, ch 1, 3 dc, ch 1, dc) in next ch sp]; repeat between first and second * 2 times, dc fp around next st; repeat between [ ], dc fp around next st, (dc, ch 1, dc) in last ch sp, turn. *(18 ch sps)*

Row 8: Ch 3, (dc, ch 1, dc) in first ch sp, *skip next st, dc bp around next st, skip next st, (dc, ch 1, dc) in next ch sp; repeat from * across, turn.

Row 9: Ch 3, (dc, ch 1, dc) in first ch sp, *skip next st, dc fp around next st, skip next st, (dc, ch 1, dc) in next ch sp; repeat from * across, turn.

Rows 10–21: Repeat rows 8 and 9 alternately. At end of last row, fasten off.

For **pom-pom (make 1 white and 1 red),** wrap yarn around two fingers 40 times, slide loops off, tie a separate strand around center of all loops; cut loops.

Trim white pom-pom to 1¼" across. Trim red pom-pom to ¾" across. Sew white pom-pom over last two rows on strap. Glue one piece of Velcro spot to end of strap on opposite side of white pom-pom. Glue other spot to right side of Bib over row 13.

Center and sew red pom-pom to row 8 of Bib.

Glue eyes directly above red pom-pom ½" apart.

For **beard,** wrap white yarn around cardboard four times, slide loops off, tie separate piece of white around center of all loops. Glue one end centered to bottom of red pom-pom. ●

Mini Display

Designed by Wilma Bonner

Finished Size: 33" tall.

Materials:
- Size 10 crochet cotton thread:
    - 440 yds. green
    - 55 yds. white
- ¼"-wide x ⅛"-thick balsa wood strips: *(frame)*
    - 2 pieces each 28" long
    - 2 pieces each 24" long
    - 4 pieces each 20½" long
    - 2 pieces each 14" long
    - 4 pieces each 10½" long
    - 2 pieces each 7" long
    - 1 piece 3¼" long
- 7" square beveled wooden plaque *(base)*
- 7⅞" x 5" x 1" wood piece (tree trunk)
- 4 wood 1" balls
- Clear 4-lb test monofilamen
- 26 decorative thumb tacks
- 24 assorted miniature hanging ornaments
- 18K gold spray paint
- Forest green and burnt umber craft paints
- Gold ceramcoat paint
- Small paint brush
- Gold glitter
- Fabric stiffener
- Rust-proof straight pins
- Plastic food wrap
- Hair blow dryer
- Two 2" wood screws
- Screw driver
- Stiff hair brush *(optional)*
- Glue gun and glue
- Wood glue *(for wood)*
- No. 7 steel hook or hook needed to obtain gauge

Gauge: 7 dc = ¾"; 4 dc rows = 1".

Basic Stitches: Ch, sl st, sc, dc.

Note: Lattice pieces are ½" longer than the corresponding balsa wood pieces for frame.

7½" Lattice (make 2)
Row 1: With green, ch 14, dc in eighth ch from hook, dc in each ch across, turn. *(7 dc, 1 ch-7 sp made)*
Rows 2–30: Ch 7, dc in each dc across, turn. At end of last row, fasten off.

11" Lattice (make 4)
Row 1: With green, ch 14, dc in eighth ch from hook, dc in each ch across, turn. *(7 dc, 1 ch-7 sp made)*

Rows 2–44: Ch 7, dc in each dc across, turn. At end of last row, fasten off.

14½" Lattice (make 2)
Row 1: With green, ch 14, dc in eighth ch from hook, dc in each ch across, turn. *(7 dc, 1 ch-7 sp made)*
Rows 2–58: Ch 7, dc in each dc across, turn. At end of last row, fasten off.

21" Lattice (make 4)
Row 1: With green, ch 14, dc in eighth ch from hook, dc in each ch across, turn. *(7 dc, 1 ch-7 sp made)*
Rows 2–84: Ch 7, dc in each dc across, turn. At end of last row, fasten off.

24½" Lattice (make 2)
Row 1: With green, ch 14, dc in eighth ch from hook, dc in each ch across, turn. *(7 dc, 1 ch-7 sp made)*
Rows 2–98: Ch 7, dc in each dc across, turn. At end of last row, fasten off.

28½" Lattice (make 2)
Row 1: With green, ch 14, dc in eighth ch from hook, dc in each ch across, turn. *(7 dc, 1 ch-7 sp made)*
Rows 2–114: Ch 7, dc in each dc across, turn. At end of last row, fasten off.

Star
Side (make 3)
Rnd 1: With white, ch 6, sl st in first ch to form ring, (ch 5, dc) in first st, ch 1, (dc, ch 2, dc, ch 1) 5 times in ring, join with sl st in third ch of ch-5. *(12 ch sps made)*
Rnd 2: Ch 1, sc in first st, (sc, ch 3, 2 dc) in next ch sp, sc in next st, sc in next ch sp, *sc in next st, (sc, ch 3, 2 dc) in next ch sp, sc in next st, sc in next ch sp; repeat from * around, join with sl st in first sc.
Rnd 3: Sl st across to top of first ch-3, (ch 6, dc) in same ch as last sl st, ch 3, (dc, ch 3, dc, ch 3) in top of each ch-3 around, join with sl st in third ch of ch-6.
Rnd 4: Ch 1, sc in first st, (sc, ch 3, 4 dc, sc) in next ch sp, sc in next st, 3 sc in next ch sp *(3-sc group made)*, *sc in next st, (sc, ch 3, 4 dc, sc) in next ch sp, sc in next st, 3 sc in next ch sp *(3-sc group made)*; repeat from * around, join with sl st in first sc.
Rnd 5: Sl st across to top of first ch-3, (ch 6, dc) in same ch as last sl st, ch 5, sc in center st of next 3-sc group, ch 5, *(dc, ch 3, dc) in top of

Continued on page 158

next ch-3, ch 5, sc in center st of next 3-sc group, ch 5; repeat from * around, join with sl st in third ch of ch-6.

Rnd 6: (Sl st, ch 3, 2 dc, ch 3, 3 dc) in first ch sp, ch 5, sc in next sc, ch 5, *(3 dc, ch 3, 3 dc) in next ch sp, ch 5, sc in next sc, ch 5; repeat from * around, join with sl st in top of first ch-3. Fasten off.

Finishing

1: Apply fabric stiffener to each Lattice and each Star Side pieces according to manufacturer's instructions. Place each piece on flat surface covered with plastic wrap. Pin in place. Remove pins when completely dried. If additional stiffening is needed, paint fabric stiffener on both sides. Let dry completely. Option: You may use a stiff hair brush to remove any caked-on stiffener.

2: Shape Star Sides folded in half, with blow dryer. Glue fold of each Star Side together forming a three-dimensional Star. Let dry completely. Spray Star with 18K gold spray paint. Sprinkle glitter on all sides. Let dry completely.

3: Paint all frame pieces with forest green paint. Let dry completely.

4: Place corresponding frame pieces on flat surface according to red placement lines on illustration (below right) spaced 3" apart; using wood glue, glue remaining frame pieces spaced 3" apart on top according to blue lines on illustration, forming a tree shape. Let dry completely.

5: Glue 3¼" strip to back of 20½" strip at green line on illustration. *(This will help the tree to lay flat against the angled edge on trunk.)*

6: Cut one 5" edge of tree trunk at an angle for top edge *(see illustration).*

7: Paint tree trunk with burnt umber paint; paint base and balls with gold paint. Let dry completely.

8: Center tree trunk on base *(see photo)*; screw wood screws in from bottom of base, up through tree trunk to secure.

9: Glue one wooden ball to each corner on bottom of base.

10: Center and glue Lattice pieces to frame. Let dry completely.

11: Glue frame to top edge on tree trunk *(see photo).*

12: Glue Star to top of tree.

13: Hang ornaments on tree using tacks *(see photo).*

14: For **added support,** place one tack at top back of frame, place another tack at top back of tree trunk directly below first tack; secure monofilament to top tack, then to bottom tack stretching taut to keep tree from leaning. ●

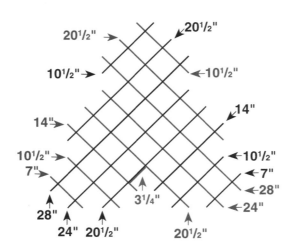

Frame Illustration

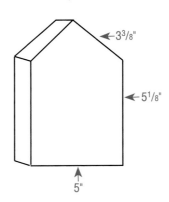

Tree Trunk Illustration

Basic Stitches

ain–ch:
, pull through lp
hook.

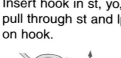

Slip stitch–sl st:
Insert hook in st, yo,
pull through st and lp
on hook.

Single Crochet–sc: Insert
hook in st, yo, pull through
st, yo, pull through both lps
on hook.

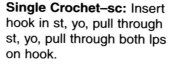

Reverse sc: Working from left
to right, insert hook in next st to
the right, complete as sc.

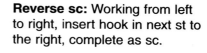

ible Crochet–dc:
insert hook in st, yo, pull
ugh st, (yo, pull through
s) 2 times.

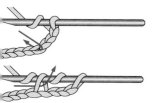

**Half Double
Crochet–hdc:** Yo,
insert hook in st, yo,
pull through st, yo,
pull through all 3 lps
on hook.

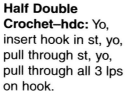
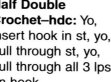

Treble Crochet–tr: Yo 2
times, insert hook in st, yo,
pull through st, (yo, pull
through 2 lps) 3 times.

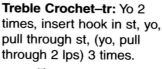

**Front Post Stitch–fp
Back Post Stitch–bp:**
Yo, insert hook from
right to left around
post of st on previous
row, complete as dc.

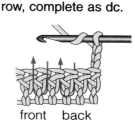

front   back

Loop Stitch

Sc Over Ring

**Front Loop
Back Loop**
front   back

**ront
oop &
eft Bar**

Back Bar of Chain

Back Bar of Sc

Embroidery Stitches

Satin Stitch

Cross Stitch

2 4 12 6 10 8

1 3 5   7 11 9

Backstitch

French Knot
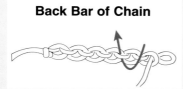

Fly Stitch
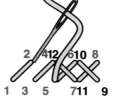

unning Stitch

Straight Stitch

Standard Abbreviations

ch, chs....chain, chains
dc.........double crochet
hdc..half double crochet
lp, lps.........loop, loops
rnd,rnds..round, rounds
sc ....single crochet
sl st..............slip stitch
sp, sps ....space, spaces
st, sts ....stitch, stitches
tog ....together
tr ....treble crochet
yo ....yarn over
sc next 2 sts tog—
   (insert hook in next
   st, yo, pull through
   st) 2 times, yo, pull
   through all 3 lps on
   hook.
hdc next 2 sts tog—
   (yo, insert hook in
   next st, yo, pull
   through st) 2 times,
   yo, pull through all 5
   lps on hook.
dc next 2 sts tog—(yo,
   insert hook in next
   st, yo, pull through
   st, yo, pull through 2
   lps on hook) 2 times,
   yo, pull through 3
   lps on hook.

Hook Sizes

U.S.	Metric	U.K.
14	0.60mm	
12	0.75mm	
10	1.00mm	
6	1.50mm	
0....5	1.75mm	
1....B	2.00mm	14
2....C	2.50mm	12
....D	3.00mm	10
4....E	3.50mm	9
5....F	4.00mm	8
6....G	4.50mm	7
	4.75mm	
8 ...H	5.00mm	6
9....I	5.50mm	5
10...J	6.00mm	4
	6.50mm	3
10½K	7.00mm	2
11	8.00mm	
13	9.00mm	
15...P	10.00mm	
....Q	16.00mm	

Ounces to Grams
1 = 28.4
2 = 56.7
3 = 85.0
4 = 113.4

Grams to Ounces
25 = 7/8
40 = 1 2/5
50 = 1 3/4
100 = 3 1/2